AMERICA'S

SECOND

CENTURY

Readings in United States
History Since 1877

Third Edition

Kenneth G. Alfers
Cecil Larry Pool
William F. Mugleston

KENDALL/HUNT PUBLISHING COMPANY
2460 Kerper Boulevard P.O. Box 539 Dubuque, Iowa 52004-0539

1. "'Master Fraud of the Century': The Disputed Election of 1876," by Roy Morris, Jr. Copyright 1988. Reprinted through the courtesy of Cowles Magazines, publisher of *American History Illustrated*.
3. "Horatio Alger: Creator of the American Success Story," by Joseph Gustaitis. Copyright 1987. Reprinted through the courtesy of Cowles Magazines, publisher of *American History Illustrated*.
4. "Andrew Carnegie: Captain of Industry," by Robert L. Heilbroner. *American Heritage*, Copyright 1960. Reprinted by permission of the author.
5. "The Haymarket Bomb," by Burton Schindler. Copyright 1986. Reprinted through the courtesy of Cowles Magazines, publisher of *American History Illustrated*.
6. "The Great Fight: Mr. Jake vs. John L. Sullivan," by James A. Cox. *Smithsonian* Magazine, December 1984. Reprinted by permission of the author.
7. "Populism and Modern American Politics," by Peter Frederick. Printed by permission of the author.
8. "Our First Southeast Asian War," by David R. Kohler and James Wensyel. Copyright 1990. Reprinted through the courtesy of Cowles Magazines, publisher of *American History Illustrated*.
9. "The Brownsville Affray," by Richard Young. Copyright 1986. Reprinted through the courtesy of Cowles Magazines, publisher of *American History Illustrated*.
10. "Hell on Saturday Afternoon," by John F. McCormack, Jr. Copyright 1976 by *Mankind* Magazine. February 1976; reprinted by permission.
11. "Mary Harris Jones: 'The Most Dangerous Woman in America,' " by Joseph Gustaitis. Copyright 1988. Reprinted through the courtesy of Cowles Magazines, publisher of *American History Illustrated*.
12. "Politics is Adjourned!" by Roy Hoopes. Copyright 1986. Reprinted through the courtesy of Cowles Magazines, publisher of *American History Illustrated*.
13. "The Real Eliot Ness," by Steven Nickel. Copyright 1987. Reprinted through the courtesy of Cowles Magazines, publisher of *American History Illustrated*.
14. "The Causes of the Great Crash," by John Kenneth Galbraith. *American Heritage*, Copyright 1958. Reprinted by permission of the author.
15. "FDR: A Practical Magician," by John Kenneth Galbraith. *American Heritage*, Copyright 1983. Reprinted by permission of the author.
16. "Prelude in the Pacific," by Edward Oxford. Copyright 1991. Reprinted through the courtesy of Cowles Magazines, publisher of *American History Illustrated*.
18. "The Fifties: A New Perspective," by William L. O'Neill. Reprinted by permission of the author.
19. "Trumpet of Conscience: A Portrait of Martin Luther King, Jr." by Stephen B. Oates. Copyright 1988. Reprinted through the courtesy of Cowles Magazines, publisher of *American History Illustrated*.
20. "Kennedy as President: A Perspective," by Robert James Maddox. Copyright 1986. Reprinted through the courtesy of Cowles Magazines, publisher of *American History Illustrated*.
21. "Remember the Ladies," by Joan Kennedy Taylor. *Reason Magazine*, Copyright 1987. Reprinted by permission of the author.
22. "Vietnam: The War That Won't Go Away," by George Herring. Reprinted by permission of the author.
23. "'I Am Not a Crook': Corruption in Presidential Politics," by Kenneth G. Alfers. Copyright 1980. Reprinted by permission of the Dallas Community College District, from *America: The Second Century Study Guide* by Kenneth G. Alfers.
24. "How the Media Seduced and Captured American Politics," by Richard C. Wade. *American Heritage*, Copyright 1983. Reprinted by permission of the author.
25. "Can We Still Afford to be a Nation of Immigrants?" by David Kennedy. Printed by permission of the author.
26. "Recent American Foreign Policy in Perspective," by Joseph S. Nye, Jr. Printed by permission of the author.
27. "Looking Backward, Looking Forward: An Interview with Carl Degler." Printed by permission of the author.

Contents

Part III (1945–Present)

Preface to Third Edition

The third edition of *America's Second Century* is an almost entirely new product but, we hope, no less useful to instructors and students than earlier editions. Our guiding principles are still readability and sound scholarship. Seven articles have been retained from the second edition; fifteen are new to this edition. In a feature that may be unique to collections of this type, we have also included interviews with five of the most prominent and provocative historians currently writing: Carl Degler, on American political and social behavior; Peter Frederick, on the Populists; George Herring, on the Vietnam War; Joseph Nye, on American foreign policy; and William O'Neill, on the 1950s. These interviews were conducted by Kenneth Alfers in 1991 in conjunction with Dallas Telecourses' production of *America in Perspective*. Also included are excerpts from a thought-provoking address on immigration given by David Kennedy at Mountain View College in 1990. We are grateful to both our students and colleagues for their compliments, criticisms, and suggestions for improvements.

Kenenth G. Alfers
Larry Pool
William F. Mugleston

Preface

We Americans living in the 1980s have had special reasons to reflect upon our nation's past. Nearly a decade ago we began celebrating the bicentennial of the Declaration of Independence. In the next few years greater attention will be focused on the 200th anniversary of our Constitution.

It is well that those special occasions serve to remind us that we do indeed have a rich and vibrant history. The technological changes occurring in the 1980s sometimes appear to be moving forward so rapidly that we do not have or take the time to gain an historical perspective on events.

A prime purpose of this reader is to help students develop that needed historical perspective. Furthermore, we acknowledge the fact that the U.S. history survey course is perhaps our only chance to reach most students in American colleges and universities. This reader, therefore, is intended to serve as an integral part of a survey of U.S. history since 1865. It can be used to supplement texts, monographs, historical novels, and/or lectures. Although organized topically, the articles can be used selectively along traditional chronological lines (see the accompanying guide).

In choosing articles, we were primarily concerned with readability and sound scholarship. Too often we have heard from our entering students that history has been boring and uninteresting. We want students to enjoy reading history while they are gaining that understanding and developing that habit of critical thinking which we think so important.

We wish to thank Raymond W. Smock of the Instructional Resources Corporation for his efficient help in securing photographs.

Kenneth G. Alfers
Larry Pool
William F. Mugleston
Mountain View College
Dallas, Texas

AMERICA'S
SECOND
CENTURY

In 1876, the United States, celebrating the centennial of the Declaration of Independence and the start of the American Revolution, entered its second century. It was a vastly different land from that known by the founding fathers. No longer a loose coalition of states along the Atlantic Coast, it was now a unified nation stretching all the way to the Pacific Ocean.

The late 19th century was the great age of the Industrial Revolution. This was the age of Andrew Carnegie, who would becone a new form of American hero. Not all Americans would experience the riches of the age, especially the new class of industrial workers. Many of these workers would turn to unionization, but unions were not a welcome development in a country that glorified individualism and idolized property and wealth.

The politics of America's second century began with the corrupt election of 1876. But the Populist crusade of 1896 would prove to be one of the greatest political contests of all time.

The America of the second century was a country that reached all the way to the Pacific Ocean, and in 1890, the census had revealed that there was no longer a discernable line of a western frontier. Faced with the closing of the frontier, the United States would expand into the Pacific and the Caribbean. The end of the frontier, the revolution of the industrial age, the struggle of American workers, the crusade of the Populists, the creation of an American empire, these were but some of the great movements and changes that took place in the last quarter of the nineteenth century.

Part 1

1877-1900

Master Fraud of the Century: The Disputed Election of 1876

by Roy Morris, Jr.

In 1876 the nation was celebrating its centennial as well as electing a president. The campaign had been filled with Democratic charges of corruption against the Republicans and with Republicans "waving the bloody shirt," accusing Democrats of being for rebellion. When the ballots were counted after the election in November, the Democratic candidate, Samuel Tilden, was the obvious winner. The Republicans were not willing, however, to accept the loss of the position their party had held for sixteen years. The story of how the results of the election changed and how Rutherford B. Hayes came to be the nineteenth president is clearly told in the following article by Roy Morris, Jr.

An angry gloom settled over the editorial office of the *New York Times* on the night of November 7, 1876. Late returns from across the country seemed to suggest, even to the staunchly Republican *Times,* that Democratic presidential nominee Samuel J. Tilden was heading for a victory over his Republican opponent, Ohio Governor Rutherford B. Hayes. Already the rival *New York Tribune,* another Republican mouthpiece, had hit the streets with the headline, "Tilden Elected." The *Chicago Tribune's* assessment was more despairing: "Lost. The Country Given Over to Democratic Greed and Plunder."

No one suffered from the news more keenly than *Times* managing editor John C. Reid. A survivor of the Civil War's notorious Libby Prison in Richmond, Virginia, Reid hated all Democrats, particularly Southern Democrats. Earlier that evening, when asked which states the *Times* was conceding to Tilden, Reid had snapped, "None." Now, with all but a few states reporting, the nation seemed to have elected its first Democratic President in twenty years. Tilden had a popular margin of more than 250,000 votes. More important, he seemed likely to win a narrow victory in the electoral college.*

---

*According to one count, unofficial returns gave Tilden 4,284,265 popular votes, with 4,033,295 going to Hayes. This tally would have assured Tilden of a 37-vote margin in the electoral college, with 203 votes to Hayes's 166.

5

But while shuffling through a pile of telegrams, Reid came across one from Democratic headquarters: "PLEASE GIVE YOUR ESTIMATE OF ELECTORAL VOTES FOR TILDEN. ANSWER AT ONCE." The wire specifically requested information on returns from Florida, Louisiana, and South Carolina—the three southern states where Republican Reconstruction governments still remained in control.

As Reid reviewed the *Times's* figures, he realized that the returns from the three states in question were still too fragmentary to call. Hayes conceivably could have carried—or could at least claim to have carried—all three. And if these states' nineteen electoral votes could be certified for Hayes (a distinct possibility in view of Republican control over the political machinery there), he would triumph in the electoral college, garnering exactly the 185 votes needed for victory. The election was not yet decided.

As the sky above the city began to lighten, Reid hurried to Republican headquarters at the Fifth Avenue Hotel. Inside, he found the rooms deserted. Republican National Committee chairman Zachariah Chandler, thinking he knew a lost cause when he saw one, had retired to his bedroom hours before with a large bottle of whiskey.

In the lobby Reid bumped into a little man wearing strangely enough, an enormous pair of goggles. William E. Chandler, no relation to Zachariah, was a Republican committeeman from New Hampshire. Recognizing the newsman, Chandler flourished a copy of the morning *Tribune* and swore, "Damn the man who have brought this disaster."

Reid assured him there had not yet been a disaster. "If you will only keep your heads up around here," he said, "there is no question of the election of President Hayes."

With Chandler in tow, Reid raced upstairs to locate the Republican chairman. After managing to rouse him, nightshirt and all, the two men explained Reid's plan for saving the election. Zachariah Chandler, sleepy and confused, told them to do whatever they thought best.

Downstairs, Reid and William Chandler grabbed a carriage and raced to the nearest Western Union office. Along the way Chandler drafted telegrams to Republican leaders in the three states. "HAYES IS ELECTED IF WE HAVE CARRIED SOUTH CAROLINA, FLORIDA, AND LOUISIANA," he advised them. "CAN YOU HOLD YOUR STATE? ANSWER IMMEDIATELY."

Across town in his Gramercy Park mansion, New York Governor Samuel Tilden slept. He had gone to bed at midnight with a seemingly insurmountable lead, the cheers of supporters ringing in his ears.

In Columbus, Ohio, Tilden's Republican opponent was also sleeping. Hayes's private victory party had ended early, spoiled by returns showing Tilden carrying New York and other doubtful eastern states. His wife, Lucy, ordinarily a vivacious hostess, had preceded him to bed, complaining of a headache.

For both candidates, and for much of the nation, the election of 1876 seemed at an end. But with William E. Chandler's telegrams now clattering across the Western Union wires, the political contest was in fact just beginning.

Americans of all political persuasions had entered the centennial year yearning for relief from the endless string of scandals emanating from Ulysses S. Grant's administration. The Whiskey Ring,* The Belknap case,** and dozens of lesser contretemps had made the term "Grantism" a much reviled insult. Grant, seemingly impervious to criticism, had clung stubbornly to hopes of a third term in office. But the criminal indictment of his personal secretary on charges of corruption and bribery effectively ended Grant's presidential pretensions; he reluctantly announced plans for a lengthy tour of Europe once his second term as president concluded.

With Grant removed from consideration, Republicans had gathered in Cincinnati to nominate a successor. By far the leading candidate had been Maine Congressman James G. Blaine. But Blaine, though undeniably charismatic, was burdened by his own scandals, including charges that while speaker of the house he had profited from the granting of federal railroad subsidies. Liberal Republicans had favored Treasury Secretary Benjamin H. Bristow, the man responsible for cracking the Whiskey Ring.

On the seventh ballot the convention had turned to Hayes, a comparative dark horse. Colorless, loyal, and untainted by scandal, Hayes was acceptable to all factions of the party. A Civil War general who had served with merit, he had subsequently demonstrated, through three terms as governor of the nation's most populous state, vote-getting prowess and an uncanny knack for winning close elections. Still, to many Republicans, Hayes's nomination "fell like a wet blanket on the party." Defeat in November was widely predicted.

The Democrats, by contrast, had confidently looked forward to victory. Not only were the Republicans at a disadvantage because of Grant's sorry record, but the General Amnesty Act of 1872 had returned the vote to thousands of former Confederates, many of whom were now sitting in Congress as a Democratic majority. Moreover, the Democrats had what they considered the perfect candidate, issue, and slogan for scandal-weary 1876; they would campaign for "Tilden and Reform."†

New York governor Tilden, at age sixty-two, was an unlikely subject for passionate support. Intellectually brilliant but personally aloof, he had made his fortune as a corporate lawyer. A confirmed bachelor and hypochondriac, he was nevertheless a tireless worker, possessing one of the best political minds of his generation. Tilden had helped expose the "Boss" Tweed Ring.‡ His national stature as a two-fisted reformer made his nomination for president a foregone conclusion.

---

*Revenue officers were robbing the Treasury of millions of dollars in internal revenue. Grant's private secretary Orville E. Babcock was among the culprits.

**Grant's Secretary of War William E. Belknap was impeached by the House of Representatives after an investigation revealed that he had accepted bribes for the sale of Indian trading posts.

†Tilden had headed the prosecution that led to conviction of New York City political machine boss William M. Tweed for bribery, graft, and fraudulent elections. (See pages 34–35).

‡New York politicians and contractors had conspired to defraud the state in the course of canal repairs.

After the candidates were chosen, the election shaped up as the closest in a generation. For the first time since Abraham Lincoln's election, the Democrats could reasonably hope to regain the White House. The corruption of the Grant years, an ongoing depression, and the voting clout of the "Solid South" gave the party a large advantage.

The Republicans, for their part, had controlled federal government for the past sixteen years, and could rightfully claim to have saved the Union. In the South, the army continued to support carpetbagger regimes in Florida, Louisiana and South Carolina, and millions of Southern blacks could be expected to offset the Democrats' huge advantage among white voters.

Tilden's personally supervised campaign ran with unprecedented efficiency. Under his directions the party prepared a 750-page *Campaign Text Book* detailing the abuses of the Grant administration. A literary bureau cranked out five million pieces of campaign literature on a private printing press, and a bureau of correspondence kept friendly newspapers well-supplied with weekly newsletters and copies of speeches. A speakers bureau coordinated campaign appearances by prominent Democratic orators.

To counter the well-oiled Democratic machine, the Republicans made ready use of campaign "assessments." By long-standing tradition, federal employees were expected to contribute 2 percent of their yearly salaries to help finance their party's political races. Liberals denounced the questionable practice, and Hayes himself mildly complained, but "voluntary" donations continued to fatten the Republican war chest.

Idealists urged Hayes and Tilden to run campaigns worthy of the centennial year. But American politics in the nineteenth century was partisan and dirty. The 1876 election was worse than most. The Democrats, as expected, hit hard at the discredited Grant administration. The Republicans struck back by "waving the bloody shirt," painting the Democrats as the party of rebellion. One of the harshest attacks came in October at a rally of the Grand Army of the Republic in Indianapolis. For two hours, Colonel Robert G. Ingersoll lashed the Democrats.

"Every enemy this great republic has had for twenty years has been a Democrat," he thundered. "Every man that shot Union soldiers . . . was a Democrat. Every man that loved slavery better than liberty was a Democrat. The man that assassinated Abraham Lincoln was a Democrat . . . Every scar you have got on your heroic bodies was given to you by a Democrat . . . Every arm that is lacking, every limb that is gone . . . is a souvenir of a Democrat."

The Democrats countered by reviving old charges that Hayes had pocketed money given to him for safekeeping by a soldier in his regiment who died in battle, and that he belonged to the American Alliance, a nationalist organization opposing political rights for foreign-born citizens.

In the South, which was still struggling to recover from the disastrous effects of the war, the presidential campaign was a serious business. Already, eight of the eleven old-line Confederate states had thrown out unpopular Reconstruction regimes and replaced them with freshly minted "Redeemers" dedicated to restoring Southern home rule. To many Northerners, "home rule" was perceived as a code name for white supremacy and the renewed subjugation of blacks. Rumors of violence and intimidation were greatly exaggerated by Republicans, but there were more than enough documented cases to inflame Northern public opinion.

In the three "unredeemed" states, the campaign was particularly nasty. Whites used threats, floggings, and outright murder to keep blacks away from the polls. The success of the so-called "Mississippi Revolution of 1875" emboldened some whites to step up their attacks. In that state a last-minute appeal for aid had been rejected by the Grant administration with the terse reply that the public was "tired of these annual autumnal outbreaks." Federal intervention in Southern elections was widely viewed as a thing of the past.

Election day dawned cold and clear in Hayes's Ohio and drizzly and gray in Tilden's New York. A record turnout thronged the polls. Tilden, uncharacteristically sporting a jaunty red carnation in his lapel, was quietly sure of victory. As state after state tumbled into Tilden's column, congratulatory telegrams flooded the private wire he had installed in his home, and excited Democrats from Texas to New England toasted "President Tilden" and "Centennial Sam."

No such expressions of confidence buoyed Hayes at his rented house in Columbus. Disappointed Republicans across the nation went home to bed.

But the next morning, while Hayes accepted defeat, a worried Tilden huddled with aides. Something, he sensed, was very wrong. Despite his huge lead in popular votes, some Republicans were acting as if the issue were still in doubt. That afternoon, Republican chairman Zachariah Chandler threw the nation into a turmoil by flatly declaring "Hayes has 185 votes and is elected." The *New York Times* exulted, "The Battle Won!"

Meanwhile, William Chandler was en route to Florida, the first in a long line of "visiting statesmen" dispatched by both parties to the three doubtful Southern states. President Grant, for good measure, ordered Army General William T. Sherman to deploy his troops to ensure a peaceful—and presumably honest—tabulation of votes. Hayes now realized "that with a few Republican states in the South to which we were fairly entitled, we would yet be victors." Tilden, as was his nature, kept his own counsel.

According to unofficial returns, Tilden had carried all three states. The election returns, however, still had to be reviewed by state certification or returning boards, which would investigate allegations of irregularities, disqualify fraudulent returns, and certify the official counts. All three boards in question had Republican majorities. South Carolina's board included three Republicans who were themselves candidates for office. Florida's board was Republican by a two-to-one margin, the swing vote in the hands of a former Confederate deserter. Louisiana's board consisted of an undertaker, a saloon-keeper, and two thoroughly disreputable carpetbaggers—all of whom would be indicted for fraud within the year.

With the visiting statesmen looking on, the boards met to determine the outcome of their states. Evidence of fraud, intimidation, and violence by partisans of both sides was undeniable. In Louisiana, where black voters gave bloodcurdlingly accounts of election-eve atrocities, Republican Senator John Sherman wrote to Hayes that the testimony "seems more like the history of hell than of civilized communities." In Florida, Republican observer General Lew Wallace, future author of *Ben Hur,* remarked, "It is terrible to see the extent to which all classes go in their determination to win. Conscience offers no restraint." The Democratic member of Florida's board hit one of his colleagues on the head with a cane.

To no one's surprise, the three boards all ruled in favor of Hayes, disallowing just enough Democratic votes to give him a razor-thin margin of victory. Newly elected Democratic governors responded by certifying and submitting minority returns in favor of Tilden.

The electoral college, meeting in December, was unable to declare a definite winner.

The nation now faced an unprecedented crisis: neither candidate, it appeared, had been elected. Tilden had 184 undisputed electoral votes and Hayes had 165; both sides claimed the nineteen contested Southern electoral votes and one in Oregon.

The people looked to Congress to resolve the dispute. Unfortunately, on the matter of contested elections the Constitution was vague and subject to conflicting interpretations. It merely stated that the president of the Senate (usually the vice president of the United States) was to open all election certificates in the presence of both houses of Congress, "and the vote shall then be counted."

With the death of Vice President Henry Wilson in 1875, Republican Senator Thomas Ferry of Michigan had become the acting vice president. If Ferry were authorized to count the votes, undoubtedly he would choose the ones for Hayes.* But if neither candidate was allowed the disputed votes, the election would be thrown into the Democratic-controlled House, and Tilden would be elected President. Hayes, understandably, favored the first recourse; Tilden the second.

Congress could reach no decision. Committees were appointed to study the situation.

As the stalemate continued, the country became increasingly restive. The threat of violence, never far from the surface, suddenly seemed especially menacing. In New Orleans, Republican gubernatorial claimant S. B. Packard was shot and wounded by a disgruntled Democrat. In Columbus, a bullet crashed through the window of Hayes's home while the family sat down to dinner. Thoughtful men on both sides worried aloud over the possibility of renewed civil war, this time pitting Republicans against Democrats.

*Considerable controversy centered on whether the president of the Senate had any discretionary power in counting the disputed votes.

In the capital, rumors ran rampant. Mysterious forces such as the Knights of the Golden Circle and Sons of Liberty were reputedly planning to march on Washington and place Tilden in the White House by force. Tilden Minutemen sprang up in several midwestern states. The Democratic sergeant-at-arms of the House threatened to deputize 100,000 men and bring them to Washington to insure Tilden's election. The phrase heard most frequently was, "Tilden or blood."

President Grant took such mutterings seriously, moving several artillery companies into the capital and letting it be known that he would meet any violence with overwhelming force.

Tilden, to his credit, discouraged such talk. "It will not do to fight," he told supporters. "We have just emerged from one civil war, and it will never do to engage in another." Southern Democrats, having recently fought and lost such a war, were noticeably lacking in martial spirit. Georgia Senator Benjamin Hill acidly remarked that those advocating violence "had no conception of the conservative influence of a 15-inch shell with the fuse in process of combustion."

Still, Democratic leaders became increasingly concerned about Tilden's reluctance to assert his rights. Throughout the deadlock he consistently rejected advice to take his case before the people. Secretive and reticent by nature, he preferred a policy of "watchful waiting." To supporters who warned that the election was being stolen, he blandly assured them that "it will come out all right." Key legislative leaders came away from meetings "uninformed and uninstructed." One group of callers at Gramercy Park emerged to complain that "Tilden won't do anything; he's cold as a damn clam."

In the meantime, with Hayes's tacit approval, talks had been going on for weeks between his representatives and leading Southern Democrats. The Southerners, while still supporting Tilden, were more concerned with preserving the newly elected Democratic governments in Florida, Louisiana, and South Carolina. In return for "not making trouble," Hayes's men hinted broadly to the Southerners that he would implicitly accept home rule and be more generous with federal aid than the notoriously tight-fisted Tilden. Powerful railroad lobbyists put added pressure on the Southern leaders. Tilden was advised of the talks, but continued to discount the threat they posed.

In January 1877, Congress hammered out a compromise that neither side wanted but neither could avoid. Despite opposition from both presidential claimants, a fifteen-man electoral commission was created with the power to rule on disputed ballots. Five senators, five congressmen, and five Supreme Court justices would serve on the commission. Seven of the members would be Democrats, seven would be Republicans, and one, presumably, would be independent.

The independent member of the commission was expected to be Justice David Davis of Illinois. In the event of a tie, he would cast the deciding vote. But on the day before the commission bill passed, Davis was unexpectedly elected to the Senate by the Democratic-controlled Illinois legislature. His place on the commission was taken by Republican Justice Joseph P. Bradley of New Jersey, the least partisan of the remaining jurists.

On February 1, 1877, the day designated to begin counting the ballots, a huge crowd packed the galleries of Congress. Looking on were the foreign ministers of England, Japan, Germany, and numerous other countries. The count proceeded smoothly until Florida, the first contested state, was called. Its conflicting returns were referred to the electoral commission.

After nine days of hearings, Florida's four electoral votes were awarded to Hayes. Voting followed party lines, Bradley siding with his fellow Republicans. Outraged Democrats openly charged that Bradley had been "reached," but they had no choice but to abide by the commission's ruling.

Tilden stoically received the news, changing the subject to his planned trip to Europe. In his mind, at least, there was no longer any doubt of Hayes's election.

When the commission ruled similarly in Hayes's favor on Louisiana's malodorous returns, all but the most partisan observers realized that Hayes would be the next President.

With Tilden's defeat a foregone conclusion, Southern Democrats prepared to fend for themselves. In return for assurances that Hayes would remove federal troops from the three unredeemed states, they agreed to work with Republicans to complete the electoral count before Inauguration Day. They further agreed to guarantee all civil rights for blacks and to oppose continued violence in the region. In turn, they were assured that Hayes would appoint a Southerner to his cabinet. The informal agreement was ratified on February 26 during a secret meeting of Hayes's representatives and a group of Southerners at Washington's Wormley Hotel. Three days later Hayes boarded a train for the nation's capital.

Die-hard Tilden supporters desperately sought to delay proceedings by parliamentary maneuvers and filibustering. The House session on March 1 was one of the stormiest in history. Members roared with disapproval as House Speaker Samuel Randall, a former Tilden supporter, stymied all efforts to stop the vote. Some congressmen waved pistols; one climbed atop his desk, screaming with anger. Adding to the pandemonium was a throng of railroad lobbyists on the House floor. Oaths and insults filled the air.

Finally, after eighteen tumultuous hours, the session ended with a telegram from Tilden graciously requesting that the vote count be completed. He knew he must accept the electoral commission's results or risk the nation erupting into civil war.

At 3:55 A.M. on March 2, 1877, weary senators filed into the House to observe the final tally of votes. A clerk entered carrying two mahogany boxes containing election returns from all thirty-eight states. An armed guard preceded him and then stood in front of the Democratic side of the House.

An exhausted Senator Ferry formally certified the final results: 185 electoral votes for Hayes, 184 for Tilden. "Wherefore," he announced in a shaky voice, "I do declare that Rutherford B. Hayes of Ohio . . . is duly elected President of the United States." Hayes, who had been sleeping aboard a train was awakened about dawn by exultant supporters. "Boys, boys," he cautioned, "you'll waken the passengers."

The next night the President-elect dined privately with Grant at a tomb-like White House. Whatever joy he may have felt at his hard-won victory was tempered by the bitterness it had provoked among many of his fellow countrymen. A Cincinnati newspaper pronounced his election "the master fraud of the century." Democratic wags suggested he change his name to "Ruth-erfraud" B. Hayes. Others dubbed him "His Fraudulency."

In 1877 the stipulated inauguration day, March 4, fell on a Sunday, requiring that the formal ceremonies be delayed until Monday. But to forestall any last-second chicanery on the part of disgruntled Tildenites, the president and his advisors agreed that Hayes should be sworn into office immediately. On Saturday evening, with a gloomy-visaged Grant looking on, Hayes took his oath of office in the secrecy of the White House Red Room.

After nearly four months of angry uncertainty, filled with blatant fraud, violence, and fears of renewed civil war, the nation finally had its nineteenth President.

The Battle of Little Bighorn

by Larry Pool

The clash between the Europeans and the American Indians in the western hemisphere created a conflict that would last for centuries and would result in violence into the twentieth century. One of the most famous of these outbursts of violence would be the battle which took place along the Little Bighorn River in the summer of 1876. It was the year of the centennial celebration of the Declaration of Independence and the year of a presidential election. It would be the year in which the lives of the Sioux Indians, seeking their freedom; George Armstrong Custer, an ambitious and glory hungry military officer; and Marcus Reno, an unknown cavalry officer, would be inextricably bound together in the pages of history.

The Sioux Indians had migrated into the area of the Black Hills in the 18th century, and after the United States purchase of the Louisiana Territory and the War of 1812, they declared their support for the Americans in 1815. In 1825 the Sioux signed their first treaty with the United States, a simple agreement of peace and friendship. Americans then began to move across the Sioux land. By 1845 there had been numerous incidents of violence between the Sioux and the American emigrants which resulted in a U.S. military display of force to quieten the situation. In 1851, a new treaty was signed between the United States and the Sioux, Arapaho and Cheyenne giving the Indians the land between the one hundredth and one hundred seventh meridians of longitude and the thirty-ninth and forty-fourth parallels of latitude. This area of about 123,000 square miles included parts of what are now the states of Colorado, South Dakota, Nebraska and much of Wyoming. The Indians agreed to stop fighting the soldiers and the emigrants and to end inter-tribal warfare.

The peace of 1851 would be short lived as trouble broke out in 1853 between the Sioux and the U.S. soldiers. For the next twenty years there would be periodic outbursts of warfare as American emigrants continued their relentless trek west across Indian land. In 1874, a U.S. military expedition went into the Black Hills region because of reports of gold in the area. They were accompanied by newspapermen and a few professional gold hunters. The party returned after sixty days with reports of abundant riches in the area. By the spring of 1875, large groups of prospectors were moving into the area. The Sioux leader Red Cloud went to Washington and arranged for a meeting between the Sioux and an American commission. This commission, including Senator W. B. Allison and Gen. Alfred Terry, asked the Sioux to give up the area of the Black Hills as well as the Powder River and Bighorn lands. The Indians asked for food for seven generations and $600 million. The commission offered $400,000 a year with the right to cancel with a two year notice or a flat $6 million. The talks, failing to reach a compromise, resulted in the commission proposal that the Indians be removed from the land either by starvation or warfare. The date for the Indians to be out of the Black Hills was set as January 31, 1876. In February, with the Indians refusing to leave, the matter was turned over to the military. The stage was set for one of the most famous battles of the Indian wars and for one of its chief players, George Armstrong Custer.

George Custer, born December 5, 1839, entered West Point in 1857. His career at the academy was not stellar as he graduated at the bottom of his class in 1861, but he left West Point to receive his first appointment to serve in the Civil War that had just erupted. By June, 1862, he was on Gen. George McClellan's staff with the rank of brevet captain. A year later he was given, at the age of twenty-three, the rank of brevet brigadier general. His first opportunity to lead his command of the First, Fifth, Sixth and Seventh Michigan Cavalry in battle came at Gettysburg. On the final day of that historic confrontation, Custer led his cavalry in a counter charge against the Confederates. He showed his penchant for braggadocio after the conflict by saying "I challenge the annals of warfare to produce a more brilliant charge of cavalry."

The remainder of the war saw Custer leading his cavalry force in frontal assaults at every opportunity. His forces helped to provide Union victories at Cedarville, Winchester, Yellow Tavern, Dinwiddie and Five Forks. Custer became a hero, a role he was well suited to play.

Custer learned early to be friendly to newspapermen. He was soon referred to in the press as "the Boy General with the Golden Locks" and "the Murat of the American Army." He played the role to the hilt, including wearing a uniform he designed for himself. On May 23, 1865, as a grand revue was held in Washington to celebrate the end of the war, Custer's horse ran away and broke through the ranks. The crowd roared with applause as Custer raced by the reviewing stand, his long, golden locks streaming behind. Custer, the hero, had made his presence known.

After the war, Custer was returned to the rank of captain and sent to the west, first to Texas and then to Kansas. In 1866, he became a lieutenant colonel in the Seventh Cavalry. In 1867, he led his force in destroying the village of the Cheyenne chief Black Kettle on the Washita River. He attacked the village from both ends without making any reconnaissance to determine the size of the encampment. The surprise attack was a success.

After Washita, Custer led his force in pursuit of Native Americans in Texas and Oklahoma. He then was stationed at Ft. Hays in 1870 and in 1871 at Elizabethtown in Kentucky. In 1872, he accompanied the Grand Duke Alexis of Russia on a buffalo hunt. Finally in 1873, Custer and the seventh Cavalry went west again to escort surveyors of the Northern Pacific Railroad into the Yellowstone country. In 1874, Custer was placed in command of Ft. Abraham Lincoln. From there he led the force into the Black Hills that year exploring for gold. A year after that expedition, Custer took a leave and went to New York, a city he had visited several times before.

As Custer was preparing to return to Ft. Lincoln in 1876, a congressional committee charged the Secretary of War, William C. Belknap, with fraud. Custer, a long time enemy of the secretary, offered to testify. His testimony would embroil him in a controversy with President Grant as he had implicated not only Belknap in wrong doing but Orville Grant, the President's brother, as well. Custer, desperately wanting to go west to join the expedition against the Sioux, was ordered to remain in Washington for possible further testimony. After failing in his attempts to see the president to get the orders changed, Custer left Washington for Chicago without permission. He avoided harsh disciplinary action through the intervention of Gen. Sheridan and Gen. Sherman and was allowed to lead the Seventh Cavalry as part of the expedition under Gen. Alfred Terry.

Gen. Terry would lead one column of a three pronged attack against the Sioux. This column of one thousand men would go west from Ft. Lincoln to the Yellowstone. Major Marcus Reno, with six companies of Seventh Cavalry, was sent to scout the forks of the Powder River and then down the Rosebud to its mouth. On June 21, 1876, Terry's column met with Reno at the Rosebud River. Reno reported that he had found a large trail leading toward the Little Bighorn River. Terry ordered Custer to take the Seventh Cavalry and follow the trail found by Reno. Any contact with the Sioux was to be reported to Gen. Terry.

Custer's force crossed the Little Bighorn River on June 24. The next morning, June 25, Custer received word that the Sioux had been sighted. Custer then divided his force. He ordered three companies under Capt. Fred Benteen to go to the first valley to the left, and if he did not find any Indians, to go to the next valley. Maj. Reno, with three companies, and Custer, with five companies, would proceed down either side of a stream leading to the Little Bighorn. When they were within a few miles of the village, Custer ordered Reno to attack down the stream and across the river. Custer would proceed down the river along a bluff, supposedly to attack the village from the other end, as he had done in his attack on the village of Black Kettle on the Washita.

Reno's attack was soon met by a fierce counter charge. He ordered his men to dismount and deployed them in a stand of timber. When it became apparent that his force would be overrun, Reno ordered his men to remount and cross the river where he was able to deploy them on the heights above the river. By the time they reached the heights, Reno's forces had lost thirty-two men killed and seven wounded. From the advantage of the heights, the troopers were able to hold off their attackers. They were soon joined by the returning forces of Capt. Benteen. The force on the hill, then numbering three hundred eighty-one men, could hear firing from beyond their position, but they could do nothing as the attack on their position continued until nine o'clock in the evening.

The firing they heard came from the fight of Custer's forces with the Indians. Custer had tried to find a place to cross the river beyond the village, but was attacked before he could do so. Two troops were attacked along a high ridge above the river. Three troops were attacked between the ridge and the river. The troopers dismounted and fought in small groups as they attempted to repel the horde of attackers. Some formed defensive barriers using their dead horses for cover. The battle lasted only about an hour. When it ended, Custer and all of his men lay dead, scattered across the field of battle. The next day, June 26, the Indians resumed their attack on the forces of Reno and Benteen. After several hours of futile assaults on the trooper's position, the Indians began to withdraw. The next day Gen. Terry arrived with a relief column. The Indians had all moved and were able to avoid the pursuing Americans. Within a few months, most of the Indians had successfully moved into Canada. By that time, efforts were being made in the east to find the blame for the disaster and to save the heroic reputation of Custer.

The initial efforts to blame Gen. Terry soon failed. The Custer partisans, led by his widow, then turned their attention to Capt. Benteen and especially Maj. Reno. In his book, *A Complete Life of Major General George A. Custer,* Frederick Whittaker accused Reno of cowardice, drunkenness and failure to obey orders. By 1878, Whittaker was asking Congress to investigate the massacre of Custer and his men, asserting that the disaster had been caused by the cowardice of Custer's subordinates. A court of inquiry was convened in Chicago in January, 1879, for the purpose of investigating Maj. Reno's conduct at the battle of Little Bighorn.

Testimony during the inquiry was received from numerous witnesses. Some accused Reno of being drunk during the fight, others labeled him a coward. There was also testimony in support of Reno, especially from other military officers. The accusations that Reno broke off his attack on the village too soon and retreated across the river in panic were disputed. The testimony indicated that had Reno continued his assault, his force would have been destroyed. Reno also testified, stating that he had expected support from Custer which never came. He also denied the allegations of drunkenness and cowardice. The court, after hearing all of the testimony, adjourned on February 11, 1879, after stating that there was no evidence to support the claims that the massacre of Custer and his men was due to the cowardice or incompetency of his subordinates. Despite being exonerated for the disaster at Little Bighorn, Reno continued to be haunted by the allegations that he had been the cause of the death of the heroic Custer.

In November, 1879, Reno was charged with conduct unbecoming an officer and a gentleman and brought before a court martial at Ft. Meade, Dakota Territory. He was accused of being drunk and disorderly in public, of engaging in a brawl in a public place and of peeping into the living quarters of his commanding officer. He was found guilty and sentenced to be dismissed from military service. In his closing remarks before the court, Reno said, "It has been my misfortune to have attained a wide-spread notoriety through this country by means of the press . . . a greater degree of attention will be called to what I do than other officers not so widely advertised." Despite its harsh sentence, the court recommended mercy for Reno from the Department Commander, Gen. Alfred Terry. Gen. Terry, although believing that the court had erred in its judgment, was reluctant to modify the findings since to do so would have left Reno with no punishment. He felt that Reno did deserve some reprimand for his conduct, but not dismissal. He felt assured that the president would modify the sentence.

In January, 1880, the General of the Army, W. T. Sherman, forwarded the proceedings to President Rutherford Hayes, recommending that the sentence be modified to suspension from command for one year with loss of half pay and confinement to his post. The president rejected the request for leniency and confirmed the sentence. Reno was dismissed from the military on April 1, 1880. Reno petitioned the Secretary of War, Robert Lincoln, but he was informed that correction of his sentence could come only through an act of Congress. Every year, until his death in 1889, Reno managed to have a bill introduced in Congress granting him restoration. The Little Bighorn disaster was still a controversial matter, and ambitious politicians, such as Military Affairs Committee Chairman Benjamin Harrison, were fearful of the consequences if they were to show charity to the man who, in the public mind, was to blame for the death of Custer. Because of his dishonorable discharge, Reno was not buried at Little Bighorn but in Glenwood Cemetery in Washington. The controversy over this matter did not end there, however.

In the spring of 1967, Charles Reno, the great-grand nephew of Marcus Reno, sought to exonerate his great-grand uncle by bringing the case before the U.S. Army Board of Correction of Military Records. The Board heard two days of testimony in defense of Maj. Reno showing that the court martial had erred in its interpretation of the Articles of War under which they had sentenced him. Finally on May 5, 1967 the Board recommended that the records of the Department of the Army be corrected to show that Marcus A. Reno was honorably discharged in the grade of major on April 1, 1880. The body of Maj. Reno was then moved and reburied at Little Bighorn.

Horatio Alger: Creator of the American Success Story

by Joseph Gustaitis

Rags to riches. The American dream. The Puritan ethic. All of these are terms associated with the stories of Horatio Alger, but such associations are the product of twentieth century intellectuals not of Alger. Emmy award winning writer Joseph Gustaitis gives a brief look in this article into the true story behind the man whose name has become mistakenly synonymous with the above terms.

A quarter of a billion books sold and still a failure.

Such a statement would not be the only contradiction in the life of Horatio Alger, Jr., American's best-selling author of "rags-to-riches" stories. He was a Harvard intellectual who wrote novels once branded "subliterary," a writer who everyone today "knows" but nobody reads, and a minister who committed what was considered to be one of the most diabolical crimes in the canon of sin.

The popular notion of an Alger novel runs like this: a poor, obnoxiously sweet lad ingratiates himself with a business mogul, marries the boss's daughter and becomes a millionaire—the whole work being a celebration of Gilded Age capitalism. Actually, none of the Alger books have this formula, nor was the author an apologist for Social Darwinism.

His heros did succeed, to be sure. Yet success meant not a Newport mansion, but a respectable middle-class job at, say ten dollars a week, and luck (such as finding a lost wallet) contributed just as much as pluck. As for romance, it was not in Alger's line. In all his stories of boy heroes, there is one kiss and not a single marriage. Some of these lads can be cloyingly moral, but usually they are reformable wise guys like "Ragged Dick" who, when told by a gentleman, "I've seen you before," whirls around and says, "P'raps you'd like to see me behind." Alger knew the slang and habits of street kids and made no secret that they nipped whiskey and smoked cheap cigars.

Alger's more than one hundred novels draw such vivid sketches of nineteenth-century New York that he is indelibly linked with that city, where he spent thirty of his sixty-seven years. But he was a Massachusetts man at heart. He was born in Chelsea, near Boston, on January 13, 1832, the first child of debt-ridden Reverend Horatio Alger and his wife.

A transfer to a more prosperous parsonage in 1844 enabled Alger senior to send his precocious though sickly sixteen-year-old son to Harvard. The younger Horatio was popular there: he was a Phi Beta Kappa student and wrote enough conventional lyrics to be reputed as a poet and to be selected "Class Odist."

Henry Wadsworth Longfellow was teaching at Harvard then, and Alger seems to have entertained notions of being his successor as national balladeer. But verse did not pay the bills, so instead he taught school, published a few stories, then bowed to the inevitable and chose to attend Harvard Divinity School. Alger fully realized that he had no true calling to the ministry, but he concluded that a clergyman's income would provide him with the financial cushion to pursue writing.

Alger took a European grand tour in 1860–61 and then came home to a nation at war with itself. He tried to enlist but was too nearsighted and too short (5′2″) for the Union forces. He then published a Civil War novel for the juvenile market. The war's end found him ministering to the flock of the First Unitarian Church in Brewster, Massachusetts.

Because Alger was a Harvard man with a clergyman father and a reputation as a writer of "moral" tales for young people, he was considered a good catch for that congregation. But a year after he assumed the post, dreadful rumors began circulating about the new pastor. A committee probed; shocking revelations surfaced. Two teenage boys averred that "Horatio Alger Jr. had been practicing on them at different times deeds that are too revolting to relate." The thirty-four-year-old minister did not deny the allegations, acknowledged he had been "imprudent," and quickly left town.

Further service in the clergy was now out of the question, and Alger escaped to the anonymity of New York City to support himself solely by writing. He struggled for nearly a year before he struck gold with his eighth novel, *Ragged Dick* (1867), the saga of a tough shoeshine boy who, through persistence and luck, heads down the road to respectability. It was the prototypical Alger story, to be recast in scores of boys' books that followed. The tale's gritty feel for the underside of Manhattan life brought it a refreshing air of unsentimentality. *Ragged Dick* quickly made the bestseller list; its author became famous.

Alger dreamed of being a serious author for adults, but the public and his publisher wanted more rags-to-riches stories, and so sequels and imitations followed at the rate of nearly three a year for the next six years. *Ragged Dick* became a series, followed by *Luck and Pluck* (1869) and *Tattered Tom* (1871).

No small measure of these books' success was due to their careful detail. Alger sublimated his sexual attraction to boys by befriending, patronizing, and studying the thousands of homeless street kids who got by through hustling, petty crime, selling newspapers, and, like "Ragged Dick," bootblacking. The author was instrumental in the success of the Newsboys' Lodging House, a shelter for homeless boys, and he sincerely tried to help the lads rise in the world as his fictional heros did.

In the next two decades Alger also wrote stories about rural America, traveled west to research details for fiction set there, and published biographies of American statesmen, namely *From Canal Boy to President* (a rush job capitalizing on the assassination of President Garfield) and lives of Webster and Lincoln.

Alger's health was never robust, and it began to decline in the winter of 1895–6. He moved to Natick, Massachusetts, and died there on July 18, 1899.

Shortly before his death, Alger had calculated that he had earned about $100,000 and sold about 800,000 books during his career—substantial, but not spectacular. It was only after he died, when his novels were republished in cheap editions, that his works began to sell in staggering quantities that have been estimated at between 100 and 400 million. This incredible boom lasted until about 1920, after which Alger's books were slowly forgotten.

The subsequent popular association of the author's name with American success and free enterprise was largely due to twentieth-century intellectuals, both conservative and liberal, who, in casting about for a symbol of *laissez-faire,* latched upon Alger. They were at least partly wrong in doing so, for his books are too full of scheming tycoons, vicious landlords, and miserly employers to be seen as a paean to American business. But by the 1930s false attention of such ideas to Alger's works was easy, because by then no one read them anymore.

Which is perhaps the final irony in Horatio Alger's career. In the nineteenth century, his books were famous. In this one, only his name is. But of how many writers can it be said that their names have become American icons?

A ndrew Carnegie:
A Captain of Industry

by Robert L. Heilbroner

One of the major reasons for the rapid industrialization of the United States during the late nineteenth century was the emergence of the entrepreneurs. Ingenuity, managerial expertise, willingness to take risks, and hard work were some of the qualities displayed in large measure by these men. None of them are more appealing than Andrew Carnegie. In him we see the personification of the American Dream. We also see what we hope the real-life Horatio Alger figures did with their money before they died.

Professor Robert Heilbroner, an economist at the New School for Social Research, is noted for his writings on economic history and thought. Among his well-known works are *The Worldly Philosophers, The Future as History, The Limits of American Capitalism,* and *An Inquiry into the Human Prospect.* In this essay he once again demonstrates his ability to enliven the study of our past.

Toward the end of his long life, at the close of World War I, Andrew Carnegie was already something of a national legend. His meteoric rise, the scandals and successes of his industrial generalship—all this was blurred into nostalgic memory. What was left was a small, rather feeble man with a white beard and pale, penetrating eyes, who could occasionally be seen puttering around his mansion on upper Fifth Avenue, a benevolent old gentleman who still rated an annual birthday interview but was even then a venerable relic of a fast-disappearing era. Carnegie himself looked back on his career with a certain savored incredulity. "How much did you say I had given away, Poynton?" he would inquire of his private secretary; "$324,657,399" was the answer. "Good Heaven!" Carnegie would exclaim. "Where did I ever get all that money?"

Where he *had* got all that money was indeed a legendary story, for even in an age known for its acquisitive triumphs, Carnegie's touch had been an extraordinary one. He had begun, in true Horatio Alger fashion, at the bottom; he had ended, in a manner that put the wildest of Alger's novels to shame, at the very pinnacle of success. At the close of his great deal with J. P. Morgan in 1901, when the Carnegie steel empire was sold to form the core of the new United States Steel Company, the banker had extended his hand and delivered the ultimate encomium of the times: "Mr. Carnegie," he said, "I want to congratulate you on being the richest man in the world."

It was certainly as "the richest man in the world" that Carnegie attracted the attention of his contemporaries. Yet this is hardly why we look back on him with interest today. As an enormous moneymaker Carnegie was a flashy, but hardly a profound, hero of the times; and the attitudes of Earnestness and Self-Assurance, so engaging in the young immigrant, become irritating when they are congealed in the millionaire. But what lifts Carnegie's life above the rut of a one-dimensional success story is an aspect of which his contemporaries were relatively unaware.

Going through his papers after his death, Carnegie's executors came across a memorandum that he had written to himself fifty years before, carefully preserved in a little yellow box of keepsakes and mementos. It brings us back to December, 1868, when Carnegie, a young man flushed with the first taste of great success, retired to his suite in the opulent Hotel St. Nicholas in New York, to tot up his profits for the year. It had been a tremendous year and the calculation must have been extremely pleasurable. Yet this is what he wrote as he reflected on the figures:

> Thirty-three and an income of $50,000 per annum! By this time two years I can so arrange all my business as to secure at least $50,000 per annum. Beyond this never earn—make no effort to increase fortune, but spend the surplus each year for benevolent purposes. Cast aside business forever, except for others.
>
> Settle in Oxford and get a thorough education, making the acquaintance of literary men—this will take three years of active work—pay especial attention to speaking in public. Settle then in London and purchase a controlling interest in some newspaper or live review and give the general management of it attention, taking part in public matters, especially those connected with education and improvement of the poorer classes.
>
> Man must have an idol—the amassing of wealth is one of the worst species of idolatry—no idol more debasing than the worship of money. Whatever I engage in I must push inordinately; therefore should I be careful to choose that life which will be the most elevating in its character. To continue much longer overwhelmed by business cares and with most of my thoughts wholly upon the way to make more money in the shortest time, must degrade me beyond hope of permanent recovery. I will resign business at thirty-five, but during the ensuing two years I wish to spend the afternoons in receiving instruction and in reading systematically.

It is a document which in more ways than one is Carnegie to the very life: brash, incredibly self-confident, chockablock with self-conscious virtue—and more than a little hypocritical. For the program so nobly outlined went largely unrealized. Instead of retiring in two years, Carnegie went on for thirty-three more; even then it was with considerable difficulty that he was persuaded to quit. Far from shunning further money-making, he proceeded to roll up his fortune with an uninhibited drive that led one unfriendly biographer to characterize him as "the greediest little gentleman ever created." Certainly he was one of the most aggressive profit seekers of his time. Typically, when an associate jubilantly cabled: "No. 8 furnace broke all records today," Carnegie coldly replied, "What were the other furnaces doing?"

It is this contrast between his hopes and his performance that makes Carnegie interesting. For when we review his life, what we see is more than the career of another nineteenth-century acquisitor. We see the unequal struggle between a man who loved money—loved making it, having it, spending it— and a man who, at bottom, was ashamed of himself for his acquisitive desires. All during his lifetime, the money-maker seemed to win. But what lifts Carnegie's story out of the ordinary is that the other Carnegie ultimately triumphed. At his death public speculation placed the size of his estate at about five hundred million dollars. In fact it came to $22,881,575. Carnegie *had* become the richest man in the world—but something had also driven him to give away ninety per cent of his wealth.

Actually, his contemporaries knew of Carnegie's inquietude about money. In 1889, before he was world-famous, he had written an article for the *North American Review* entitled "The Gospel of Wealth"—an article that contained the startling phrase: "The man who dies thus rich dies disgraced." It was hardly surprising, however, if the world took these sentiments at a liberal discount: homiletic millionaires who preached the virtues of austerity were no novelty; Carnegie himself, returning in 1879 from a trip to the miseries of India, had been able to write with perfect sincerity, "How very little the millionaire has beyond the peasant, and how very often his additions tend not to happiness but to misery."

What the world may well have underestimated, however, was a concern more deeply rooted than these pieties revealed. For, unlike so many of his self-made peers, who also rose from poverty, Carnegie was the product of a *radical* environment. The village of Dunfermline, Scotland, when he was born there in 1835, was renowned as a center of revolutionary ferment, and Carnegie's family was itself caught up in the radical movement of the times. His father was a regular speaker at the Chartist rallies, which were an almost daily occurrence in Dunfermline in the 1840's, and his uncle was an impassioned orator for the rights of the working class to vote and strike. All this made an indelible impression on Carnegie's childhood.

"I remember as if it were yesterday," he wrote seventy years later, "being awakened during the night by a tap at the back window by men who had come to inform my parents that my uncle, Bailie Morrison, had been thrown in jail because he dared to hold a meeting which had been forbidden. . . . It is not to be wondered at that, nursed amid such surroundings, I developed into a violent young Republican whose motto was 'death to privilege.' "

From another uncle, George Lauder, Carnegie absorbed a second passion that was also to reveal itself in his later career. This was his love of poetry, first that of the poet Burns, with its overtones of romantic egalitarianism, and then later, of Shakespeare. Immense quantities of both were not only committed to memory, but made into an integral—indeed, sometimes an embarrassingly evident—part of his life: on first visiting the Doge's palace in Venice he thrust a companion in the ducal throne and held him pinioned there while he orated the appropriate speeches from *Othello*. Once, seeing Vanderbilt walking on Fifth Avenue, Carnegie smugly remarked, "I would not exchange his millions for my knowledge of Shakespeare."

But it was more than just a love of poetry that remained with Carnegie. Virtually alone among his fellow acquisitors, he was driven by a genuine respect for the power of thought to seek answers for questions that never even occurred to them. Later, when he "discovered" Herbert Spencer, the English sociologist, Carnegie wrote to him, addressing him as "Master," and it was as "Master" that Spencer remained, even after Carnegie's lavishness had left Spencer very much in his debt.

But Carnegie's early life was shaped by currents more material than intellectual. The grinding process of industrial change had begun slowly but ineluctably to undermine the cottage weaving that was the traditional means of employment in Dunfermline. The Industrial Revolution, in the shape of new steam mills, was forcing out the hand weavers, and one by one the looms which constituted the entire capital of the Carnegie family had to be sold. Carnegie never forgot the shock of his father returning home to tell him, in despair, "Andra, I can get nae mair work."

A family council of war was held, and it was decided that there was only one possible course—they must try their luck in America, to which two sisters of Carnegie's mother, Margaret, had already emigrated. With the aid of a few friends the money for the crossing was scraped together, and at thirteen Andrew found himself transported to the only country in which his career would have been possible.

It hardly got off to an auspicious start, however. The family made their way to Allegheny, Pennsylvania, a raw and bustling town where Carnegie's father again sought work as an independent weaver. But it was hopeless to compete against the great mills in America as in Scotland, and soon father and son were forced to seek work in the local cotton mills. There Andrew worked from six in the morning until six at night, making $1.20 as a bobbin boy.

After a while his father quit—factory work was impossible for the traditional small enterpriser—and Andrew got a "better" job with a new firm, tending an engine deep in a dungeon cellar and dipping newly made cotton spools in a vat of oil. Even the raise of $3 a week—and desperately conjured visions of Wallace and the Bruce—could not overcome the horrors of that lonely and foul-smelling basement. It was perhaps the only time in Carnegie's life when his self-assurance deserted him: to the end of his days the merest whiff of oil could make him deathly sick.

Yet he was certain, as he wrote home at sixteen, that "anyone could get along in this Country," and the rags-to-riches saga shortly began. The telegraph had just come to Pittsburgh, and one evening over a game of checkers, the manager of the local office informed Andrew's uncle that he was looking for a messenger. Andy got the job and, in true Alger fashion, set out to excel in it. Within a few weeks he had carefully memorized the names and the locations, not only of the main streets in Pittsburgh, but of the main firms, so that he was the quickest of all the messenger boys.

He came early and stayed late, watched the telegraphers at work, and at home at night learned the Morse code. As a result he was soon the head of the growing messenger service, and a skilled telegrapher himself. One day he dazzled the office by taking a message "by ear" instead of by the commonly used tape printer, and since he was then only the third operator in the country able to turn the trick, citizens used to drop into the office to watch Andy take down the words "hot from the wire."

One such citizen who was especially impressed with young Carnegie's determination was Thomas A. Scott, in time to become one of the colorful railway magnates of the West, but then the local superintendent of the Pennsylvania Railroad. Soon thereafter Carnegie became "Scott's Andy"—telegrapher, secretary, and general factotum—at thirty-five dollars a month. In his *Autobiography* Carnegie recalls an instance which enabled him to begin the next stage of his career.

> One morning I reached the office and found that a serious accident on the Eastern Division had delayed the express passenger train westward, and that the passenger train eastward was proceeding with a flagman in advance at every curve. The freight trains in both directions were standing on the sidings. Mr. Scott was not to be found. Finally I could not resist the temptation to plunge in, take the responsibility, give "train orders" and set matters going. "Death or Westminster Abbey" flashed across my mind. I knew it was dismissal, disgrace, perhaps criminal punishment for me if I erred. On the other hand, I could bring in the wearied freight train men who had lain out all night. I knew I could. I knew just what to do, and so I began.

Signing Scott's name to the orders, Carnegie flashed out the necessary instructions to bring order out of the tangle. The trains moved; there were no mishaps. When Scott reached the office Carnegie told him what he had done. Scott said not a word but looked carefully over all that had taken place. After a little he moved away from Carnegie's desk to his own, and that was the end of it. "But I noticed," Carnegie concluded good-humoredly, "that he came in very regularly and in good time for some mornings after that."

It is hardly to be wondered at that Carnegie became Scott's favorite, his "white-haired Scotch devil." Impetuous but not rash, full of enthusiasm and good-natured charm, the small lad with his blunt, open features and his slight Scottish burr was every executive's dream of an assistant. Soon Scott repaid Andy for his services by introducing him to a new and very different kind of opportunity. He gave Carnegie the chance to subscribe to five hundred dollars' worth of Adams Express stock, a company which Scott assured Andy would prosper mightily.

Carnegie had not fifty dollars saved, much less five hundred, but it was a chance he could ill afford to miss. He reported the offer to his mother, and that pillar of the family unhesitatingly mortgaged their home to raise the necessary money. When the first dividend check came in, with its ornate Spencerian flourishes, Carnegie had something like a revelation. "I shall remember that check as long as I live," he subsequently wrote. "It gave me the first penny of revenue from capital—something that I had not worked for with the sweat of my brow. 'Eureka!' I cried, 'Here's the goose that lays the golden eggs.' " He was right; within a few years his investment in the Adams Express Company was paying annual dividends of $1,400.

It was not long thereafter that an even more propitious chance presented itself. Carnegie was riding on the Pennsylvania line one day when he was approached by a "farmer-looking" man carrying a small green bag in his hand. The other introduced himself as T. T. Woodruff and quite frankly said that he wanted a chance to talk with someone connected with the railroad. Whereupon he opened his bag and took out a small model of the first sleeping car.

Carnegie was immediately impressed with its possibilities, and he quickly arranged for Woodruff to meet Scott. When the latter agreed to give the cars a trial, Woodruff in appreciation offered Carnegie a chance to subscribe to a one-eighth interest in the new company. A local banker agreed to lend Andy the few hundred dollars needed for the initial payment—the rest being financed from dividends. Once again Andy had made a shrewd investment: within two years the Woodruff Palace Car Company was paying him a return of more than $5,000 a year.

Investments now began to play an increasingly important role in Carnegie's career. Through his railroad contacts he came to recognize the possibilities in manufacturing the heavy equipment needed by the rapidly expanding lines, and soon he was instrumental in organizing companies to meet these needs. One of them, the Keystone Bridge Company, was the first successful manufacturer of iron railway bridges. Another, the Pittsburgh Locomotive Works, made engines. And most important of all, an interest in a local iron works run by an irascible German named Andrew Kloman brought Carnegie into actual contact with the manufacture of iron itself.

None of these new ventures required any substantial outlay of cash. His interest in the Keystone Bridge Company, for instance, which was to earn him $15,000 in 1868, came to him "in return for services rendered in its promotion"—services which Carnegie, as a young railroad executive, was then in a highly strategic position to deliver. Similarly the interest in the Kloman works reflected no contribution on Carnegie's part except that of being the human catalyst and buffer between some highly excitable participants.

By 1865 his "side" activities had become so important that he decided to leave the Pennsylvania Railroad. He was by then superintendent, Scott having moved up to a vice presidency, but his salary of $2,400 was already vastly overshadowed by his income from various ventures. One purchase alone—the

Storey farm in Pennsylvania oil country, which Carnegie and a few associates picked up for $40,000—was eventually to pay the group a million dollars in dividends in *one* year. About this time a friend dropped in on Carnegie and asked him how he was doing. "Oh, I'm rich, I'm rich!" he exclaimed.

He was indeed embarked on the road to riches, and determined, as he later wrote in his *Autobiography,* that "nothing could be allowed to interfere for a moment with my business career." Hence it comes as a surprise to note that it was at this very point that Carnegie retired to his suite to write his curiously introspective and troubled thoughts about the pursuit of wealth. But the momentum of events was to prove far too strong for these moralistic doubts. Moving his headquarters to New York to promote his various interests, he soon found himself swept along by a succession of irresistible opportunities for money-making.

One of these took place quite by chance. Carnegie was trying to sell the Woodruff sleeping car at the same time that a formidable rival named George Pullman was also seeking to land contracts for his sleeping car, and the railroads were naturally taking advantage of the competitive situation. One summer evening in 1869 Carnegie found himself mounting the resplendent marble stairway of the St. Nicholas Hotel side by side with his competitor.

"Good evening, Mr. Pullman," said Carnegie in his ebullient manner. Pullman was barely cordial.

"How strange we should meet here," Carnegie went on, to which the other replied nothing at all.

"Mr. Pullman," said Carnegie, after an embarrassing pause, "don't you think we are making nice fools of ourselves?" At this Pullman evinced a glimmer of interest: "What do you mean?" he inquired. Carnegie quickly pointed out that competition between the two companies was helping no one but the railroads. "Well," said Pullman, "what do you suggest we do?"

"Unite!" said Carnegie. "Let's make a joint proposition to the Union Pacific, your company and mine. Why not organize a new company to do it?" "What would you call it?" asked Pullman suspiciously. "The Pullman Palace Car Company," said Carnegie and with this shrewd psychological stroke won his point. A new company was formed, and in time Carnegie became its largest stockholder.

Meanwhile, events pushed Carnegie into yet another lucrative field. To finance the proliferating railway systems of America, British capital was badly needed, and with his Scottish ancestry, his verve, and his excellent railroad connections Carnegie was the natural choice for a go-between. His brief case stuffed with bonds and prospectuses, Carnegie became a transatlantic commuter, soon developing intimate relations both with great bankers like Junius Morgan (the father of J. P. Morgan), and with the heads of most of the great American roads. These trips earned him not only large commissions— exceeding on occasion $100,000 for a single turn—but even more important, established connections that were later to be of immense value. He himself later testified candidly on their benefits before a group of respectfully awed senators:

> For instance, I want a great contract for rails. Sidney Dillon of the Union Pacific was a personal friend of mine. Huntington was a friend. Dear Butler Duncan, that called on me the other day, was a friend. Those and other men were presidents of railroads. . . . Take Huntington; you know C. P. Huntington. He was hard up very often. He was a great man, but he had a great deal of paper out. I knew his things were good. When he wanted credit I gave it to him. If you help a man that way, what chance has any paid agent going to these men? It was absurd.

But his trips to England brought Carnegie something still more valuable. They gave him steel. It is fair to say that as late as 1872 Carnegie did not see the future that awaited him as the Steel King of the world. The still modest conglomeration of foundries and mills he was gradually assembling in the Allegheny and Monongahela valleys was but one of many business interests, and not one for which he envisioned any extraordinary future. Indeed, to repeated pleas that he lead the way in developing a steel industry for America by substituting steel for iron rails, his reply was succinct: "Pioneering don't pay."

What made him change his mind? The story goes that he was awe-struck by the volcanic, spectacular eruption of a Bessemer converter, which he saw for the first time during a visit to a British mill. It was precisely the sort of display that would have appealed to Carnegie's mind—a wild, demonic, physical process miraculously contained and controlled by the dwarfed figures of the steel men themselves. At any rate, overnight Carnegie became the perfervid prophet of steel. Jumping on the first available steamer, he rushed home with the cry, "The day of iron has passed!" To the consternation of his colleagues, the hitherto reluctant pioneer became an advocate of the most daring technological and business expansion; he joined them enthusiastically in forming Carnegie, McCandless & Company, which was the nucleus of the empire that the next thirty years would bring forth.

The actual process of growth involved every aspect of successful business enterprise of the times: acquisition and merger, pools and commercial piracy, and even, on one occasion, an outright fraud in selling the United States government overpriced and underdone steel armor plate. But it would be as foolish to maintain that the Carnegie empire grew by trickery as to deny that sharp practice had its place. Essentially what lay behind the spectacular expansion were three facts.

The first of these was the sheer economic expansion of the industry in the first days of burgeoning steel use. Everywhere steel replaced iron or found new uses—and not only in railroads but in ships, buildings, bridges, machinery of all sorts. As Henry Frick himself once remarked, if the Carnegie group had not filled the need for steel another would have. But it must be admitted that Carnegie's company did its job superlatively well. In 1885 Great Britain led the world in the production of steel. Fourteen years later her total output was 695,000 tons less than the output of the Carnegie Steel Company alone.

Second was the brilliant assemblage of personal talent with which Carnegie surrounded himself. Among them, three in particular stood out. One was Captain William Jones, a Homeric figure who lumbered through the glowing fires and clanging machinery of the works like a kind of Paul Bunyan of steel, skilled at handling men, inventive in handling equipment, and enough of a natural artist to produce papers for the British Iron and Steel Institute that earned him a literary as well as a technical reputation. Then there was Henry Frick, himself a self-made millionaire, whose coke empire naturally complemented Carnegie's steelworks. When the two were amalgamated, Frick took over the active management of the whole, and under his forceful hand the annual output of the Carnegie works rose tenfold. Yet another was Charles Schwab, who came out of the tiny monastic town of Loretto, Pennsylvania, to take a job as a stake driver. Six months later he had been promoted by Jones into the assistant managership of the Braddock plant.

These men, and a score like them, constituted the vital energy of the Carnegie works. As Carnegie himself said, "Take away all our money, our great works, ore mines and coke ovens, but leave our organization, and in four years I shall have re-established myself."

But the third factor in the growth of the empire was Carnegie himself. A master salesman and a skilled diplomat of business at its highest levels, Carnegie was also a ruthless driver of his men. He pitted his associates and subordinates in competition with one another until a feverish atmosphere pervaded the whole organization. "You cannot imagine the abounding sense of freedom and relief I experience as soon as I get on board a steamer and sail past Sandy Hook," he once said to Captain Jones. "My God!" replied Jones. "Think of the relief to us!"

But Carnegie could win loyalties as well. All his promising young men were given gratis ownership participations—minuscule fractions of one per cent, which were enough, however, to make them millionaires in their own right. Deeply grateful to Jones, Carnegie once offered him a similar participation. Jones hemmed and hawed and finally refused; he would be unable to work effectively with the men, he said, once he was a partner. Carnegie insisted that his contribution be recognized and asked Jones what he wanted. "Well," said the latter, "you might pay me a hell of a big salary." "We'll do it!" said Carnegie. "From this time forth you shall receive the same salary as the President of the United States." "Ah, Andy, that's the kind of talk," said Captain Bill.

Within three decades, on the flood tide of economic expansion, propelled by brilliant executive work and relentless pressure from Carnegie, the company made immense strides. "Such a magnificent aggregation of industrial power has never before been under the domination of a single man," reported a biographer in 1902, describing the Gargantuan structure of steel and coke and ore and transport. Had the writer known of the profits earned by this aggregation he might have been even more impressed: three and a half million dollars in 1889, seven million in 1897, twenty-one million in 1899, and an immense forty million in 1900. "Where is there such a business!" Carnegie had exulted, and no wonder—the majority share of all these earnings, without hindrance of income tax, went directly into his pockets.

Nevertheless, with enormous success came problems. One of these was the restiveness of certain partners, under the "Iron-Clad" agreement, which prevented any of them from selling their shares to anyone but the company itself—an arrangement which meant, of course, that the far higher valuation of an outside purchaser could not be realized. Particularly chagrined was Frick, when, as the culmination of other disagreements between them, Carnegie sought to buy him out "at the value appearing on the books." Another problem was a looming competitive struggle in the steel industry itself that presaged a period of bitter industrial warfare ahead. And last was Carnegie's own growing desire to "get out."

Already he was spending half of each year abroad, first traveling, and then, after his late marriage, in residence in the great Skibo Castle he built for his wife on Dornoch Firth, Scotland. There he ran his business enterprises with one hand while he courted the literary and creative world with the other, entertaining Kipling and Matthew Arnold, Paderewski and Lloyd George, Woodrow Wilson and Theodore Roosevelt, Gladstone, and of course, Herbert Spencer, the Master. But even his career as "Laird" of Skibo could not remove him from the worries—and triumphs—of his business: a steady flow of cables and correspondence intruded on the "serious" side of life.

It was Schwab who cut the knot. Having risen to the very summit of the Carnegie concern he was invited in December, 1900, to give a speech on the future of the steel industry at the University Club in New York. There, before eighty of the nation's top business leaders he painted a glowing picture of what could be done if a super-company of steel were formed, integrated from top to bottom, self-sufficient with regard to its raw materials, balanced in its array of final products. One of the guests was the imperious J. P. Morgan, and as the speech progressed it was noticed that his concentration grew more and more intense. After dinner Morgan rose and took the young steel man by the elbow and engaged him in private conversation for half an hour while he plied him with rapid and penetrating questions; then a few weeks later he invited him to a private meeting in the great library of his home. They talked from nine o'clock in the evening until dawn. As the sun began to stream in through the library windows, the banker finally rose. "Well," he said to Schwab, "if Andy wants to sell, I'll buy. Go and find his price."

Carnegie at first did not wish to sell. Faced with the actual prospect of a withdrawal from the business he had built into the mightiest single industrial empire in the world, he was frightened and dismayed. He sat silent before Schwab's report, brooding, loath to inquire into details. But soon his enthusiasm returned. No such opportunity was likely to present itself again. In short order a figure of $492,000,000 was agreed on for the entire enterprise, of which Carnegie himself was to receive $300,000,000 in five per cent gold bonds and preferred stock. Carnegie jotted down the terms of the transaction on a slip of paper and told Schwab to bring it to Morgan. The banker glanced only briefly at the paper. "I accept," he said.

After the formalities were in due course completed, Carnegie was in a euphoric mood. "Now, Pierpont, I am the happiest man in the world," he said. Morgan was by no means unhappy himself: his own banking company had made a direct profit of $12,500,000 in the underwriting transaction, and this was but a prelude to a stream of lucrative financings under Morgan's aegis, by which the total capitalization was rapidly raised to $1,400,000,000. A few years later, Morgan and Carnegie found themselves aboard the same steamer en route to Europe. They fell into talk and Carnegie confessed, "I made one mistake, Pierpont, when I sold out to you."

"What was that?" asked the banker.

"I should have asked you for $100,000,000 more than I did." Morgan grinned. "Well," he said, "you would have got it if you had."

Thus was written *finis* to one stage of Carnegie's career. Now it would be seen to what extent his "radical pronouncements" were serious. For in the *Gospel of Wealth*—the famous article combined with others in book form—Carnegie had proclaimed the duty of the millionaire to administer and distribute his wealth *during his lifetime*. Though he might have "proved" his worth by his fortune, his heirs had shown no such evidence of their fitness. Carnegie bluntly concluded: "By taxing estates heavily at his death, the State marks its condemnation of the selfish millionaire's unworthy life."

Coming from the leading millionaire of the day, these had been startling sentiments. So also were his views on the "labor question" which, if patronizing, were nonetheless humane and advanced for their day. The trouble was, of course, that the sentiments were somewhat difficult to credit. As one commentator of the day remarked, "His vision of what might be done with wealth had beauty and breadth and thus serenely overlooked the means by which wealth had been acquired."

For example, the novelist Hamlin Garland visited the steel towns from which the Carnegie millions came and bore away a description of work that was ugly, brutal, and exhausting: he contrasted the lavish care expended on the plants with the callous disregard of the pigsty homes: "the streets were horrible; the buildings poor; the sidewalks sunken and full of holes. . . . Everywhere the yellow mud of the streets lay kneaded into sticky masses through which groups of pale, lean men slouched in faded garments. . . ." When the famous Homestead strike erupted in 1892, with its private army of Pinkerton detectives virtually at war with the workers, the Carnegie benevolence seemed revealed as shabby fakery. At Skibo Carnegie stood firmly behind the company's iron determination to break the strike. As a result, public sentiment swung sharply and suddenly against him; the St. Louis *Post-Dispatch* wrote: "Three months ago Andrew Carnegie was a man to be envied.

Today he is an object of mingled pity and contempt. In the estimation of nine-tenths of the thinking people on both sides of the ocean he has . . . confessed himself a moral coward."

In an important sense the newspaper was right. For though Carnegie continued to fight against "privilege," he saw privilege only in its fading aristocratic vestments and not in the new hierarchies of wealth and power to which he himself belonged. In Skibo Castle he now played the role of the benign autocrat, awakening to the skirling of his private bagpiper and proceeding to breakfast to the sonorous accompaniment of the castle organ.

Meanwhile there had also come fame and honors in which Carnegie wallowed unshamedly. He counted the "freedoms" bestowed on him by grateful or hopeful cities and crowed. "I have fifty-two and Gladstone has only seventeen." He entertained the King of England and told him that democracy was better than monarchy, and met the German Kaiser: "Oh, yes, yes," said the latter worthy on being introduced. "I have read your books. You do not like kings." But Mark Twain, on hearing of this, was not fooled. "He says he is a scorner of kings and emperors and dukes," he wrote, "whereas he is like the rest of the human race: a slight attention from one of these can make him drunk for a week. . . ."

And yet it is not enough to conclude that Carnegie was in fact a smaller man than he conceived himself. For this judgment overlooks one immense and irrefutable fact. He did, in the end, abide by his self-imposed duty. He did give nearly all of his gigantic fortune away.

As one would suspect, the quality of the philanthropy reflected the man himself. There was, for example, a huge and sentimentally administered private pension fund to which access was to be had on the most trivial as well as the most worthy ground: if it included a number of writers, statesmen, scientists, it also made room for two maiden ladies with whom Carnegie had once danced as a young man, a boyhood acquaintance who had once held Carnegie's books while he ran a race, a merchant to whom he had once delivered a telegram and who had subsequently fallen on hard times. And then, as one would expect, there was a benevolent autocracy in the administration of the larger philanthropies as well. "Now everybody vote Aye," was the way Carnegie typically determined the policies of the philanthropic "foundations" he established.

Yet if these flaws bore the stamp of one side of Carnegie's personality, there was also the other side—the side that, however crudely, asked important questions and however piously, concerned itself with great ideals. Of this the range and purpose of the main philanthropies gave unimpeachable testimony. There were the famous libraries—three thousand of them costing nearly sixty million dollars; there were the Carnegie institutes in Pittsburgh and Washington, Carnegie Hall in New York, the Hague Peace Palace, the Carnegie Endowment for International Peace, and the precedent-making Carnegie Corporation of New York, with its original enormous endowment of $125,000,000.

In his instructions to the trustees of this first great modern foundation, couched in the simplified spelling of which he was an ardent advocate, we see Carnegie at his very best:

> Conditions on erth [*sic*] inevitably change; hence, no wise man will bind
> Trustees forever to certain paths, causes, or institutions. I disclaim any intention
> of doing so. . . . My chief happiness, as I write these lines lies in the thot [*sic*]
> that, even after I pass away, the welth [*sic*] that came to me to administer as a
> sacred trust for the good of my fellow men is to continue to benefit
> humanity. . . .

If these sentiments move us—if Carnegie himself in retrospect moves us at last to grudging respect—it is not because his was the triumph of a saint or a philosopher. It is because it was the much more difficult triumph of a very human and fallible man struggling to retain his convictions in an age, and in the face of a career, which subjected them to impossible temptations. Carnegie is something of America writ large; his is the story of the Horatio Alger hero *after* he has made his million dollars. In the failures of Andrew Carnegie we see many of the failures of America itself. In his curious triumph, we see what we hope is our own steadfast core of integrity.

The Haymarket Bomb

by Burton Schindler

In the late nineteenth century, American workers were struggling for the rights that modern workers take for granted, such as the eight hour day. Chicago was the scene of a lot of labor unrest. It was the home of the McCormick Reaper Works which was engaged in a bitter labor dispute with its workers in the spring of 1886. After Chicago police broke up a fight between union and non-union workers outside the plant, a mass meeting of workers was called for May 4 in Haymarket Square. The tragic events of that evening would see seven policemen die with scores more injured and untold numbers of civilians killed and wounded. The tragedy would then be compounded by the legal events that would follow. Newspaper reporter and free lance writer Burton Schindler recounts in this article the horror of that evening in Chicago and the ensuing controversy over the trials and executions of anarchists accused of the crime.

A trail of sparks followed the small dark object as it soared over the throng. A few in the shoving, scrambling, shouting crowd looked up. But most were trying to avoid rank after rank of policemen who were marching steadily toward them. In the dimness of the few gas lights, only twinkles from the police badges could be seen.

Then the bomb exploded.

The repercussions from that blinding flash in Haymarket Square in Chicago one hundred years ago, May 4, 1886, were far-reaching. Eventually the bomb blast and its aftereffects would leave seven policemen dead and sixty others wounded, an unknown number of civilians killed and injured, four men hanged, another a suicide, a judge and a lawyer disgraced, a governor's career wrecked, and a mighty labor union destroyed. Its echoes can still be faintly heard today.

Haymarket—like Watergate eight-six years later—was a place that lent its name to a particular event in time and to the violent emotions accompanying that event. Haymarket Square was, as it is today, a wide place on Randolph Street just west of Desplaines Avenue, near Chicago's open-air produce market. It gained its place in history because it happened to be a convenient location for a mass-meeting of workers who were protesting the long hours, low pay, and oppression they claimed were the results of unfair government action.

The circumstances that would set the stage for the events of May 1886 had been taking form for more than a decade. America's working class had been hard-hit by economic severity and depression during the 1870s. Especially apparent was the wide gulf between the world of a few industrial millionaires and that of three million unemployed and fifteen million others who lived in poverty. Such conditions led to riots, the starting of labor union organizations, and the questioning by some of the viability of the capitalist system.

By 1886 one national labor union, the Knights of Labor, had grown to over seven hundred thousand members, and workers all around the country were demanding improved conditions. In particular, they were marching and striking for an eight-hour workday. A deadline for making the eight-hour day a reality was set for May 1, 1886.

Chicago, especially, was a hotbed of labor unrest. In 1871 much of Chicago had been destroyed by fire, and within three years thousands of workers who had come to rebuild the city were unemployed. Making the situation even worse over the next several years was an influx of thousands of Irish and German immigrants. The result was that there were simply not enough jobs to go around, and many of those who did have work labored under poor conditions. In addition, a group of radicals had taken over much of the labor and union leadership, especially among the German immigrant workers, who had seen employers use other immigrant groups as strikebreakers against them whenever they attempted to enforce demands.

But the Germans who headed the most vocal groups were not just seeking changes in the number of working hours—they wanted an end to the entire capitalist system that seemed to create millionaires at the expense of the poverty-stricken. And they saw violence as the means to that end. They called themselves Socialists sometimes, but they often preferred the name the newspapers used: Anarchists.

Two men were the leaders of this group: August Spies, who was editor of the German-language Socialist newspaper *Arbeiter-Zeitung* ("Workers' Newspaper"), and Albert Parsons, editor of another activist newspaper, *The Alarm.*

Spies, born in Germany in 1855, had emigrated to the United States in 1872. He moved to Chicago the following year and in 1876 opened a furniture store. Spies soon made enough money to bring his widowed mother, sister, and three brothers to America. His interest in socialism began in the mid-1870s, when he felt the irony of his own success in the face of the poverty around him.

Parsons was born in Montgomery, Alabama, in 1848 and was orphaned at an early age. He served in the Confederate Army during the Civil War but became a strong believer in black civil rights, a cause he addressed in *The Spectator,* a newspaper he started in Texas in 1867. Parson's marriage to a woman of mixed racial background made him unwelcome in Texas, and in 1873 the couple moved to Chicago to become involved with the labor struggle that was centered there.

By 1886 both men had been politically active for years, making speeches throughout the country to any group that would listen, expounding their ideas of a new society without property rights, in which every man would be equal. Only a year earlier Parsons had spoken at a workingman's picnic attended by more than ten thousand, calling for a society in which there would be "neither masters nor slaves, neither governors nor governed, no law but the natural law."

As the drive for an eight-hour workday gained momentum, the anarchists saw it as an opportunity for promoting their own militant causes, and Spies and Parsons became the leading spokesmen for the campaign in the Chicago area. The two men frequently issued calls for violence in the columns of the *Arbeiter-Zeitung* and *The Alarm;* later these words would help to place nooses around their necks.

With the arrival of the May deadline for an eight-hour day, more than forty thousand Chicago workers went on strike. No violence occurred on May 1, as had been feared by officials, but it erupted just two days later at the McCormick Reaper Works on Blue Island Avenue. During a bitter labor struggle that had begun at McCormick several months earlier, the plant management had locked out striking union workers and hired nonunion men.

On the afternoon of May 3, August Spies was asked to speak to a group of striking lumber shovers a few blocks from the McCormick works. While he was addressing a crowd of some six thousand men, nonunion workers began leaving the nearby plant at the end of their shift, and strikers there attacked them with rocks. Police quickly moved in; shots were fired; and within minutes two men were dead. Early newspaper reports erroneously claimed that six had been killed.

Spies rushed to the scene following his speech and witnessed some of the violence. Infuriated by what he saw as police brutality, he returned to his office and printed up leaflets, in English and German, with the headlines "Revenge!" and "Workingmen, to Arms!!!" The following morning other anarchists associated with Spies printed up additional handbills calling for a mass meeting of workers that night in Haymarket Square. Because of the emotions that were building up over the McCormick deaths, they expected a crowd of twenty thousand, and Haymarket was the only spot that could accommodate such numbers. The organizers knew that the Desplaines Avenue police station was only a half-block from the site, but though there would be angry speeches they neither planned nor expected violence.

The night of May 4 was mild, but the skies were heavy with clouds and an intermittent mist blew through the square where a few groups were beginning to gather. At about 8:15 P.M., Spies arrived on the scene and found only about two thousand people waiting. There was no organization and no speeches were yet in progress, just small clumps of people talking together around the intersection. Spies headed a few yards up Desplaines Avenue, away from the square, to a wagon that he selected as a speakers' platform. Calling the crowd over, he began his talk while hoping that other speakers would soon arrive. He continued for an hour. Eventually, a few others of his group began to arrive.

While Spies was speaking, Chicago Mayor Carter Harrison wandered through the crowd. Earlier he had personally given permission for the rally and now he made himself conspicuous by lighting and relighting his cigar. "I want the people to know their mayor is here," he said to a bystander, who warned him that his action might bring him harm. Harrison new that Police Captain William Ward and Inspector John Bonfield were waiting with 176 officers at the nearby station in case of trouble. After listening a while, Harrison strolled down to the alley where the police were assembled and told Bonfield that although the speech was angry, there seemed to be nothing dangerous in the situation. With that, he left and rode to his home on Ashland Avenue.

As Spies finished, another speaker arrived. Albert Parsons had been hurriedly located and brought to the wagon before the crowd could leave. Parsons spoke for an hour more, and while most of his speech supported the eight-hour day and the usual calls for an end to oppression, a *Chicago Tribune* reporter recalled later that he also told the listeners, although in a calm voice, to "arm, arm yourselves." He also referred to a "Gatling gun ready to mow you down." A *New York Times* story over the weekend had mentioned that members of Chicago's Commercial Club, an association of business leaders, had raised over two thousand dollars among themselves to purchase a Gatling machine gun for the local militia regiment to be used in the event of disorder.

Parsons then introduced Samuel Fielden as the last speaker. Parsons and his wife Lucy soon headed up Desplaines Avenue to a beer hall, Zepf's, to await the end of the rally.

Fielden, who was born in 1847 in Lancashire, England, had begun working in a cloth mill at age eight—an experience that would have a formative influence on his later involvement in labor and union causes. Emigrating to the United States in 1868, he found employment as a stonehauler in Chicago. One of the more radical activists, Fielden was nevertheless popular and respected among workers for his eloquent and impassioned speeches on labor issues.

As Fielden started to speak, the skies rumbled and drops of rain began to pelt the crowd in Haymarket Square. Most of the listeners drifted away, until fewer than three hundred remained around the speakers' wagon. As Spies listened from the back of the wagon, Fielden said that the law was nothing of value. He told his listeners "to lay hands on it and throttle it until it makes its last kick."

Two detectives who had been mingling with the crowd hurried away from the wagon as Fielden spoke these words. They rushed down the street to Inspector Bonfield at the Desplaines Street station and told him that the atmosphere was growing violent. Bonfield and Ward mustered their squads and ordered them forward. The men moved out of the darkened alley next to the police station, filling the street and heading across the half-block of Randolph to a spot just north of the corner where Fielden was speaking.

At first the crowd was unaware of the approaching policemen. As the ranks of officers began to shove into their midst, Captain Ward shouted, "I command you, in the name of the people of the State of Illinois, immediately and peaceably to disperse!" Fielden saw the police and responded, "But we are peaceable," and began to climb down from the wagon. At just that moment the trail of sparks flew overhead. The bomb landed just in front of the first police rank. It burst with a roar that was heard by Mayor Harrison, who was preparing for bed in his home blocks away.

For an instant afterward there was silence. Then shouts, screams, and soon the roar of shots as the police fired into the crowd. Most of the crowd started to run up the street, away from the police. The shots followed them, dropping some blocks or more away. The scene around the explosion was one of horror. Maimed and dying policemen lay scattered along the pavement. Injured and shot workers lay moaning against the darkened buildings. The firing continued for almost five minutes.

Many of those who were injured by the bullets or the trampling crowd burst into saloons and stores along Desplaines and other streets, ignoring the threats of the owners, and piled up tables and boxes for protection. The police, meanwhile, began to drag their injured comrades back toward the station. Soon the floor there was covered with mangled and bleeding men, some calling for help, others pale and silent in shock and approaching death. Eventually, seven policemen would die and more than sixty would recover from wounds. According to the *Chicago Tribune,* "a very large number of the police were wounded by each other's revolvers."

Of the civilian casualties, no exact count was ever made. Many of the injured were hauled away by their friends, some riding streetcars to get away from the scene. Others treated themselves as best they could, fearing to report their wounds lest they be arrested.

As the night descended on the city, police raced from rumor to rumor of impending riot and rebellion. Alarmed, Mayor Harrison issued orders approaching martial law. Suspects were routed out of bed, often without the legality of a warrant. Men were jailed without evidence, and questioning was often harsh. Over the next days, all meetings would be banned. The city trembled in fear. Even display of the color red was prohibited because of its association with the anarchists.

Newspapers and civic leaders across the country demanded action and revenge. The *New York Times* headlined its lead story the next morning, "Anarchy's Red Hand." And, from the respected *Albany Law Review* came demands for punishment "for the few long-haired, wild-eyed, bad-smelling, atheistic, reckless foreign wretches."

By midmorning on May 5, the Chicago police had arrested dozens. Among them were seven who would eventually stand trial. August Spies and Adolph Fischer, a typesetter at Spies's newspaper, were arrested just after nine o'clock in their office. Samuel Fielden was taken from his home early in the morning. He was wearing a bandage and told police he had been wounded in the knee and needed treatment. According to his testimony, a detective responded that "they ought to put strychnine in it." While Fielden was being rushed to a cell, the police turned his house inside-out, but found nothing incriminating. Other activists arrested included George Engel, Oscar Neebe, Michael Schwab, and Louis Lingg.

Albert Parsons was not found. While he and his wife were waiting at Zepf's Hall they heard the explosion and shots. Knowing that her husband would be a prime suspect, Lucy urged him to leave the city. Borrowing five dollars from a friend, Parsons made his way to the Chicago & Northwestern Railroad station and took the next train to Wisconsin.

After staying one night with a friend in Lake Geneva, Parsons went to Waukesha, were he remained in hiding while the search continued in Chicago. His escape caused even further outrage.

While Chicago seethed in fear and rumor, other cities, too, reacted with alarm. According to many historians, this was America's first actual terrorist bombing. For many, the threat of true anarchy now was made real. The Knights of Labor sought to distance themselves from the unknown bomb-thrower and issued statements denouncing the act and urging the conviction of Parsons, Fielding, and Spies. The demands for swift justice were heard everywhere.

Indictments were handled quickly and the trial began on June 21, only a few weeks after the Haymarket explosion. It lasted until August 19 and, despite the heat of a Chicago summer, the courtroom was continually packed. Judge Joseph E. Gary was chosen to preside. His actions—such as refusing to allow the case to be postponed until public hysteria had died down and refusing to disqualify clearly prejudiced jurors—would eventually become cause for the claims of bias.

The Cook County state's attorney was Julius S. Grinnell. For a time, the defendants were without a lawyer. No one in Chicago was willing to risk his career in their behalf. Finally, after being asked to find an attorney for the seven, William P. Black, a respected corporation lawyer and Civil War veteran, decided to handle the case himself even though he, too, feared that it might cause him damage.

Meanwhile, hiding out in Wisconsin, Albert Parsons considered his situation. There he was safe. But his conscience demanded that he join his comrades on the dock, even though he guessed the outcome of the trial. Before the trial began, after talking with his friends and on the advice of William Black, Parsons decided to return and to be tried. Black had hoped that Parson's voluntary surrender would improve the court's attitude. Unfortunately for Parsons, his return only sealed his fate.

Both the prosecution and defense had difficult jobs ahead of them. Grinnell's first problem was to connect the defendants with the bomb itself. One witness, Harry L. Gilmer, told the police that he had seen August Spies actually lighting the fuse at the rear of the wagon. But others discounted that testimony, saying that they had seen the bomb coming from a spot near the northeast corner of Desplaines Avenue and Randolph.

Each of the defendants turned out to have a clear alibi for his whereabouts, which meant that none of those on trial could have actually thrown the bomb. Samuel Fielden was actually talking with Captain Ward as the bomb flew overhead. August Spies was seen by the crowd and policemen at the back of the wagon. Louis Lingg was on the north side of town, George Engel and Oscar Neebe were at home, and Michael Schwab was five miles away. Adolph Fischer and Albert Parsons were known to have been in Zepf's Hall when the explosion occurred.

Determined to obtain a conviction nevertheless, Grinnell now changed his tactics, going for a charge of conspiracy. "Although perhaps none of these men personally threw the bomb," he argued, "they each and all abetted, encouraged and advised the throwing of it and are therefore as guilty as the individual who in fact threw it."

Judge Gary aided the prosecutor's cause mightily with his charge to the jury that if any of the men had "by print or speech advised, or encouraged the commission of murder, without designating time, place or occasion at which it should be done . . . then all of such conspirators are guilty of such murder." August Spies's handbills and the speeches of the others were coming back to convict them of a crime they did not commit.

After dozens of witnesses (many of whom gave conflicting testimony that was later discredited) and extensive exhibited evidence that told of the defendants' years of inciting anarchy, the trial came to a close. The jury received its instructions and retired to deliberate on the afternoon of August 19. It needed only three hours to reach its verdict.

On the following morning Judge Gary convened the court, and the verdict was read. Oscar Neebe was considered to have played a minor role in the alleged conspiracy and was sentenced to fifteen years in prison; all of the other defendants were found guilty of murder and sentenced to death. The verdict exceeded even the expectations of state's attorney Grinnell, who had anticipated at most four death sentences.

According to defense attorney William Black, "not a [defendant's] face blanched" as the verdict was read. Albert Parsons, who was standing near an open window, coolly waved a red handkerchief to the hostile crowd waiting in the street below. Then, to advise them of the penalty, he tied the cords of the widow shade to form a noose. His action was greeted by wild cheers.

Black immediately filed for a retrial, but Judge Gary denied all motions on October 7, the day set for formal sentencing. Prior to his statements, Gary allowed each prisoner the right to speak. They all took full advantage of the opportunity: their speeches lasted for three days.

The defendants remained unrepentant regarding both their beliefs and actions. "I am an Anarchist," Albert Parsons loudly stated. "I declare again, openly and frankly," said Louis Lingg, "that I am in favor of using force." "I am sorry that I am not to be hung with the rest of the men," said Oscar Neebe. Nevertheless the men maintained that they had been tried for their radical political beliefs, not their actions; that they had been found guilty by public opinion from the beginning; and that they were innocent of the crime for which they had been convicted.

Gary told the condemned men that their trial had been "unexampled for these days, in the patience with which an outraged people have extended you every protection and privilege of the law which you have derided and defied." He then set December 3, 1886, for their execution.

Black promptly filed an appeal with the Supreme Court of Illinois. On November 25, Chief Justice John M. Scott ordered a stay of execution until the appeal was decided. That body took months to deliberate, but in the end, its decision on September 14, 1887, confirmed the verdict. On November 2, 1887, the United States Supreme Court refused to consider the case as it lacked jurisdiction. A new date, November 11, 1887, was set for the executions.

In the interim, however, emotions had subsided a bit. Some of those who had earlier been crying for instant vengeance now were wondering if the trial had been completely fair. Petitions began to pour into the office of Governor Richard J. Oglesby in Springfield. After an Amnesty Association was formed, the mass of petitions and personal appeals for clemency for the seven condemned men grew even more. Among the powerful petitioners was Samuel Gompers, the first president of the new American Federation of Labor (AFL) that had been founded in 1886. The fledgling organization would eventually supplant Terence Powderly's faltering Knights of Labor as the strongest organization behind labor reform. "I abhor anarchy," stated Gompers, "but I also abhor injustice when meted out even to the most despicable being on earth."

Illinois law required that a condemned man had to ask personally for clemency before the governor could legally act in the matter. Only Samuel Fielden, August Spies, and Michael Schwab did so. After many hours and a full day devoted to listening to petitions, Oglesby prepared to make his decision. But two events intervened before he could make a statement.

On November 6, guards at the Cook County Jail conducted a surprise search of the cells. They discovered four dynamite bombs hidden under the bunk in Louis Lingg's cell. Reports that the prisoners had planned a mass suicide attempt ran through the city. Lingg was moved to another cell and the other prisoners were separated from each other. Visitors, however, were permitted.

Then, at about 9:00 A.M. on November 10, a loud explosion resounded through the cell block. Guards rushed into Lingg's cell to find him slumped on his cot in a mass of blood and torn flesh. He had exploded a dynamite cap in his mouth and blown the lower half of his face away. Despite attempts by doctors to sew up the shattered face, Lingg continued to bleed and he died at 2:50 P.M. His body was dumped into a tub to await the execution of his comrades the following day.

Governor Oglesby was told of Lingg's suicide. It is not known how the event weighed on his decision. His final announcement on November 10 was that Michael Schwab and Samuel Fielden would have their sentences commuted to life in prison. The others would hang.

At 11:30 A.M. on the following day, November 11, 1887, Sheriff Canute R. Matson entered the prison with a squad of armed guards. Outside, Chicago was an armed camp: the Cook County Jail was ringed with armed officers, and police and soldiers were on alert at key points throughout the city. They feared not only a possible attempt to rescue the prisoners, but citywide rebellion.

Robed in white shrouds, the four condemned men were led to a scaffold that had been erected in a corridor of the jail building. Rows of benches, occupied by 170 witnesses, faced the scaffold. As each man was brought forward to stand under a hangman's rope, his ankles were bound with a leather strap. The noose was then placed around his neck and a hood put over his head.

From behind one hood, the muffled voice of Adolph Fischer cried out in German, "Hurrah for Anarchy!" George Engel echoed his cry in English. The witnesses strained to hear August Spies who shouted through his hood, "The day will come when our silence will be more powerful than the voices you strangle today!" Albert Parsons, too, attempted to speak, but as he started, the trap was sprung and the four dropped. Eight minutes later they were declared dead; all four had died from strangulation.

Afterward, the bodies were taken to their respective homes for mourning by their friends. (The remains of Louis Lingg, because he had no relatives in America, were taken to Engel's house.) On Sunday, November 13, a funeral procession wound through downtown Chicago to the central railroad station. By this time public opinion had reversed itself; many now viewed the five men as martyrs who had died unjustly. More than twenty thousand people followed the caskets to the depot, while over two hundred thousand others lined the streets. Then a special train carried the bodies and ten thousand mourners toward the German village of Forest Park on Chicago's west side and its Waldheim Cemetery. It was the largest funeral in the city's history.

Six years later, on June 25, 1893, anther eight thousand people assembled at Waldheim Cemetery for the dedication of a monument to the condemned men. The memorial featured a bronze sculpture by Albert Weinert, depicting

Suggested additional reading: *The Haymarket Tragedy* by Paul Avrich (Princeton University Press, 1984).

a hooded woman placing a wreath on the head of a fallen worker. August Spies's last words from the scaffold were carved into the base of the memorial.

On the following day the new governor of Illinois, John Peter Altgeld, announced that he was pardoning the three remaining members of the "Haymarket Eight." At the same time he issued a strong worded, detailed statement condemning the Haymarket trial as blatantly unfair and the actions there by the police, prosecuting attorneys, and judge as prejudiced. Michael Schwab, Samuel Fielden, and Oscar Neebe were free men.

Governor Altgeld's actions, however, drew hostile reactions from many newspapers around the country and ignited a storm of controversy. Later the governor would be defeated in his bid for a second term—a result at least in part attributed to his stand on the Haymarket trial.

Altgeld was not the only one to suffer from association with the Haymarket controversy. Corporation lawyer William P. Black, who had defended the anarchists at the risk of his reputation, saw his worse fears realized. Following the trial Black was ostracized by the city's business community, lost most of his clients, and his once-thriving law partnership dissolved.

Even more far-reaching in consequence was Haymarket's effect on the labor movement. Although labor unions had had no direct connection with the bombing—and sought to distance themselves from it—such association in the public mind was nevertheless inevitable. The campaign for an eight-hour workday suffered a severe setback, and the powerful Knights of Labor, which had boasted seven hundred thousand members in 1886, soon shriveled to a shadow of its former strength.

And what of the man who should have been convicted, the actual bomb-thrower? He was never caught or identified. Some suspected that he was an *agent provocateur* against the eight-hour movement. The police, and many others, suspected that the killer was Michael Schwab's brother-in-law, Rudolph Schnaubelt. Although no proof was ever presented, many have claimed that it was indeed Schnaubelt who stood in a darkened doorway near the corner of Randolph and Desplaines and hurled the bomb ninety-two feet to its point of impact. It would have taken a very strong man to toss it that far. Schnaubelt was a big man, standing over six feet tall and weighing about two hundred pounds. He was arrested and questioned during the furor following the bombing, but claimed innocence. Shortly after Schnaubelt was released he fled to England and then to Argentina. Eventually he married, became a prosperous manufacturer, and faded into anonymity.

The true identify of the person responsible will probably never be known. However, research by historian Paul Avrich indicates that Dyer Lum, an anarchist who committed suicide in 1893, knew who the bomb-thrower was. Lum's letters give tantalizing hints—but no specific name—about the man: he was a militant activist and anarchist, he was probably German, and he was not one of the men tried and convicted of the crime.

Thirteen years after the tragic day, on Memorial Day in 1899, a monument was dedicated to the fallen policemen of Haymarket Square. The bronze figure of a policeman with his arm raised, demanding peace, was placed on a granite base about a block from the site of the actual events. Twice, in 1969 and 1970, the policeman's figure was blown from its pedestal by bombs put there by modern anarchists. After the second explosion, Chicago's Mayor Richard Daley denounced the acts and pledged a full-time police guard over the monument. But a year later, this measure having proved too costly, the figure was removed from its base and placed in the lobby of the main Chicago police station.

Today the site of the bombing is a desolate corner of rubble and decrepit buildings. Traffic roars down the nearby Kennedy Expressway, and fruit and vegetable vendors fill the marketplace with activity. The empty pedestal for the police memorial stands in Haymarket Square, visited only by pigeons and an occasional vacant-eyed drunk from nearby Skid Row.

But twice each year at Waldheim Cemetery, on May 4 and November 11 (the anniversaries of the bombing and executions), someone places a single, long-stemmed red rose at the base of the memorial for the condemned men. After one hundred years, the controversy still lingers on over the anarchists . . . or the martyrs . . . depending on the point of view.

Burton Schindler is a newspaper reporter and feature writer who also does extensive free lance writing for business and general interest publications.

The Great Fight: Mr. Jake vs. John L. Sullivan

by James A. Cox

As the United States was moving from a rural-agrarian society to an urban-industrialized nation in the late 19th century, more was changing than demographics and economics. America was experiencing social change as well, including the emergence of spectator sports as a new found passion for city dwellers. Vicarious thrills were available by watching sporting events and from reading about them in the new sports pages of a few newspapers such as the *National Police Gazette.*

One of the most popular sports of the era was boxing. With its violence and rugged individual effort this brutal form of sporting encounter appealed to the hordes of Americans now trapped in the big cities and deprived of the adventure of the frontier. The great hero of these new boxing fans was the Boston Strong Boy, John L. Sullivan. Although Queensbury rules were coming into favor, in 1889 the Great John L. agreed to defend his championship title in a bare knuckles fight. In what would be the last major bare knuckles bout in America, Sullivan would fight Jake Kilrain. On a hot July day in Mississippi, these two men would give the nation a last glimpse of a violent, bloody, hand-to-hand style struggle. America was changing, but on that day in July, sports fans would love the last of the frontier style fights.

James A. Cox, a free lance writer from New Jersey and the author of other sports related articles, gives us a vivid and entertaining look at this last great championship fight of its kind in the United States.

At a few minutes past 4 P.M. on July 7, 1889, a special three-car train chugs out of the Queen and Crescent Yards in New Orleans. In theory, the time of departure is known only to a privileged few, among them Bud Renaud, New Orleans sportsman and fight promoter, Col. Charles W. Rich, Mississippi gambler and sawmill operator, and, of course, the parties of the principals—John L. Sullivan, the celebrated "Boston Strong Boy" and heavyweight champion of the world, and challenger Jake Kilrain.

The train's destination is supposed to be secret, too. New Orleans has been seething with rumors for days, and the governors of Louisiana, Alabama, Mississippi and Texas in concert have vowed that no barbaric bare-knuckles contest—illegal in all 38 states—will take place within the borders of their fair constituencies. In fact, Governor Lowry of Mississippi has put out what almost amounts to a contract on Sullivan. He is still burning over indignities suffered seven years before when John L., a brash boozy youth, ignored his prohibitions and stripped the title from Paddy Ryan after nine brutal rounds in full view of the verandah of the gracious Barnes Hotel in Mississippi City. With vengeful spirit but no legal justification, he has offered a flat $1,500 reward for the arrest of the champion.

But now, somehow, the location of the fight site has leaked out: in Mississippi, somewhere in the 10,000-acre tract of pinelands surrounding Charlie Rich's place in Richburg, near Hattiesburg, about 100 miles north of New Orleans.

The telegraph chatters and Governor Lowry summons the militia to guard all the main roads and rail lines from Louisiana into Mississippi. In the Queen & Crescent rail yards, a mob scene takes place. Two cars of the special train are taken over by the fighters and their parties. A third car, the boxcar, separates them. A smiling Sullivan rides in the rear car with a handful of cronies, plus fighting gear—shoes, towels and sponges. In the front car with Kilrain are Richard K. Fox, publisher of the *National Police Gazette* of pink-sheet fame, Bat Masterson, former marshal of Dodge City, and various solemn-looking men who talk softly without moving their lips much. The crowd continues to gather, trying to clamber aboard. But before the militia catch them, the fighters' train pulls out, forcing its way through the crowds. Word spreads that the fight is scheduled now to start soon after dawn to avoid the heat. The operators of the Q & C, knowing a good thing when they see it, hastily assemble additional trains to accommodate the thousands left behind.

Two trains leave in the early morning, jammed so tight with gambling men, sports enthusiasts, pickpockets, armed thugs and opportunists—including Renaud, Charley Johnston, who was "a very important gentleman" from New York City, and Steve Brodie, still basking in the glory of his alleged leap off the Brooklyn Bridge—that a man can't reach for the pint flask in his own hip pocket without risk of starting a border war.

The ride, often through mist-shrouded swamps, is slow, with long delays, in sweltering boxes, over slippery tracks. There is some confusion as to what happens next. According to one version, when the trains reach the Mississippi state line, a company of Governor Lowry's militia is waiting, bayonets stacked in a barricade across the track. The fireman piles on the coal and the train barrels through, sending bayonets whizzing past the ears of the militiamen as they dive for the safety of trackside ditches. The other, more likely, version is that the railroad dispatcher reroutes the train along the ghost run through southwestern Mississippi—where gaunt cypress trees wade into dark grottoes, and frogs never hush—and then northeast to Hattiesburg.

Finally, at about 9 A.M., the engines wheeze to a stop at Charlie Rich's lumber camp. Carriages have been provided for the important people. Half of the rest scatter urgently into the underbrush, while the other half trail the carriages to a clearing in the woods where Charlie's crew has been working all night by the sputtering orange glare of pine-knot torches, erecting a ring, several tiers of wooden seats and spreading sawdust liberally on the ground.

While the fighters and their corner men are readying themselves for the upcoming fray (there'll be no steins of bourbon this time, John L., not with William Muldoon, a wrestling champion and physical-conditioning fanatic in charge of training), let's take a moment to look at the circumstances and personalities in the unfolding drama.

Richard Kyle Fox could have been a hero in the Horatio Alger stories. He arrived in New York City from Dublin in 1874, a penniless 29-year-old, got a job on a newspaper, saved his money and two years later purchased the *National Police Gazette,* a weekly heavy with scandal and sensation that had fallen on evil days. The first thing Fox did when he took over was to emblazon his name, "Richard K. Fox, Editor & Proprietor," on the masthead. The second thing was to add to the *Gazette's* pink pages a sports section, a feature unheard of in newspapers of the time. Baseball and football were just getting started and the first ball hadn't been tossed through a peach basket yet. But there were many races and prizefights, the latter growing in public interest despite—or because of—the proscriptions against them.

To add to the excitement and at the same time boost the *Gazette*'s circulation, Fox promoted competitions of every kind imaginable, awarding "championship" belts, cups and trophies (which usually featured his mustachioed visage) with a lavish hand. There were contests for steeple climbing, oyster opening, hair cutting, one-legged dancing, sculling and female pugilism. There was a special trophy for one George A. Sampson, who supported a scale-model Ferris wheel on his chest; one for the bartender who could make a pousse-café with the most layers; and another one for poor Billy Wells, who balanced a block of iron on his head while somebody went at it with a sledge hammer.

The *Gazette,* avidly read by men and boys all over the country, soon became the sportsman's Bible. Its circulation zoomed and Richard K. Fox, now a dapper millionaire in his mid-30s, found himself the most influential figure in the sports world.

One evening in the spring of 1881, Fox was sitting at his usual table in Harry Hill's Dance Hall and Boxing Emporium, located on the edge of New York's Bowery. Harry Hill's was known as "the best of the worst places," and everybody who was anybody made it a point to be seen there—Diamond Jim Brady, Lillian Russell, P. T. Barnum, James Gordon Bennett Jr., Thomas A. Edison (ostensibly to see how his new light bulbs were working), even Oscar Wilde and the noted Brooklyn divine, Henry Ward Beecher.

The entertainment on this particular evening had been supplied by a muscular 22-year-old brawler from Boston named John Lawrence Sullivan. This was the same cocky young man who had been touring the vaudeville circuit, offering $50 to anyone who could last four rounds with him in "sparring exhibitions," so called in order to stay within the law. In fact, John L. would simply climb into the ring, glower at the audience and roar, "I can lick any sonovabitch in the house!"

The Boston Strong Boy knew little about ring science, but he carried 195 pounds of solid muscle on a 5-foot-10½-inch frame and packed a mighty wallop in either hand. "It was like being hit by a runaway horse," said Professor Mike Donovan, later to become famous as the sparring partner of Teddy Roosevelt. The professor was one of the few who managed to last for three rounds with Sullivan.

Now, at Harry Hill's place, John L. put away Steve Taylor, a good boxer with a local reputation, in the middle of the second round. Following his established pattern, he helped drag the fallen gladiator back to his corner, fussed over him until he came to and slipped him a couple of dollars for his trouble. Then, raising his arms for silence, he made a few remarks suitable to the occasion, ending up with the quaintly formal sign-off that was to become his trademark: "Always on the level, yours very truly, John L. Sullivan."

A short time later, back in his street clothes, he took over one of Harry Hill's tables and busied himself using the $50 he had kept from Steve Taylor to buy drinks for a crowd of friends and hangers-on.

"So that's Sullivan," said Richard K. Fox, seated a few tables away. He stroked his silky handlebar mustache with one beringed hand and raised a manicured finger on the other. "Tell Sullivan," he said to the waiter who materialized, "to come over here. I want to talk to him."

Surrounded by sycophants, pulling lustily on his stein of bourbon and very full of himself, John L. was in no mood to tug his forelock and play lackey to anyone. "You tell Fox," he bellowed, loud enough to be heard all over the room, "that if he wants to see me he can goddamn well come over to *my* table!"

No one had ever talked to the great Fox like that before. He never forgot it. And he never forgave it.

Time passed. The following February Sullivan took only ten minutes and 30 seconds to wrest the championship from Paddy Ryan, a husky immigrant bartender who enjoyed the support of Richard K. Fox. "When Sullivan struck me," Ryan confessed, "I thought a telegraph pole had been shoved against me endways." Game to the end, Paddy showed up at Sullivan's victory party at the St. James in New Orleans and, as John L. himself later put it, "partook of our festivities."

John L. Sullivan, champion of America, went on an eight-month tour across the country, now offering $1,000 to anyone who could stay four rounds with him, Marquis of Queensberry Rules. These rules, then coming into favor, were substantially the same as they are now: padded gloves, three-minute rounds with a one-minute recess, the count of ten for a knockout. In the old London Prize-Ring Rules, still in force when Sullivan began his career, the fighters fought bareknuckle or with skin-tight leather gloves. They wrestled, too, grabbing anywhere above the waist, which is why the old-time fighters shaved their heads. A round lasted until one fighter was knocked down by a punch, thrown by a wrestling hold or slipped. He then got a 30-second rest, after which "time" was called, giving him eight more seconds to come to the "scratch," a line marked in the middle of the ring. If he couldn't make it, he was declared "knocked out of time," which phrase was later shortened to "knocked out." There was no specified number of rounds—a bare-knuckle fight was a fight to the finish.

Sullivan much preferred the Queensberry Rules. But he took on anybody, any time, any rules. In exhibitions and official bouts his first two years as champ, he knocked out 34 men, failing to deck only Tug Wilson—an experienced pugilist backed by Fox—who managed to last the required four rounds by running, clinching, and slipping to the floor without being hit. In ensuing years hundreds more fell before the terrible power of Sullivan's fists, including a number of hopefuls handpicked by Fox in his vendetta to "get" Sullivan. By 1887, the Boston Strong Boy had grown into the Great John L., an international figure who shook the hands of princes and presidents and was lionized wherever he went.

Meantime, Fox had come up with a new pretender, a solid heavyweight born John Killion on Long Island, who fought under the name of Jake Kilrain. Jake had battled some of the best fighters around and had gone to a draw with Charlie Mitchell, the little Englishman who was growing into such a large thorn in John L.'s side. Somewhere along the line—the facts are unclear—Fox apparently goaded Sullivan into agreeing verbally to meet Kilrain for the championship. Later, John L. refused to acknowledge the agreement, if indeed there was one. Furious, Fox declared that Sullivan had forfeited the title. He announced that Jake Kilrain was champion of America, and awarded him a special diamond-studded silver *Police Gazette* championship belt, then matched Jake with the British champion Jem Smith for the world title.

Sullivan's loyal Boston admirers were not going to sit still for that. A committee was set up (by Pat Sheedy, John L.'s manager, some cynics claim) and contributions were solicited for a tribute that would make Fox look like a piker. From the proceeds came "The $10,000 Belt." It was reported to be the largest piece of flat gold ever seen in the country, 50 inches long and 12 inches wide. The center panel spelled out John L.'s name in tiny diamonds; eight other panels carried his portraits, the U.S. Seal and assorted American eagles and Irish harps. To top everything off, the entire bauble was studded with still more diamonds, 397 of them in all.

The presentation of the belt at the old Boston Theater on August 8, 1887, was attended by 3,500 fans, among them the mayor of the city and other local politicians. It was there that Sullivan probably uttered one of his most memorable statements: "I wouldn't put Fox's belt around the neck of a goddamn dog!" The crowd loved it. Somebody passed the hat. John L. took home $4,000.

A victorious six-month tour of England and the Continent followed. But returning home in April 1888, he embarked on another long toot. And this time the high living—night after night on the town, huge steaks, magnums of champagne, steins of bourbon and big black cigars without number—began to take its toll. From 195 pounds, his best fighting weight, he ballooned to 240, all flab. Worse, the booze accomplished what no man had been able to do— put him down for the count. For nine weeks Sullivan took to his bed, as he later noted in his autobiography, with "typhoid fever, gastric fever, inflammation of the bowels, heart trouble, and liver complaint all combined," which seemed to some cynics a rather elaborate way of describing the D.T.'s. Five physicians tapped and dosed him, and he thought he was going to die. Even when he got up he had incipient paralysis, whatever that is, and went on crutches for six weeks. There also were rumors of a "mysterious itch."

Never would there be a better time to "get" the bloated Boston boaster, Richard Kyle Fox reasoned. In barber shops, saloons, livery stables, firehouses and police stations all over the country, *Gazette* readers were told that Sullivan was near death's door and would probably never be able to fight again; and, conversely, that he was using his sickness as an excuse for evading a fight with the "real champion," Jake Kilrain.

Week after week the refrain grew, and at last John L., who still had his pride if not his health, rose to the bait. In January he agreed to meet Kilrain in New Orleans in July—London Prize-Ring Rules, no gloves, at Fox's insistence—for a purse of $20,000 winner take all, with a side bet of $1,000.

Sullivan's backers quickly called in icy-eyed Billy Muldoon, a trainer who, for a fee of $10,000, agreed to put John L. back into fighting shape (fee forfeited if Kilrain won). With one ironclad proviso: Muldoon was to be absolute boss. Sullivan would follow the regimen set up for every minute of every hour, 24 hours a day, without question or temperamental display. It was agreed, and one of the backers, the tough, pistol-packing gambler out of Brooklyn named Charley Johnston, vowed that he would answer for John L. But first they had to find him, because he was off on another bender. Inside his lavishly appointed offices, with their Turkish carpets, plush chairs and inlaid mother-of-pearl tables, Fox learned of all this and contentedly stroked his mustache. Muldoon had six months to whip Sullivan into shape, but what good came of flogging a dead horse? Sullivan was finished, washed up. Physical conditioning was Muldoon's stock-in-trade, not making miracles.

Six months passed and it is July 8, 1889. For weeks all across America, urchins and schoolboys, who are not the final arbiters in matters of sport, have been chanting a loyal battle cry: "Sull-i-van will KILLrain!"—and the *Gazette* be damned. But at ringside, where the sun is beating down mercilessly already, the smart-money men are worried. Can the Big Fellow still fight? And even if he can, how long can he possibly last? Kilrain isn't known as a slugger, but he's strong and he has great endurance. He's also a good wrestler, and in bareknuckle fighting a wrestling fall can be nearly as effective as a knockdown punch. "Sullivan is no wrestler," announces the New York *World* on the day of the fight, expressing the reservation that is in everybody's mind: "According to the history of all such drunkards as he, his legs ought to fail him after 20 minutes of fighting."

Ringside seats are snapped up at premium prices: 722 fans pay $15 each to perch on campstools, while 1,400 more part with a sawbuck for the privilege of standing behind them. There are grandstand seats ranging in price from 50 cents to $2, but the rowdy element in the crowd overruns them and the man who passes the hat doesn't get much. In all, more than 3,000 men and boys are in attendance. Ann Livingston, John L.'s beefy, bosomy, showgirl inamorata of many years, who sometimes went to his fights dressed in men's clothing, does not attend. But at least one woman does. She is a black lady named Aunt Mattie, who was elderly when she helped to raise Mississippi poet James H. Street in pre-Depression America, but is spry enough in 1889 to perch in the lower branches of an oak tree behind the grandstand.

It is Hades-hot. The sun is a burnished brass disk in the sky, the temperature at ringside 100 degrees F. And rising. It will be 110 degrees before the day is over. The crowd chews on rumors that the militia will show up at any moment. Newspapermen fume when they learn that most of their free seats have been sold by the managers, and that no special telegraphic facilities are furnished. The only wire, belonging to the railroad company, is taken up by railroad business. It is said that there is a rush for carrier pigeons, but none can be found. The reporters must go back to New Orleans to reach a telegraph station.

Shortly before 10 A.M., Jake Kilrain, his corner men Charlie Mitchell and Mike Donovan, and his timekeeper, Bat Masterson, push through the crowd to the ring. Jake tosses his hat over the ropes and follows it in, shouting in the prize ring's time-honored gesture of defiance, "Me hat's in the ring!" He looks New York pale but fit. His face, though, has a sour cast this morning, and the sweat that beads out over his body may not be entirely from the temperature and humidity.

Moments later, the champion strides down to the ring. He is wearing a long robe, and when he shrugs it off the ringsiders inhale appreciatively. Not for the emerald-green tights, flesh-colored stockings and glossy-black high-topped boots, as resplendent as they are, but for the miracle that William Muldoon has wrought. For there before them stands the Big Fellow of legend, down to 207 pounds and, except for a slight bulge that girdles his midriff, looking surprisingly fit.

In the ring, the fighters shake hands and each gives $1,000 in cash—the side bet—to the referee, John Fitzpatrick, who soon after will be elected mayor of New Orleans. Their boots are fitted with metal spikes to prevent them from slipping on the earthen floor of the ring. Then their seconds also shake hands, as is the custom, and return to their corners.

At 10:15, Fitzpatrick hollers "Time!" The two adversaries advance to the mark. They circle for an instant. Then Kilrain rushes in, grabs Sullivan by the shoulders and backheels him to the ground. The ringsiders cheer excitedly. First fall to Kilrain. Money changes hands. The round has lasted exactly five seconds.

The second round is Sullivan's. He lands a heavy blow on Jake's ribs and throws him. Thirty seconds. They clinch in the third round and Kilrain lands several foul blows. The crowd hisses. Sullivan pulls away and sends Kilrain tumbling with a right to the heart followed by a left to the head.

By the fourth round the strategy of the Kilrain corner becomes clear. Jake refuses to swap punches with Sullivan head on, instead jabbing and backing away until he sees an opportunity to clinch and throw his opponent to the ground. This is Charlie Mitchell's style—wear your opponent down. Charlie also maintains a steady stream of foul abuse from the corner, trying to goad John L. into blind anger. He seems to be succeeding. The round is approaching 15 minutes when the frustrated Sullivan lowers his fists and grasps, "Why don't you stand and fight like a man, you sonovabitch? Are you a fighter or a sprinter?"

Jake laughs, tauntingly.

In the seventh, Kilrain suddenly comes out of his shell and lands a vicious right on John L.'s ear, tearing it open. "First blood, Kilrain!" the referee cries out and a lot more money changes hands.

This is the last time Jake's supporters have much to cheer about. By the tenth round, Kilrain stumbles backward until Sullivan catches up with him, then falls to the ground without being hit to gain the automatic 38-second respite. Sullivan is enraged, the more so a round or two later when Jake steps on his foot, piercing it with one of his shoe spikes and drawing blood.

As the fight wears on, it becomes apparent that it is Kilrain, not Sullivan, who is wilting under the terrible heat. The steep wooden grandstands cut off any movement of air; the ring becomes a sun-scorched inferno. Men keel over like ninepins. The fighters continue their grotesque dance, one backpedaling, the other advancing and swinging ponderous blows. Their backs and shoulders are blistered crimson by the sun; blood, most of it Kilrain's, streaks their bodies. Sullivan's fists are beginning to swell.

Kilrain's seconds have a quart of whiskey and he takes sips and nips to keep his strength up. Sullivan is drinking tea. He refuses even to sit during the 38-second breaks. "What the hell is the use?" he asks his anxious seconds. "I just have to get back up again, don't I?" Muldoon asks him how long he thinks he can stay. "Till tomorrow morning, if it's necessary," Sullivan snarls.

In the 44th round, somebody—possibly even Muldoon—spikes the champion's tea with whiskey. John L. takes a huge gulp, goes out to toe the mark and gets sick. Instead of lacing into him, Jake asks if he wants to call it a draw. John L., still vomiting, responds by knocking him down. A wag at ringside starts a witticism that whirlwinds throughout the crowd: John L.'s stomach is getting rid of the tea but hanging on for dear life to the whiskey.

Kilrain's seconds carry him to his corner after every round now, and as he comes back out to the mark his head rolls loosely on his shoulders as if his neck has been broken. Charley Johnston offers $500 to $50 at ringside, with no takers. After the 75th round a physician from the New York Athletic Club pulls Mike Donovan aside and says, "Your fighter will die if you keep sending him out there. Think of the heat, man!"

At the same time, Mitchell sends a message to Sullivan's corner: if Kilrain retires, will Big John give him $2,000? His object apparently is to show that Sullivan is as eager to stop the fight as Kilrain. But before a deal can be struck, Donovan, who has seen two men die in the ring, throws in the sponge. Mitchell raves and Kilrain blubbers like a babe. Without waiting for congratulations, Sullivan bounds across the ring and challenges Charlie Mitchell to climb in and have it out to a finish right then and there. Charlie is more than willing, and it takes a half-dozen stout men to keep them apart.

So, after two hours, 16 minutes and 25 seconds, the last bareknuckle championship bout in history goes into the record books. A wad of $100 bills is counted out into John L.'s hands, swollen to three times their normal size, and somebody remembers to pass him the *Police Gazette* belt. The story goes around that he tossed it to Charley Johnston "for his bulldog." If so, he may have lived to regret the gesture, for in later, leaner days he will pawn his own belt for $175—after the diamonds have been pried out.

The country's newspapers carried the story the next day. The headline writers for the *New York Times* waxed smugly righteous: "The Bigger Brute Won." Literally accurate, but not in fact very significant. Jake weighed 190 pounds to John L.'s 207. Years later, poet James Street preferred Aunt Mattie's version of the fight, recited to him when he was a boy on her knee, calling it the best piece of sports reporting he had ever heard. "They knocked each other down so many times I quit countin' them," she said. "Mr. John started a sweatin' about the second round. He grunted and snorted a heap. Mr. Jake danced like a bridegroom at his weddin' dinner. Finally Mr. John hit Mr. Jake so hard Mr. Jake just didn't get up and that's all it was to it."

Well, not quite. Mr. John was tried by the State of Mississippi, convicted and sentenced to a year in jail. His lawyers appealed and at the retrial agreed to plead guilty in return for a $500 fine. Sullivan paid the fine and hotfooted it back to New York and a monumental celebratory binge. Jake Kilrain, cast aside by Richard K. Fox and broke, was paroled under a quaint old Mississippi law to work off his fine to a respectable private citizen of the state—in this case Charlie Rich, who kept him busy shooting pool in a place he owned in Hattiesburg. Jake, incidentally, so near death's door after the fight, managed to live long enough to serve as a pallbearer at John L.'s funeral in 1918. He didn't get counted out himself until 1937, when he was 78.

Populism and Modern American Politics

by Peter Frederick

In the midst of the terrible depression of the 1890s, the second worst in the nation's history, the Populist Party was born and showed extraordinary vitality in expressing the grievances of small farmers and rural debtors. The Populists reached their climax in the election of 1896 when their presidential candidate, William Jennings Bryan, also the nominee of the Democratic Party, drew almost six and one-half million votes nationwide, more than any other candidate, win or lose, had ever received. Yet Bryan lost the election in a landslide, the Populist Party soon faded away (as most third parties do in America), and the Democratic Party slid into a long period of decline nationally. The Populist experience shows the enormous difficulty of making fundamental changes in the American political system.

But in this interview, Peter Frederick, Professor of History at Wabash College, argues that the influence of the Populists should not be measured solely by how well or poorly they did at the polls. They proposed many innovations which citizens today take for granted, such as direct election of U.S. senators, the graduated income tax, and the secret ballot. They forced the two major parties to address serious economic and social issues that had been ignored for a generation. And the challenge to the political system that the Populists mounted a century ago has shaped the nature of the Republican and Democratic parties down to our times. Peter Frederick is the author of *Knights of the Golden Rule: The Intellectual as Christian Social Reformer in the 1890s* (1976).

Interview with Peter Frederick

Q. Were the Populists at all perceived to be a threat to the political and economic establishment in 1892?

A. They're going to do pretty well in the election of 1892. Populists will get a million votes in a third party candidacy in 1892 and win a few state representatives and three governors. So they become finally a threat because they are forcing issues to the American people that have been ignored for 20 years by the two major parties. And that's scary, and that's threatening. You get the two major parties beginning to recognize and notice. Here is a grassroots people's movement that's threatening because the two major parties are avoiding the issues.

Q. Sort of a follow-up to that, how successful was the Populist party in 1892? What factors limited their success? And how did the Populist leaders themselves respond to the 1892 election results?

A. Populists were, by their expectations, enormously successful in 1892. They won a million votes. Won a few state houses, governors, state representatives and senators. They were hopeful that they could look to doing even better in '94 and '96 and they began to say, "Hey, politics is the way we're going to be heard." And they see the emergence of a third party as a strong force. It was not known then that third parties were anathema in American politics. The last third party had been the Republican party and it had become one of the two dominant ones. So, they had every expectation that they might work. One of the problems with the Populists as they moved into the post '92 election was the depression.

Q. What factors limited the success of the Populist party in 1892?

A. Populists were limited in '92 by the fact that they just did [not] make a dent into the labor vote in the cities. Nor did they make a big dent in the black vote. Not many blacks are voting. But there were issues of race, particularly among southern Populists between white and black. There were differences between the perspectives of northern Populists and southern Populists. They began to see rifts in their own movement on political issues. The biggest failure really was not connecting with urban workers.

Q. How did the depression of 1893 affect the Democratic, the Republican and the Populist parties?

A. The depression of 1893 was devastating. First of all, it was devastating to people's lives. But it especially had its impact on politics, as depressions will. And Populists saw the depression as a chance to expand their membership and expand their power. And they saw urban workers unemployed and hurting and they thought perhaps they could undo the failures of '92 in reaching the urban workers and add them to their rolls for '94 and '96. The depression had a big effect on the Democratic party. Cleveland was in power and he was totally immobilized. He turned to gold. He'd always been [as] conservative as the Republican party had been on issues. He was a sound money man. He repealed the Silver Purchase Act, and just went wholesale towards sound money politics. That wasn't going to do him any good. The Democrats were split into gold and silver parts of the party.

They were in shambles. The Republicans gained enormously in the election of 1894. And 1894 is a very significant election even before the presidential election, because the Republican party emerges as a dominant party and it's going to be dominant until the 1930s.

Q. Why did the Populists endorse Bryan in 1896? Did they have any alternatives? To what extent had they accomplished their mission when the Democrats picked up on so many of their issues in 1986?

A. Approaching the election of 1896, the Populists had a serious dilemma. They had not made [an] impact in connection with urban workers. They were divided on race questions between white and black farmers and sharecroppers. The basic question the Populists faced was to continue to push their many issues, to keep pushing a multiple issue campaign, or to focus increasingly on a single issue with a lot of popular appeal, the coinage of free silver. Populists increasingly in '93, '94, '95, even in '96 were a party captured by western silver miners. And it was the power of simplicity, a single issue, an issue that could be turned into a moral issue. They lost the power of focusing on the complex array of a capitalist society that was trampling on the rights of the people as they saw it, and turned increasingly to silver. They saw elements in [the] Democratic party also pushing toward silver, and there was some pressure among the leadership as they moved toward their own political convention in '96 to go along with the Democrats. So the big question they faced was fusion on one issue, that is connect with the Democratic party, or maintain their autonomy and their integrity as a third party with the many issues that had defined the culture that had been emerging in the late 1880s. They are going to make a very disastrous choice for their future.

Q. Why did Bryan lose the 1896 presidential election? Why did McKinley win? Why was this election significant?

A. The election of 1896 is one of the most significant elections in the history of American politics. It changes the shape of politics. It does in third party movements and mass democratic movements in a very significant and thorough way. Populists didn't just shoot themselves in the foot, they self-destructed by the decision to fuse with the Democrats and with the very popular young [William Jennings] Bryan of Nebraska. Bryan didn't lose the election so much as the Republicans won it. And they won it by conducting the first modern highly financed political campaign. McKinley sat home in Ohio and just let the money from Standard Oil and J. P. Morgan and the corporations flow in and he spent enormous amounts of money. And he also wrapped himself in the flag. It was very much like the election of '88 with Bush. McKinley was quite silent, but the McKinley people talked about peace, prosperity, progress and patriotism. And every one of his campaign posters had the American flag and a big gold symbol. They just poured money into that campaign. Bryan, who had very little money, traveled a lot and spoke and spoke and spoke. And it wasn't enough to counteract a really thoroughly modern campaign.

Q. What was the legacy of the Populist party?

A. The Populist party died as a result of the election of 1896. They joined the Democrats and they were already dead by the time they decided at their own convention to fuse. And yet in many ways, they forced the two major parties to try and address some of the issues. In a sense, the Populists set the agenda for American politics for the next 20 to 30 years. A number of the items in the Omaha platform become implemented in the next 20 years, direct election of senators, graduated income tax, women's suffrage, [recall and] referendum, a number of the direct democracy programs, and so they had an impact on American politics. And yet in a fundamental way, they failed, because what the two major parties do, and what they learn is that when a third party forces issues on us that we've been ignoring, one of the two major parties or both will adapt those issues, but they adapt them to maintain the current established order and the dominant forces in society at an even stronger level. So the Populists, like a bee, they sting and leave a little stinger, but the body is unharmed and essentially unchanged, in fact, strengthened.

Q. What did the Populist experience show us about how political change comes about in America, and what does it show us about the limits of bringing about political change?

A. The Populist experience shows that change comes about in America very, very slowly, and that it is always inherently limited. For example, [the] women's movement for the right to vote began in 1848. It's 1920 before they even get that little piece of the agenda. Change also works to further entrench the unequal distribution of wealth and power in the hands of the two major parties and of the established order, in this case, the corporations and the railroads [which emerge] even stronger than when the third party began making so much noise. Also, the Populist experience shows that serious structural changes in American society are impossible. The changes that are made in the aftermath of the Populists further strengthen the established order and the unequal distribution of power, and the underclass remains an underclass in even worse relationship to what they consider their oppressors.

Q. To what extent was the Populist movement the last serious challenge to the dominance of big corporations in American life?

A. The Populist movement was really the last serious challenge to the two major parties and to the two party system in America. It was a moment of a very highly energized and idealistic optimism about the power of the people to shape their own destinies. And it's sad that its ultimate fate was to show that that power was not going to happen, and that they couldn't do that. And [there] has not been a significant attempt at a democratic grassroots political movement with as much potential as the Populists in the last 90 years.

Q. In further analyzing the 1896 election, why didn't more lower and middle income voters support the Populist/Democratic ticket? Why do such voters tend to vote against what we might perceive to be their self-interests?

A. In 1896, the American voters voted against their self-interests as people often do. Race, for example. Southern white Democrats are going to vote against blacks, against their self-interests because race is a more powerful influence on their lives than economic issues are. Populists in 1896 and the Democrats did not win the votes of the workers. They didn't win the votes of the midwest. Silver had nothing to say to a worker in a factory. And silver was all that Bryan was talking about throughout that campaign, and it scared the workers who saw it as inflating prices. And so the interests ultimately between the farmer and the urban worker were too dissimilar.

Q. To what extent were the philosophical positions and the constituencies of the two major parties set after the 1896 election?

A. After 1896, the Republican party entrenched itself as a party of whites, Yankee northerners, rich corporations, Protestants, and the Democratic party became a sectional southern party. Bryan won electoral votes only in the south [and the west]. The Republican swept the north, the northeast and the midwest and so a solid south Democratic party was entrenched and a party that represented Irish, Catholic southerners. A more significant outcome of the election, I think, is that, even though Bryan won more votes than any Democrat had in twenty years, the Republican established themselves as the dominant party in the White House until the 1930s. And the Democrats established themselves as the really out party and a sectional party and a minority party.

Q. Is it fair to say that the Democratic party from the time of 1896, even though they did become a minority party for a long time, did they in some ways become a party of reform because they had picked up on some of the reform ideas of the Populists?

A. It's interesting. Another outcome of the election of 1896 is that until that point, the Republicans, insofar as they had any claim to moral issues, were the party of Lincoln and the party that supported the freedmen and Reconstruction and the Reconstruction amendments. And it was the party of morality. It had really started before, but after 1896 it lost its moral claims, and becomes the party of established interests. Interestingly enough, the Democratic party, because Bryan was such a moralist, such a pious person, becomes a party that has the promise of reform in it. Now, it's going to be a restrained reform because that's the nature of American politics, but Bryan's moralism and Protestant piety [pervade] the Democratic party and his stance and style are going to dominate it for the next twenty years. Woodrow Wilson will emerge as the president in many ways in the style of Bryan. And there are reforms, admittedly non-structural ones, not fundamental ones, but insofar as [there is] a party that looks to the interests of the workers and the farmers it's going to be the Democratic party. That will come about in a big way in the 1930s.

Chapter 8

Our First Southeast Asian War

by David R. Kohler and James Wensyel

The war in Vietnam was not the first the United States has fought in the jungles of southeast Asia against rebels fighting for their independence. The Philippine-American War, which started in 1898, would be one of the least known conflicts in United States history, even though it would involve over 125,000 men and cost nearly 4,000 American lives. The struggle began in the aftermath of the Spanish-American War, which had been started to help Cuba gain its freedom from Spain. At the start of that war, the United States attacked the Spanish in the Philippines where the Filipinos, under the leadership of Generalissimo Aguinaldo, had been fighting for their independence from the Spanish for over two years. By the time the war with Spain was over, the Filipinos had declared their nation to be independent, but the United States refused to recognize that declaration. In February 1899 a battle broke out between American soldiers and Filipino *insurrectos* signaling the start of this tragic war. This article gives a vivid account of that war and presents intriguing comparisons between the conflict in the Philippines and the war in Vietnam.

Guerrilla warfare . . . jungle terrain . . . search and destroy missions . . . benevolent pacification . . . strategic hamlets . . . terrorism . . . ambushes . . . free-fire zones . . . booby traps . . . waning support from civilians at home. These words call forth from the national consciousness uncomfortable images of a war Americans fought and died in not long ago in Southeast Asia. But while the phrases may first bring to mind America's painful experience in Vietnam during the 1960s and '70s, they also aptly describe a much earlier conflict—the Philippine Insurrection—that foreshadowed this and other insurgent wars in Asia.

The Philippine-American War of 1898–1902 is one of our nation's most obscure and least-understood campaigns. Sometimes called the "Bolo War" because of the Filipino insurgents' lethally effective use of razor-sharp bolo knives or machetes against the American expeditionary force occupying the islands, it is often viewed as a mere appendage of the one-hundred-day Spanish-American War. But suppressing the guerilla warfare waged by Philippine nationalists seeking self-rule proved far more difficult, protracted, and costly for American forces than the conventional war with Spain that had preceded it.

America's campaign to smash the Philippine Insurrection was, ironically, a direct consequence of U.S. efforts to secure independence for other *insurrectos* halfway around the world in Cuba. On May 1, 1898, less than a week after Congress declared war against Spain, a naval squadron commanded by Commodore George Dewey steamed into Manila Bay to engage the Spanish warships defending that nation's Pacific possession. In a brief action Dewey achieved a stunning victory, sinking all of the enemy vessels with no significant American losses. Destroying the Spanish fleet, however, did not ensure U.S. possession of the Philippines. An estimated 15,000 Spanish soldiers still occupied Manila and the surrounding region. Those forces would have to be rooted out by infantry.

President William McKinley had already ordered a Philippine Expeditionary Force of volunteer and regular army infantry, artillery, and cavalry units (nearly seven thousand men), under the command of Major General Wesley Merritt, to "reduce Spanish power in that quarter [Philippine Islands] and give order and security to the islands while in the possession of the United States."

Sent to the Philippines in the summer of 1898, this limited force was committed without fully considering the operation's potential length and cost. American military and government leaders also failed to anticipate the consequences of ignoring the Filipino rebels who, under Generalissimo Don Emilio Aguinaldo y Famy, had been waging a war for independence against Spain for the past two years. And when American insensitivity toward Aguinaldo eventually led to open warfare with the rebels, the American leaders grossly underestimated the determination of the seemingly ill-trained and poorly armed insurgents. They additionally failed to perceive the difficulties involved in conducting military operations in a tropical environment and among a hostile native population, and they did not recognize the burden of fighting at the end of a seven-thousand-mile-long logistics trail.

Asian engagements, the Americans learned for the first time, are costly. The enterprise, so modestly begun, eventually saw more than 126,000 American officers and men deployed to the Philippines. Four times as many soldiers served in this undeclared war in the Pacific as had been sent to the Caribbean during the Spanish-American War. During the three-year conflict, American troops and Filipino insurgents fought in more than 2,800 engagements. American casualties ultimately totaled 4,234 killed and 2,818 wounded, and the insurgents lost about 16,000 men. The civilian population suffered even more; as many as 200,000 Filipinos died from famine, pestilence, or the unfortunate happenstance of being too close to the fighting. The Philippine war cost the United States $600 million before the insurgents were subdued.

The costly experience offered valuable and timeless lessons about guerrilla warfare in Asia; unfortunately, those lessons had to be relearned sixty years later in another war that, despite the modern technology involved, bore surprising parallels to America's first Southeast Asian campaign.

Origins

America's war with Spain, formally declared by the United States on April 25, 1898, had been several years in the making. During that time the American "yellow press," led by Joseph Pulitzer's *New York World* and William Randolph Hearst's *New York Journal,* trumpeted reports of heroic Cuban *insurrectos* revolting against their cruel Spanish rulers. Journalists vividly described harsh measures taken by Spanish officials to quell the Cuban revolution. The sensational accounts, often exaggerated, reminded Americans of their own uphill fight for independence and nourished the feeling that America was destined to intervene so that the Cuban people might also taste freedom.

Furthermore, expansionists suggested that the revolt against a European power, taking place less than one hundred miles from American shores, offered a splendid opportunity to turn the Caribbean into an American sea. Businessmen pointed out that $50 million in American capital was invested in the Cuban sugar and mining industries. Revolutions resulting in burned cane fields jeopardized that investment. As 1898 opened, American relations with Spain quickly declined.

In January 1898 the U.S. battleship *Maine* was sent to Cuba, ostensibly on a courtesy visit. On February 15 the warship was destroyed by a mysterious explosion while at anchor in Havana harbor, killing 262 of her 350-man crew. The navy's formal inquiry, completed on March 28, suggested that the explosion was due to an external force—a mine.

On March 29, the Spanish government received an ultimatum from Washington, D.C.: Spain's army in Cuba was to lay down its arms while the United States negotiated between the rebels and the Spaniards. The Spanish forces were also told to abolish all *reconcentrado* camps (tightly controlled areas, similar to the strategic hamlets later tried in Vietnam, where peasants were regrouped to deny food and intelligence to insurgents and to promote tighter security). Spain initially rejected the humiliation of surrendering its arms in the field but then capitulated on all points. The Americans were not satisfied.

On April 11, declaring that Spanish responses were inadequate, President McKinley told a joint session of Congress that "I have exhausted every effort to relieve the intolerable condition . . . at our doors. I now ask the Congress to empower the president to take measures to secure a full and final termination of hostilities in Cuba, to secure . . . the establishment of a stable government, and to use the military and naval forces of the United States . . . for these purposes. . . ."

Congress adopted the proposed resolution on April 19. Learning this, Spain declared war on the 24th. The following day, the United States responded with its own declaration of war.

The bulk of the American navy quickly gathered on the Atlantic coast. McKinley called for 125,000 volunteers to bolster the less than eighty-thousand-man regular army. His call was quickly oversubscribed; volunteers fought to be the first to land on Cuba's beaches.

The first major battle of the war, however, was fought not in Cuba but seven thousand miles to the west—in Manila Bay. Dewey's victory over Spanish Admiral Patrico Montojo y Pasarón (a rather hollow victory as Montojo's fleet consisted of seven unarmored ships, three of which had wooden hulls and one that had to be towed to the battle area) was widely acclaimed in America.

American leaders, believing that the Philippines would now fall into America's grasp like a ripe plum, had to decide what to do with their prize. They could not return the islands to Spain, nor could they allow them to pass to France or Germany, America's commercial rivals in the Orient. The American press rejected the idea of a British protectorate. And, after four hundred years of despotic Spanish rule in which Filipinos had little or no chance to practice self-government, native leaders seemed unlikely candidates for managing their own affairs. McKinley faced a grand opportunity for imperialistic expansion that could not be ignored.

The debate sharply divided his cabinet—and the country. American public opinion over acquisition of the Philippines divided into two basic factions: imperialists versus antiimperialists.

The imperialists, mostly Republican, included such figures as Theodore Roosevelt (then assistant secretary of the navy), Henry Cabot Lodge (Massachusetts senator), and Albert Beveridge (Indiana senator). These individuals were, for the most part, disciples of Alfred Thayer Mahan, a naval strategist who touted theories of national power and acquisition of overseas colonies for trade purposes and naval coaling stations.

The anti-imperialists, staunchly against American annexation of the Philippines, were mainly Democrats. Such men as former presidents Grover Cleveland and Rutherford B. Hayes, steel magnate Andrew Carnegie, William Jennings Bryan, union leader Samuel Gompers, and Mark Twain warned that by taking the Philippines the United States would march the road to ruin earlier traveled by the Roman Empire. Furthermore, they argued, America would be denying Filipinos the right of self-determination guaranteed by our Constitution. The more practical-minded also pointed out that imperialistic policy would require maintaining an expensive army and navy there.

Racism, though demonstrated in different ways, pervaded the arguments of both sides. Imperialists spoke of the "white man's burden" and moral responsibility to "uplift the child races everywhere" and to provide "orderly development for the unfortunate and less able races." They spoke of America's "civilizing mission" of pacifying Filipinos by "benevolent assimilation" and saw the opening of the overseas frontier much as their forefathers had viewed the western frontier. The "subjugation of the Injun" (wherever he might be found) was a concept grasped by American youth—the war's most enthusiastic supporters (in contrast to young America's opposition to the war in Vietnam many years later).

The anti-imperialists extolled the sacredness of independence and self-determination for the Filipinos. Racism, however, also crept into their argument, for they believed that "protection against race mingling" was a historic American policy that would be reversed by imperialism. To them, annexation of the Philippines would admit "alien, inferior, and mongrel races to our nationality."

As the debate raged, Dewey continued to hold Manila Bay, and the Philippines seemed to await America's pleasure. President McKinley would ultimately cast the deciding vote in determining America's role in that country. McKinley, a genial, rather laid-back, former congressman from Ohio and one-time major in the Union army, remains a rather ambiguous figure during this period. In his Inaugural Address he had affirmed that "We want no wars of conquest; we must avoid the temptation of territorial aggression." Thereafter, however, he made few comments on pacifism, and, fourteen weeks after becoming president, signed the bill annexing Hawaii.

Speaking of Cuba in December 1897, McKinley said, "I speak not of forcible annexation, for that cannot be thought of. That, by our code of morality, would be criminal aggression." Nevertheless, he constantly pressured Madrid to end Spanish rule in Cuba, leading four months later to America's war with Spain.

McKinley described experiencing extreme turmoil, soul-searching, and prayer over the Philippine annexation issue until, he declared, one night in a dream the Lord revealed to him that "there was nothing left for us to do but to take them all [the Philippine Islands] and to educate the Filipinos, and uplift, and civilize, and Christianize them." He apparently didn't realize that the Philippines had been staunchly Roman Catholic for more than 350 years under Spanish colonialism. Nor could he anticipate the difficulties that, having cast its fortune with the expansionists, America would now face in the Philippines.

Prosecuting the War

Meanwhile, in the Philippine Islands, Major General Wesley Merritt's Philippine Expeditionary Force went about its job. In late June, General Thomas Anderson led an advance party ashore at Cavite. He then established Camp Merritt, visited General Aguinaldo's rebel forces entrenched around Manila, and made plans for seizing that city once Merritt arrived with the main body of armed forces.

Anderson quickly learned that military operations in the Philippines could be difficult. His soldiers, hastily assembled and dispatched with limited prior training, were poorly disciplined and inadequately equipped. Many still wore woolen uniforms despite the tropical climate. A staff officer described the army's baptism at Manila: ". . . the heat was oppressive and the rain kept falling. At times the trenches were filled with two feet of water, and soon the men's shoes were ruined. Their heavy khaki uniforms were a nuisance; they perspired constantly, the loss of body salts inducing chronic fatigue. Prickly heat broke out, inflamed by scratching and rubbing. Within a week the first cases of dysentery, malaria, cholera, and dengue fever showed up at sick call."

During his first meeting with Dewey, Anderson remarked that some American leaders were considering annexation of the Philippines. "If the United States intends to hold the Philippine Islands," Dewey responded, "it will make things awkward, because just a week ago Aguinaldo proclaimed the independence of the Philippine Islands from Spain and seems intent on establishing his own government.

A Filipino independence movement led by Aguinaldo had been active in the islands since 1896 and, within weeks of Dewey's victory, Aguinaldo's revolutionaries controlled most of the archipelago.

Aguinaldo, twenty-nine years old in 1898, had taken over his father's position as mayor of his hometown of Kawit before becoming a revolutionary. In a minor skirmish with Spanish soldiers, he had rallied the Filipinos to victory. Thereafter, his popularity grew as did his ragtag but determined army. Aguinaldo was slight of build, shy, and soft-spoken, but a strict disciplinarian.

As his rebel force besieged Manila, Aguinaldo declared a formal government for the Philippines with himself as president and generalissimo. He proclaimed his "nation's" independence and called for Filipinos to rally to his army and to the Americans, declaring that "the Americans . . . extend their protecting mantle to our beloved country . . . When you see the American flag flying, assemble in numbers: they are our redeemers!" But his enthusiasm for the United States later waned.

Merritt put off Aguinaldo's increasingly strict demands that America recognize his government and guarantee the Filipino's independence. Aguinaldo perceived the American general's attitude as condescending and demeaning.

On August 13, Merritt's forces occupied Manila almost without firing a shot; in a face-saving maneuver the Spanish defenders had agreed to surrender to the Americans to avoid being captured—and perhaps massacred—by the Filipino insurgents. Merritt's troops physically blocked Aguinaldo's rebels, who had spent weeks in the trenches around the city, from participating in the assault. The Filipino general and his followers felt betrayed at being denied a share in the victory.

Further disenchanted, Aguinaldo would later find his revolutionary government unrepresented at the Paris peace talks determining his country's fate. He would learn that Spain had ceded the Philippines to the United States for $20 million.

Officers at Merritt's headquarters had little faith in the Filipinos' ability to govern themselves. "Should our power . . . be withdrawn," an early report declared, "The Philippines would speedily lapse into anarchy, which would excuse . . . the intervention of other powers and the division of the islands among them."

Meanwhile, friction between American soldiers and the Filipinos increased. Much of the Americans' conduct betrayed their racial bias. Soldiers referred to the natives as "niggers" and "gu-gus," epithets whose meanings were clear to the Filipinos. In retaliation, the island inhabitants refused to give way on sidewalks and muscled American officers into the streets. Men of the expeditionary force in turn escalated tensions by stopping Filipinos at gun point, searching them without cause, "confiscating" shopkeepers' goods, and beating those who resisted.

On the night of February 4, 1899 the simmering pot finally boiled over. Private William "Willie" Walter Grayson and several other soldiers of Company D, 1st Nebraska Volunteer Infantry, apprehended a group of armed insurgents within their regimental picket line. Shots were exchanged, and three Filipino *insurrectos* fell dead. Heavy firing erupted between the two camps.

In the bloody battle that followed, the Filipinos suffered tremendous casualties (an estimated two thousand to five thousand dead, contrasted with fifty-nine Americans killed) and were forced to withdraw. The Philippine Insurrection had begun.

Guerrilla Warfare

The Americans, hampered by a shortage of troops and the oncoming rainy season, could initially do little more than extend their defensive perimeter beyond Manila and establish a toehold on several islands to the south. By the end of March, however, American forces seized Malolos, the seat of Aguinaldo's revolutionary government. But Aguinaldo escaped, simply melting into the jungle. In the fall, using conventional methods of warfare, the Americans first struck south, then north of Manila across the central Luzon plain. After hard marching and tough fighting, the expeditionary force occupied northern Luzon, dispersed the rebel army, and barely missed capturing Aguinaldo.

Believing that occupying the remainder of the Philippines would be easy, the Americans wrongly concluded that the war was virtually ended. But when the troops attempted to control the territory they had seized, they found that the Filipino revolutionaries were not defeated but had merely changed strategies. Abandoning western-style conventional warfare, Aguinaldo had decided to adopt guerrilla tactics.

Aguinaldo moved to a secret mountain headquarters at Palanan in northern Luzon, ordering his troops to disperse and avoid pitched battles in favor of hit-and-run operations by small bands. Ambushing parties of Americans and applying terror to coerce support from other Filipinos, the insurrectionists now blended into the countryside, where they enjoyed superior intelligence information, ample supplies, and tight security. The guerrillas moved freely between the scattered American units, cutting telegraph lines, attacking supply trains, and assaulting straggling infantrymen. When the Americans pursued their tormentors, they fell into well planned ambushes. The insurgents' barbarity and ruthlessness during these attacks were notorious.

The guerrilla tactics helped to offset the inequities that existed between the two armies. The American troops were far better armed, for example, carrying .45-caliber Springfield single-shot rifles, Mausers, and then-modern .30-caliber repeating Krag-Jorgensen rifles. They also had field artillery and machine guns. The revolutionaries, on the other hand, were limited to a miscellaneous assortment of handguns, a few Mauser repeating rifles taken from the Spanish, and antique muzzle-loaders. The sharp-edged bolo knife was the revolutionary's primary weapon, and he used it well. Probably more American soldiers were hacked to death by bolos than were killed by Mauser bullets.

As would later be the case in Vietnam, the guerrillas had some clear advantages. They knew the terrain, were inured to the climate, and could generally count on a friendly population. As in Vietnam, villages controlled by the insurgents provided havens from which the guerrillas could attack, then fade back into hiding.

Americans soon began to feel that they were under siege in a land of enemies, and their fears were heightened because they never could be sure who among the population was hostile. A seemingly friendly peasant might actually be a murderer. Lieutenant Colonel J. T. Wickham, commanding the 26th Infantry Regiment, recorded that "a large flag of truce enticed officers into ambushes . . . Privates Dugan, Hayes, and Tracy were murdered by town authorities . . . Private Nolan [was] tied up by ladies while in a stupor; the insurgents cut his throat . . . The body of Corporal Doneley was dug up, burned, and mutilated . . . Private O'Hearn, captured by apparently friendly people was tied to a tree, burned over a slow fire, and slashed up . . . Lieutenant Max Wagner was assassinated by insurgents disguised in American uniforms."

As in later guerrilla movements, such terrorism became a standard tactic for the insurgents. Both Filipinos and Americans were their victims. In preying on their countrymen, the guerrillas had a dual purpose: to discourage any Filipinos disposed to cooperate with the Americans, and to demonstrate to people in a particular region that they ruled that area and could destroy inhabitants and villages not supporting the revolution. The most favored terroristic weapon was assassination of local leaders, who were usually executed in a manner (such as beheading or burying alive) calculated to horrify everyone.

By the spring of 1900 the war was going badly for the Americans. Their task forces, sent out to search and destroy, found little and destroyed less.

The monsoon rains, jungle terrain, hostile native population, and a determined guerrilla force made the American soldier's marches long and miserable. One described a five-week-long infantry operation: ". . . our troops had been on half rations for two weeks. Wallowing through hip-deep muck, lugging a ten-pound rifle and a belt . . . with 200 rounds of ammunition, drenched to the skin and their feet becoming heavier with mud at every step, the infantry became discouraged. Some men simply cried, others slipped down in the mud and refused to rise. Threats and appeals by the officers were of no avail. Only a promise of food in the next town and the threat that if they remained behind they would be butchered by marauding bands of insurgents forced some to their feet to struggle on."

News reports of the army's difficulties began to erode the American public's support of the war. "To chase barefooted insurgents with water buffalo carts as a wagon train may be simply ridiculous," charged one correspondent, "but to load volunteers down with 200 rounds of ammunition and one day's rations, and to put on their heads felt hats used by no other army in the tropics . . . to trot these same soldiers in the boiling sun over a country without roads, is positively criminal . . . There are over five thousand men in the general hospital."

Another reported that the American outlook "is blacker now than it has been since the beginning of the war . . . the whole population . . . sympathizes with the insurgents. The insurgents came to Pasig [a local area whose government cooperated with the Americans] and their first act was to hang the 'Presidente' for treason in surrendering to Americans. 'Presidentes' do not surrender to us anymore."

New Strategies

Early in the war U.S. military commanders had realized that, unlike the American Indians who had been herded onto reservations, eight million Filipinos (many of them hostile) would have to be governed in place. The Americans chose to emphasize pacification through good works rather than by harsh measures, hoping to convince Filipinos that the American colonial government had a sincere interest in their welfare and could be trusted.

As the army expanded its control across the islands, it reorganized local municipal governments and trained Filipinos to take over civil functions in the democratic political structure the Americans planned to establish. American soldiers performed police duties, distributed food, established and taught at schools, and built roads and telegraph lines.

As the war progressed, however, the U.S. commanders saw that the terrorism practiced by Aguinaldo's guerrillas was far more effective in controlling the populace than was their own benevolent approach. Although the Americans did not abandon pacification through good works, it was thereafter subordinated to the "civilize 'em with a Krag" (Krag-Jorgensen rifle) philosophy. From December 1900 onward, captured revolutionaries faced deportation, imprisonment, or execution.

The American army also changed its combat strategy to counter that of its enemy. As in the insurgents' army, the new tactics emphasized mobility and surprise. Breaking into small units—the battalion became the largest maneuver force—the Americans gradually spread over the islands until each of the larger towns was occupied by one or two rifle companies. From these bases American troops began platoon-and company-size operations to pressure local guerrilla bands.

Because of the difficult terrain, limited visibility, and requirement for mobility, artillery now saw limited use except as a defensive weapon. The infantry became the main offensive arm, with mounted riflemen used to pursue the fleeing enemy. Cavalry patrols were so valued for their mobility that American military leaders hired trusted Filipinos as mounted scouts and cavalrymen.

The Americans made other efforts to "Filipinize" the war—letting Asians fight Asians. (A similar tactic had been used in the American Indian campaigns twenty years before; it would resurface in Vietnam sixty years later as "Vietnamization.") In the Philippines the Americans recruited five thousand Macabebes, mercenaries from the central Luzon province of Pampanga, to form the American-officered Philippine Scouts. The Macabebes had for centuries fought in native battalions under the Spanish flag—even against their own countrymen when the revolution began in 1896.

Just as a later generation of American soldiers would react to the guerrilla war in Vietnam, American soldiers in the Philippines responded to insurgent terrorism in kind, matching cruelty with cruelty. Such actions vented their frustration at being unable to find and destroy the enemy. An increasing number of Americans viewed all Filipinos as enemies.

"We make everyone get into his house by 7 P.M. and we only tell a man once," Corporal Sam Gillis of the 1st California Volunteer Regiment wrote to his family. "If he refuses, we shoot him. We killed over 300 natives the first night . . . If they fire a shot from the house, we burn the house and every house near it."

Another infantryman frankly admitted that "with an enemy like this to fight, it is not surprising that the boys should soon adopt 'no quarter' as a motto and fill the blacks full of lead before finding out whether they are friends or enemies.

That attitude should not have been too surprising. The army's campaigns against the Plains Indians were reference points for the generation of Americans that took the Philippines. Many of the senior officers and noncommissioned officers—often veterans of the Indian wars—considered Filipinos to be "as full of treachery as our Arizona Apache." "The country won't be pacified," one soldier told a reporter, "until the niggers are killed off like the Indians." A popular soldier's refrain, sung to the tune of "Tramp, tramp, tramp, the boys are marching," began, "Damn, damn, damn the Filipinos," and again spoke of "civilizing 'em with a Krag."

Reprisals against civilians by Americans as well as insurgents became common. General Lloyd Wheaton, leading a U.S. offensive southeast of Manila, found his men impaled on the bamboo prongs of booby traps and with throats slit while they slept. After two of his companies were ambushed, Wheaton ordered that every town and village within twelve miles be burned.

The Americans developed their own terrorist methods, many of which would be used in later Southeast Asian wars. One was torturing suspected guerrillas or insurgent sympathizers to force them to reveal locations of other guerrillas and their supplies. An often-utilized form of persuasion was the "water cure," placing a bamboo reed in the victim's mouth and pouring water (some used salt water or dirty water) down his throat, thus painfully distending the victim's stomach. The subject, allowed to void this, would, under threat of repetition, usually talk freely. Another method of torture, the "rope cure," consisted of wrapping a rope around the victim's neck and torso until it formed sort of a girdle. A stick (or Krag rifle) placed between the ropes and twisted, then effectively created a combination of smothering and garroting.

The anti-imperialist press reported such American brutality in lurid detail. As a result, a number of officers and soldiers were courtmartialed for torturing and other cruelties. Their punishments, however, seemed remarkably lenient. Of ten officers tried for "looting, torture, and murder," three were acquitted; of the seven convicted, five were reprimanded, one was reprimanded and fined $300, and one lost thirty-five places in the army's seniority list and forfeited half his pay for nine months.

Officers and soldiers, fighting a cruel, determined, and dangerous enemy, could not understand public condemnation of the brutality they felt was necessary to win. They had not experienced such criticism during the Indian wars, where total extermination of the enemy was condoned by the press and the American public, and they failed to grasp the difference now. Press reports, loss of public support, and the soldier's feeling of betrayal—features of an insurgent war—would resurface decades later during the Vietnam conflict.

Success

Although U.S. military leaders were frustrated by the guerrillas' determination on one hand and by eroding American support for the war on the other, most believed that the insurgents could be subdued. Especially optimistic was General Arthur MacArthur, who in 1900 assumed command of the seventy thousand American troops in the Philippines. MacArthur adopted a strategy like that successfully used by General Zachary Taylor in the Second Seminole War in 1835; he believed that success depended upon the Americans' ability to isolate the guerrillas from their support in the villages. Thus were born "strategic hamlets," "free-fire zones," and "search and destroy" missions, concepts the American army would revive decades later in Vietnam.

MacArthur strengthened the more than five hundred small strong points held by Americans throughout the Philippine Islands. Each post was garrisoned by at least one company of American infantrymen. The natives around each base were driven from their homes, which were then destroyed. Soldiers herded the displaced natives into *reconcentrado* camps, where they could be "protected" by the nearby garrisons. Crops, food stores, and houses outside the camps were destroyed to deny them to the guerrillas. Surrounding each camp was a "dead line," within which anyone appearing would be shot on sight.

Operating from these small garrisons, the Americans pressured the guerrillas, allowing them no rest. Kept off balance, short of supplies, and constantly pursued by the American army, the Filipino guerrillas, suffering from sickness, hunger, and dwindling popular support, began to lose their will to fight. Many insurgent leaders surrendered, signaling that the tide at last had turned in the Americans' favor.

In March 1901, a group of Macabebe Scouts, commanded by American Colonel Frederick "Fighting Fred" Funston, captured Aguinaldo. Aguinaldo's subsequent proclamation that he would fight no more, and his pledge of loyalty to the United States, sped the collapse of the insurrection.

As in the past, and as would happen again during the Vietnam conflict of the 1960s and '70s, American optimism was premature. Although a civilian commission headed by William H. Taft took control of the colonial government from the American army in July 1901, the army faced more bitter fighting in its "pacification" of the islands.

As the war sputtered, the insurgent's massacre of fifty-nine American soldiers at Balangiga on the island of Samar caused Brigadier General Jacob W. "Hell-Roaring Jake" Smith, veteran of the Wounded Knee massacre of the Sioux in 1890, to order his officers to turn Samar into a "howling wilderness." His orders to a battalion of three hundred Marines headed for Samar were precise: "I want no prisoners. I wish you to kill and burn, the more you kill and burn the better it will please me. I want all persons killed who are capable of bearing arms against the United States." Fortunately, the Marines did not take Smith's orders literally and, later, Smith would be courtmartialed.

On July 4, 1902 the Philippine Insurrection officially ended. Although it took the American army another eleven years to crush the fierce Moros of the southern Philippines, the civil government's security force (the Philippine Constabulary), aided by the army's Philippine Scouts, maintained a fitful peace throughout the islands. The army's campaign to secure the Philippines as an American colony had succeeded.

American commanders would have experienced vastly greater difficulties except for two distinct advantages: 1) the enemy had to operate in a restricted area, in isolated islands, and was prevented by the U.S. Navy from importing weapons and other needed supplies; and 2) though the insurgents attempted to enlist help from Japan, no outside power intervened. These conditions would not prevail in some subsequent guerrilla conflicts in Asia.

In addition to the many tactical lessons the army learned from fighting a guerrilla war in a tropical climate, other problems experienced during this campaign validated the need for several military reforms that were subsequently carried out, including improved logistics, tropical medicine, and communications.

The combination of harsh and unrelenting military force against the guerrillas, complemented by the exercise of fair and equitable civil government and civic action toward those who cooperated, proved to be the Americans' most effective tactic for dealing with the insurgency. This probably was the most significant lesson to be learned from the Philippine Insurrection.

Lessons for the Future

Vietnam veterans reading this account might nod in recollection of a personal, perhaps painful experience from their own war.

Many similarities exist between America's three-year struggle with the Filipino *insurrectos* and the decade-long campaign against the Communists in Vietnam. Both wars, modestly begun, went far beyond what anyone had foreseen in time, money, equipment, manpower, casualties, and suffering.

Both wars featured small-unit infantry actions. Young infantrymen, if they had any initial enthusiasm, usually lost it once they saw the war's true nature; they nevertheless learned to endure their allotted time while adopting personal self-survival measures as months "in-country" lengthened and casualty lists grew.

Both wars were harsh, brutal, cruel. Both had their Samar Islands and their My Lais. Human nature being what it is, both conflicts also included acts of great heroism, kindness, compassion, and self-sacrifice.

Both wars saw an increasingly disenchanted American public withdrawing its support (and even disavowing its servicemen) as the campaigns dragged on, casualties mounted, and news accounts vividly described the horror of the battlefields.

Some useful lessons might be gleaned from a comparison of the two conflicts. Human nature really does not change—war will bring out the best and the worst in the tired, wet, hungry, and fearful men who are doing the fighting. Guerrilla campaigns—particularly where local military and civic reforms cannot be effected to separate the guerrilla from his base of popular support— will be long and difficult, and will demand tremendous commitments in resources and national will. Finally, before America commits its armed forces to similar ventures in the future, it would do well to recall the lessons learned from previous campaigns. For, as the Spanish-born American educator, poet, and philosopher George Santayana reminded us, those who do not learn from the past are doomed to repeat it.

People living in the United States through the first half of the twentieth century witnessed some of the most startling, if not revolutionary, changes in American history. The automobile replaced the horse as the everyday means of transportation and totally reshaped the face of the land. Labor unions rose to a position of unprecedented influence and helped create the huge American middle class. The United States had become an industrial giant by 1900. It then plunged into the most catastrophic depression in its history in the 1930's, only to re-emerge by 1945, tempered by war, poised on the brink of an unparalleled postwar economic boom.

A leading role in two world wars made the United States a world superpower. American women earned a new degree of social and legal independence, and their contributions to the nation's war efforts won them a place in the workforce from which they would not be dislodged. African-Americans, in search of their portion of the American dream, participated wholeheartedly in the two world wars, uprooted themselves from the South and, like other Americans, moved to the city. Other minorities also sought their recognition as Americans.

In presidential politics, Americans witnessed within one generation the extremes of success and failure, from the depths of corruption under Harding to the soaring leadership of Woodrow Wilson and two Roosevelts. To a great extent the events of these years created the nation we know today.

$100 WILL BUY THIS CAR. MUST HAVE CASH LOST ALL ON THE STOCK MARKET

1900-1945

T he Brownsville Affray

by Richard Young

In the summer of 1906, Brownsville, Texas, in the era of Jim Crow, was filled with tension because of the stationing of black soldiers at Fort Brown. The black troopers were not welcomed by the white residents of this small town on the southern tip of the Texas coast. The soldiers were subjected to ridicule and even physical abuse when they entered the town. They were also falsely accused by the townsfolk of criminal action. At the height of this tension, shortly after midnight on August 13, a group of men went through the town shooting into houses and businesses. The shooting left one man dead. Many in the town quickly blamed the black soldiers and demanded that President Theodore Roosevelt take action. The story of this incident and its tragic consequences is vividly told by Richard Young in this article.

August 13, 1906: It was just past midnight on a sultry summer night. Fred Combe, the mayor of Brownsville, Texas, was falling asleep on his back porch. Army Major Charles Penrose, the commanding officer of nearby Fort Brown, was preparing for bed. A late birthday party was breaking up at the Cowen residence near the fort. Downtown, players anted up in a poker game at the Crixell Saloon. It was, from all appearances, a typical Sunday night in the sleepy Texas border town.

But someone had no intention of letting the town rest. A group of armed men—perhaps ten, perhaps as many as twenty—had quietly gathered in Cowen Alley, near a low fence that separated Fort Brown from the town.

Suddenly the silence was shattered as the men began moving rapidly up the alley toward the center of town, firing at windows as they ran. As bullets peppered the houses, startled residents dropped to the floors next to their beds. Downtown, police lieutenant M. Y. Dominguez rant out of a saloon and mounted his horse to investigate the disturbance. When he suddenly rode into range of the shadowy figures firing weapons, Dominguez wheeled his horse to escape, but he was shot just as he made the turn. (His arm would later be amputated.) Minutes later the men loosed a volley into the Ruby Saloon, killing barkeep Frank Natus, who was reaching out to close the alley door.

After the shooting at the saloon, the killers melted back into the night, leaving chaos in their wake. Mayor Combe ran out of his house to investigate the explosion of gunfire and was told that "the Negroes are shooting up the town."

The firing in Brownsville ended after just ten minutes, but repercussions from the incident were destined to continue for many years afterwards. Because of the racial implications involved, such eminent leaders as then-Secretary of War William Howard Taft, U.S. Senator Joseph B. Foraker, black leader Booker T. Washington, and President Theodore Roosevelt would become ensnared in a mystery that has never really been solved and in a controversy that has never been fully laid to rest.

It had all started when the government announced that the all-white Twenty-sixth Infantry Regiment, then stationed at Fort Brown would be replaced by three companies of the all-black Twenty-fifth Infantry Regiment, then stationed at Fort Niobara, Nebraska. The black troopers had compiled a long and honorable tradition of service in the Indian wars, in the Spanish-American War, and in the Philippines. To the citizens of Brownsville, however, the service record of the men of the Twenty-fifth meant far less than the color of their skin.

The news of the transfer of the Twenty-fifth to Fort Brown was met immediately with angry talk and threats. First Sergeant Nelson Huron of the departing Twenty-sixth overheard a resident say, "The people of Brownsville don't want them damned niggers here and they won't have them." Victorio Fernandez, one of Brownsville's Mexican police officers, reportedly said, "I want to kill a couple of them when they get here." At a rail station in San Antonio, a man heard some Brownsville residents say they would "shoot over the barracks" of the Negro troops to frighten them.

The black soldiers arrived by rail on Saturday, July 28, and marched to Fort Brown past sullen townspeople. Situated at the mouth of the Rio Grande near the Gulf of Mexico, Brownsville had seen its heyday around the time of the Civil War, when it had been one of the principal seaports of the Confederacy. The end of the war and the coming of the railroad had spelled the end for Brownsville as a center of commerce. In 1906, Brownsville was a small town awash with racial hatred. Some businesses and drinking establishments refused to serve the black soldiers. Certain saloons opened up segregated back rooms for the blacks, Jim-Crow fashion.

In the most serious of several incidents that took place following the arrival of the black soldiers, Privates James W. Newton and Frank J. Lipscomb were taking a Sunday evening stroll through Brownsville on August 5. As they walked down Elizabeth Street they approached a group of whites on the sidewalk—among them U.S. customs inspector Fred Tate and his wife, who were conversing with a half-dozen women. Tate later claimed that the two black soldiers had continued walking straight down the sidewalk, plowing right through the ladies congregated there. The soldiers claimed that they had stepped aside into the street and that Tate had come after them. In any case, what followed was not in dispute. Tate pulled out a .45-caliber Colt six-shooter and shouted, "I will learn you how to get off the sidewalk when you see a party of white ladies standing there." He proceeded to pistol-whip Newton.

The soldiers were paid on Saturday, August 11, and passed what many in town considered the most peaceful soldiers' payday ever seen in Brownsville. Not one soldier was arrested, and there were no cases of excessive drunkenness. But later that weekend, a Mrs. Lon Evans reported that a soldier tried to crawl through a window in her home. The next day, the headlines in the *Brownsville Daily Herald* trumpeted:

INFAMOUS OUTRAGE
Negro Soldiers Invaded Private Premises Last Night
and Tried to Seize a White Lady

That night, a climate of rumor and hysteria gripped Brownsville. Several men from the town were ready to go to the fort with weapons to precipitate a fight. Because of the excitement, Mayor Combe rode out to talk with Major Penrose. The mayor requested that the black soldiers be confined to quarters for the evening because of "a great deal of danger in town."

Major Penrose prudently decided to order his men in, setting a curfew of 8:00 P.M Captain Macklin sent out patrols to fetch the men still in town. Sergeant Taliafero, one of the soldiers on patrol, later reported that a townsman called out to him, "It is a good thing your C.O. has ordered you all in tonight because some of you were going to get killed."

The soldiers spent the remainder of the evening on the post, fishing in a lagoon, talking on the barracks porches, and playing cards and billiards in the dayroom. The moon was down when "Taps" sounded at 11:00 P.M., and all was quiet.

At midnight, Major Penrose heard two shots that he thought were pistol shots, then six or seven reports that he knew were from high-powered rifles. The attack had begun—and confusion reigned. Ambrose Littlefield, who was at the corner of Cowen Alley and Thirteenth Street, saw the raiders standing under a streetlamp on the corner of Washington and Thirteenth. He later identified them as black soldiers. However, George Thomas Porter, who lived at Thirteenth and Washington, looked out of his window and did not see anyone turn out of Thirteenth, nor did he see anyone under the streetlamp.

Police Lieutenant Dominguez said that from his vantage point at Washington and Fourteenth he looked toward Cowen Alley and saw eight men cross Fourteenth in the dark. Another policeman, Officer Padron, said he met Dominguez in a different place at that time.

Paulino Preciado, who was drinking in the Ruby Saloon when the shots killed the barman, said that he saw soldiers in the alley. But he later recanted, saying that "I could not see anybody in the alley, as it was dark out there, and I was in the light."

At Fort Brown, according to the testimony of Captain Macklin, the chain of sentinels stationed along the wall were unable to see men just ten to fifteen feet away in the dark because "everything was a blank." Major Penrose assumed that someone was firing on the fort and ordered his men into emergency formation.

According to the noncommissioned officers, all the men were in formation and accounted for—*while* the firing could still be heard in town. Later that night, Penrose sent a patrol to town under the command of Captain Samuel Lyon. Lyon reported back, to the surprise of Penrose, that the townspeople thought the soldiers had done the firing. The next morning, Penrose ordered a check of the weapons and ammunition. All rifles were clean and all ammunition accounted for.

On August 13, that same Monday morning, the town began an investigation. The major himself retraced the line of attack and found fifty to sixty expended Army shells along the way. He appointed an investigating committee composed of leading citizens of the town. They heard the testimony of twenty-two witnesses, eight of whom implicated black soldiers as the raiders. Five of those witnesses said they actually saw blacks; three others said they recognized that the men were black from the sound of their voices. The tenor of the investigation can be surmised from one typical question: Q. "We know that this outrage was committed by Negro soldiers. We want any information that will lead to a discovery of who did it."

On August 15, after two days of investigation, the citizens' committee sent a telegraph message to President Theodore Roosevelt in Washington, in which they informed him that the town was terrorized and under constant alarm. They asked "to have the troops at once removed and replaced by white soldiers." The War Department complied, sending the Twenty-fifth Infantry from Fort Brown to Fort Reno, Oklahoma.

Meanwhile, Texas authorities were conducting their own investigation: on August 23, warrants were issued for the arrest of twelve members of the black battalion for murder and conspiracy to commit murder. The twelve were selected by Texas Rangers after questioning. Although the investigation uncovered no solid allegations against the twelve and no witnesses could conclusively put them at the scene of the crime, they were removed to Fort Sam Houston in San Antonio.

Army General William S. McCaskey, Commanding General of the Department of Texas, said that the "manner by which their names were procured is a mystery. As far as is known there is no evidence that the majority of them were in any way directly connected with the affair."

The Army's investigation of the incident hit a brick wall. President Roosevelt sent Major August P. Blackson, Inspector General of the Southwest Division, to check into the matter. Blackson reported that the involvement of the men of the Twenty-fifth "cannot be doubted" but that the men of the battalion would not testify against their comrades.

Blackson contended that those who refused to "peach" or "squeal" on their comrades should "be made to suffer with the others more guilty, as far as the law will permit" because of their "conspiracy of silence." He recommended that "all of the enlisted men of the three companies present on the night of August 13 be discharged from service and be debarred from reenlistment." It appears that almost no one involved in the official Army investigation seriously addressed the notion that the men might actually be innocent and that they were saying nothing because they had nothing to say.

President Roosevelt ordered General Ernest A. Garlington to get information from the twelve soldiers incarcerated at Fort Sam Houston and from the rest of the men of the Twenty-fifth at Fort Reno. Garlington reported that each man "assumed a wooden, stolid look [and] denied any knowledge of the affair," which confirmed his belief that "the secretive nature of the race, where crimes charged to members of their color are made, is well known." Garlington wrote that he knew that many men without direct knowledge would suffer, but that they had stood together during the investigation and so should "stand together when the penalty falls."

On November 5, Roosevelt instructed Secretary of War William H. Taft to carry out the recommendation. Taft waited until after November 9 congressional elections, then began discharge proceedings against all of the men of the three companies. The process was completed within ten days—without a court-martial or a hearing. Many of the men wept as they turned in their weapons and equipment. In all, 167 men, including many who had served with honor on the frontier, in Cuba, and in the Philippines were released, making this the largest mass punishment in U.S. Army history. One of the discharged men was a twenty-six year veteran, and thirteen of the soldiers had been decorated for bravery in the Spanish-American War. Six men were Medal of Honor recipients.

The pro-Roosevelt *Outlook* editorialized that there was "no doubt" that some of the soldiers of the Twenty-fifth Regiment were guilty of murder in the first degree, and that the president's decision had been "both wise and just, notwithstanding the fact that some who are innocent suffer with the guilty." The *Outlook* concluded that there was "no reason whatever for regarding this action as having any relation to the race issue."

But blacks throughout the land saw it differently. Many felt betrayed by Roosevelt, whom they had perceived to be a friend of the black people. He was, after all, the leader of the party of Lincoln—and most black people still voted for the Republicans in 1906. Beyond that, during the Spanish-American War Roosevelt had fought with black troopers on his flank, and they had rescued him on more than one occasion. He had always spoken highly of their courage and ability as soldiers, which made it particularly galling when he contended that this case should convince black people not to "band together to shelter their own criminals."

Debate in the black community grew so heated that the nation's foremost black leader, Booker T. Washington, urged his people to tone down their attacks on the president. Because Washington had never spoken in defense of the soldiers, his stand was perceived to be justification of Roosevelt's action at the expense of the Negro movement. Other black leaders, most notably W. E. B. DuBois, were quick to capitalize on the issue—and they gained power in their community as Washington fell from favor.

The Constitutional League (a civil rights organization and precursor to the National Association for the Advancement of Colored People) lodged an official protest over the dismissal of the black soldiers on December 10, 1906. More importantly, the U.S. Senate began its own investigation. The hearings lasted from February 4 through June 14, 1907, and were resumed on November 18, 1907, and continued through March 10, 1908.

The Senate listened to the testimony of more than one hundred and sixty witnesses. The Majority Report concluded that the shooting had been done by some eight to twenty soldiers, who were never identified. The guns used had been 1903 Springfield rifles, according to the report, and the ammunition had been government issue. Of the witnesses, fifteen said they saw the attackers clad in soliders' uniforms.

During the hearings the black soldiers acquired a powerful champion, Senator Joseph B. Foraker of Ohio, a politician from within Roosevelt's own Republican party and a long-time foe of the president. Senator Foraker and three other senators wrote the minority opinion. They pointed out that there had been no indictments, despite the administration's desperate measures to secure them. This was no small matter, as the *New York Evening Post* pointed out in an editorial: "When a Texas grand jury cannot find an indictment against a hated 'nigger' it looks as if the President of the United States had a pretty poor case when he discharged those men."

The dissenters also wrote that if anyone had a motive to shoot up the town of Brownsville, it was the white gambling-house owners, not the black soldiers. Their reason was financial: the houses were segregated, and the owners were losing most of the revenue they would have been taking in if Fort Brown had been manned by white soldiers. It was the contention of Foraker and the other dissenters that the owners had probably staged the incident in order to effect the removal of the black troops.

Foraker and the others charged that the black soldiers had been punished without access to their right to a fair public trial. They further stated that the soldiers had been loyal for years and that even if some were guilty, all should not have been discharged. Furthermore, no conspiracy had been proven, and much of the testimony had been contradictory and unreliable.

These new investigations brought prior assumptions into question and raised new questions that would never be satisfactorily answered. An editorial in the March 19, 1908, *Independent* stated: "The investigation by the Senate leaves it somewhat doubtful whether the shooting was actually done by the soldiers."

Many of the witnesses claimed to have identified the attackers as black soldiers from a distance of thirty to one hundred feet, but in a firing conducted at night by the Army under conditions similar to those of the night of August 13, witnesses as close as fifty feet could see only the flash of weapons and nothing of the person firing. At a distance of just two paces on such a night, it was not possible to distinguish the race of men standing quietly in a line.

The forty Government-Issue shells found immediately outside the fort wall had been piled neatly in a circle approximately ten inches in diameter. Because a Springfield-rifle ejects expended cartridges a distance of ten feet, it would have been necessary for the men firing the rifles to find and retrieve the spent shells in the dark and neatly pile them, an action that would have been not only bizarre but nearly impossible on a moonless night. The piles of cartridges suggest that they were left there as "evidence"—scattered by someone who wanted to make it look as if the soldiers had fired them.

According to the dissenters, the rounds *had* been fired by the men of the Twenty-fifth—but on the range at Fort Niobara, sometime prior to their transfer to Fort Brown. A microscopic study conducted at the Springfield Armory proved that all of the expended cartridges had been fired by the same four rifles, all of which belonged to members of Company B. In the check of weapons ordered by Major Penrose on Monday morning, three of the four rifles were found to be clean and covered with cosmoline, a thick lubricant that would have rendered it nearly impossible to fire them. It is possible that these three rifles could have been fired and then cleaned and oiled during the night, but it is almost certain that the fourth rifle was not fired on the night of August 13. It was found buried deep in a footlocker in the locked supply room. In order to retrieve the weapon, the investigators had to remove bunks and baggage that had been piled on the locker after the move from Fort Niobara.

The dissenters theorized that the empty shells were policed up at Fort Niobara and put into boxes, and then were transported along with other equipment to Fort Brown. The boxes containing the empty shells were left unguarded on the porches of the barracks there. It would have been easy for a civilian who worked on post to pocket these rounds without anyone noticing.

The live military rounds fired into the house could be explained by the fact that the departing Twenty-sixth Infantry had often bartered with civilians, trading ammunition for whiskey and other items. The Twenty-sixth had also left a great deal of used equipment, including old uniforms, in the barracks when they left camp. Scavengers from town were frequent visitors to the post in the time between the departure of the Twenty-sixth and the arrival of the Twenty-fifth. It was not uncommon to see townspeople wearing articles of military clothing, and it certainly would not have been difficult to put together "uniforms" for the raiders.

All of these possible contradictions to the official version of the incident came to light after the men had been discharged. The mystery was never solved. No one was ever tried for the murder of Frank Natus. But the Roosevelt administration remained adamant in insisting that it had followed the right course in dismissing the men, and neither Theodore Roosevelt nor his successor, William Howard Taft, wanted anything to do with reopening the investigation.

An Army Court of Inquiry did convene to hear evidence on the issue of reinstatement of the 167 men, but the hearings were not public. On May 4, 1909, for reasons never disclosed, the Court of Inquiry reinstated fourteen of the soldiers to full honors and rank. The other 153 accused men remained pariahs, discharged without honor or chance of redemption. They had never been convicted of a crime, nor was any evidence produced against them—yet they remained outcasts.

Sixty-six years after the Brownsville incident, in 1972, U.S. Representative Augustus Hawkins initiated legislation to restore honor to the men of the Twenty-fifth Infantry. Senator Hubert H. Humphrey backed the motion in the Senate, saying, "We in government have a duty to demonstrate that we can admit an error and can correct a terrible wrong." Eventually, Secretary of the Army Robert F. Kroehlke issued an executive order that gave the 153 men honorable discharges, albeit without back pay or allowances. Congress in turn authorized a twenty-five-thousand-dollar pension for any of the discharged men still living and ten thousand dollars to any surviving spouse.

Only one of the men, eighty-six-year-old Dorsey Willis, lived to collect the money. Willis claimed that the dishonorable discharge had ruined his life, saying, "To take a person's rights from them is bad, you know. They had no right to eliminate me without trying me and finding me guilty, but they did . . . None of us said anything because we didn't have anything to say. It was a frame-up through and through."

Chapter 10

Hell on Saturday Afternoon

by John F. McCormack, Jr.

Workers at the Triangle Shirtwaist Company in New York City had much in common with other laborers. Hours were long, wages were low, and working conditions were poor. Employer resistance to unionism was equally bitter. Tragically, working at the factory also proved to be dangerous.

John F. McCormack, Jr., graphically describes the conditions of the shirtwaist workers, the factors which contributed to the disaster, and the short- and long-term effects of the fire. His commentary also provides us with insights regarding the status of women in the work force in the early twentieth century and illustrates the connection between industrialization, immigration, and urbanization. Lastly, it is interesting to note how many prominent political careers were touched and how much legislation was formulated by the investigations surrounding "the worst factory fire in history."

It was payday for the girls working at the Triangle Shirtwaist Company. A gentle early spring breeze wafted in the open windows of the ten-story Asch Building, situated on the northwest corner of Greene Street and Washington Place, New York City. The machines hummed along as they stitched the lace, lawn and silk into shirtwaists. At 4:30 p.m. they were shut down and the garment workers prepared to leave. Suddenly, flames burst forth from a cluttered rag bin. Efforts to extinguish the fire failed and hell on Saturday afternoon, March 25, 1911 was less than minutes away for over 500 factory employees.

As the eighth story fire began to spread, a bookkeeper alerted the New York City Fire Department at approximately 4:45 p.m. She also tried to warn those on the two floors above to evacuate the building. At first some of the girls thought the message was a prank. After all, the building was fire-proof. However, flames drawn in the open windows from the eighth floor below soon brought panic to the disbelievers. A babble of foreign languages added to the confusion since a large proportion of the workers were Jewish and Italian immigrants. There were 146 lives lost in what National Fire Protection Association figures show to be the worst factory fire in history.

Life was difficult for all blue collar workers at the beginning of the twentieth century. Organized labor had made few gains and these concerned skilled laborers. Semi-skilled garment workers spent their lives living in tenements and working in sweatshops. One of these girls who worked in Brownsville (Brooklyn) described her work:

> The machines go like mad all day, because the faster you work the more money you get. Sometimes in my haste I get my finger caught and the needle goes right through it. It goes so quick though, that it does not hurt much. I bind the finger up with a piece of cotton and go on working. We all have accidents like that. Where the needle goes through the nail it makes for a sore finger, or where it splinters a bone it does much harm. Sometimes a finger has to come off. . . .

This same woman earned $4.50 per week, paying out $2.00 of that for room and board near the factory.

The shirtwaist industry at the time of the Triangle fire employed over 40,000 workers in about 450 New York City factories. About eighty percent of these were single women between the ages of eighteen and twenty-five. These girls worked between fifty-six and fifty-nine hours a week and as high as seventy during the busy season. Wages ranged from $4.00 to as high as $10.00 per week. Idle periods, however, could last as long as three months.

Moreover, substantial reductions were made in the workers' wages for use of electric power, needles and thread. If an operator was a few minutes late to work, she was docked a half-day's pay. Frequently, factory managers would actually lock employees in to force them to work overtime. Very few ill workers were permitted to leave before the day's work was finished. Lunch hours were habitually cut short and known union members were summarily dismissed.

It was the latter action which led to an unexpected and spectacular strike against Triangle Shirtwaist Company and another firm in 1909. The Shirtwaist Makers Union ordered the strike when some of its members were fired because of their union affiliation. The strike spread to the whole industry. The Triangle Company then decided to physically break the union by hiring toughs with criminal records as "special police" to "protect" its property. The *Jewish Daily Forward* printed some photos of the brutalized strikers and public opinion forced Triangle to find a new solution. It did. The company now came up with one of the most unique solutions ever employed to settle a strike. The toughs were replaced outside the factory by prostitutes!

Meanwhile, the shirtwaist makers managed to secure some powerful allies of their own: Mary Dreier, President of the Women's Trade Union League, Mrs. Alva E. Belmont, Mrs. Mary Beard, Anne Morgan, Inez Milholland, Lenora O'Reilly, Victoria Pike, John Mitchell of the United Mine Workers, Rabbi Stephen S. Wise and lawyer Samuel Untermeyer. Rallies and benefits were held under the guidance of these persons and others. The girls from Vassar

College worked on behalf of the strikers. After a delegation of New Yorkers visited Philadelphia, the shirtwaist makers there walked off the job. The Philadelphians were visited by Helen Taft, the U.S. President's daughter, a student at nearby Bryn Mawr College. She felt sorry for them and would "speak to papa about the terrible conditions" there. She then left for the opera.

The strike ended with the employees gaining much of what they had asked: better working conditions, a fifty-two hour week with no more than two hours per day overtime and time and a half for that with a fixed wage scale. Unfortunately, the issue of union recognition was never accepted by the manufacturers and there were no guarantees that the employers would not revert to form when they felt they could get away with it.

Among the most obstinate of the employers were Isaac Harris and Max Blanck, owners of the Triangle Shirtwaist Co. The firing of union members by their firm had precipitated the great strike of 1909. As the largest shirtwaist manufacturers, they intended to maintain their leadership in the field by any means possible. For instance, during the strike they hired strike breakers, thugs and prostitutes to cow the strikers. They also set up a phonograph on the ninth floor of the Asch Building so that their workers could dance during lunch time. Blanck even gave out prizes to the best dancers. When the strike ended, so did the dancing.

The owners were constantly concerned that their employees were trying to steal yard goods. In 1907 an incident occurred which indicated the great lengths to which the management would go to safeguard the company from such thefts. Two sisters were accused of taking materials by Samuel Bernstein, superintendent. They were returned to the building and forced to disrobe before two female employees. The sisters further charged that three men watched the proceedings through a transom. No stolen items were found. Nevertheless, this obsession that employees were stealing was to cost many lives in the fire. As a matter of course, the eighth and ninth floor doors on the Washington Place side of the building were locked. This forced the girls to go through a narrow passageway to the freight elevators on the Greene Street side. It also afforded an opportunity for the management to make certain no one was pilfering yard goods.

Other factors contributed to the disaster. There were large bins filled with scraps of cloth waiting for the rag man to come for them. He had last appeared in January. Wicker baskets filled with finished goods lined the aisles. Finished garments hung on racks. Cardboard and wooden boxes were stacked on the tenth floor. Gasoline, used to heat the pressing irons, was stored on the eighth floor. The ninth floor tables had wooden wells where oil drippings from the machines collected just above the knees of the operators. In addition, a large barrel of oil was stored by a door. Stairwells were not illuminated. A small fire escape led to a back courtyard. Fire officials later estimated that it would have taken three hours for the five hundred people on the top three floors to go down this way. Water valves were corroded shut with their attached hoses rotting in the folds. The Asch Building was fire proof, yet events showed it to be as fire proof as any furnace is, consuming all combustibles within it.

When the bookkeeper tried to alarm the two floors above her, the workday had just ended. The unbelieving girl who answered on the tenth floor finally comprehended and reported the fire to Mr. Blanck. On the ninth floor Max Hochfield was the first one to learn of the fire. He worked near the forelady. As she reached out to ring the quitting bell, he dashed past her into the stair-well and down the stairs. He saw the flames as he passed the eighth floor. He turned to go back for his sister when a hand grabbed him and pushed him downward. The first fireman had penetrated the burning building.

Flames had lapped in the open windows of the two floors above and panic gripped those frantically trying to escape. Girls tried in vain to leave by the locked doors. Others bunched up against the doors to the elevator shafts. Still others horrified the crowds now gathering on the street below by appearing on window ledges. "Don't jump!" "Don't jump!" they screamed. The horses of Hook and Ladder Company 20 soon appeared pulling their apparatus behind them. Quickly the firemen raised their ladders, the tallest in New York City. The crowds gasped! The ladders, when fully extended, could only reach the sixth story. Other firemen and citizen volunteers grasped life nets. Garment workers jumped for them. The men were simply bowled over by the impact of the plummeting figures, some of them already aflame. It was of little use since the distance was too great for the life nets to perform their purpose. Bodies had to be removed from atop fire hoses as these were stretched into the building.

At one point a man emerged at a ninth floor window. He helped a young woman to the window then lifted her outwards and let go. He performed this act three times before the horrified onlookers below. A fourth girl came to the window. The two figures embraced and kissed. He then held her out and dropped her. Thereupon, he climbed upon the window sill and leaped to the pavement. It was an act of love never to be forgotten by the witnesses to the Triangle holocaust.

There were others amidst the panic that Saturday afternoon who kept their wits about them. Among these no praise too high could be extended to the elevator operators. In grave danger, themselves, they continued to operate their life-saving machinery until no longer able to raise the elevators. Joseph Zito guessed he had personally brought over a hundred people to safety. Gaspar Mortillalo had his elevator jam when too many forced their way into it and atop it. Men and women slid down the cables to safety while others jumped down the shafts to serious injury and death. One, Herman Meshel, had slid down the cables under an elevator. He was found almost four hours later in water up to his neck still in the shaft, dazed, bleeding and whimpering pathetically.

Those trapped on the tenth floor owed their lives to a quick thinking college professor and his students. Professor Frank Sommer, former Essex County, N.J., sheriff, was lecturing to a class of fifty New York University Law School students on the tenth floor of the New York University-American Bank Company building next door to the Triangle concern. The fire gongs disrupted the class and Sommer rushed to the faculty room which looked across an areaway at the Asch Building. What he saw he described as a "building that was fast becoming a roaring furnace." He swiftly led his students to the roof of the N.Y.U. structure, which was about fifteen feet higher than its neighbor. They found two ladders left around by painters who were redecorating the building. These were lowered to the roof of the Asch Building. Some fifty persons, including Harris and Blanck and the latter's two children, who were visiting their father, were saved by the college students. Several rooms in the college building were scorched and firemen had to be directed there. Hundreds of valuable books were carried to safety by the students before the firemen put out the smoldering college rooms.

By this time all who could get out of the Asch Building had left. Only the doomed remained to be found by shaken fire fighters.

The Edison Company of New York strung lights along Greene Street and Washington Place and throughout the burned-out floors of the Asch Building. Firemen slowly lowered the wrapped bundles which had once been human beings. Bodies were removed to the Twenty-sixth Street pier where the city's morgue attendants and a number of derelicts were pressed into service. Soon grieving families came to identify, if possible, their loved ones. The police were hard-pressed to keep back the grief-stricken. When the latter were let in, the officers had to watch out for suicides and the hysterical. Seven victims would remain unidentified. Meanwhile, the ghouls were at work near the Asch Building. Among other sounds on Monday morning were those of young street hawkers selling alleged "dead girls' earrings" and "finger rings from the fire."

However, most Americans were stunned by the disaster. Officials sought to place the blame—somewhere, anywhere. Charitable organizations appealed for aid for families of the victims. Mayor William J. Gaynor issued a call for public contributions. The respondents ranged from the great of the land to the insignificant. Andrew Carnegie immediately gave $5,000. A little boy and his cousin donated $10, the proceeds of their "savings bank . . . to use it for somebody whose littel (sic) girl jumped out of a window. . . ." The Red Cross was the official agency designated by the mayor to receive funds through its well-known treasurer, investment banker Jacob H. Schiff. As frequently happens, the theatrical community in New York City was quick to respond. Marcus Loew, Guilio Gatti-Casazza, the Shuberts, the Hammersteins, Sam Harris, Al Jolson and George M. Cohan among others responded at once. Their benefit performances raised $15,000. In all, the gigantic sum (for those days) of $120,000 was raised. The major difficulty was getting the people to accept the money. The Red Cross found even the most destitute to be maddeningly independent.

Several protest meetings were held during the days following the tragedy. These ranged from threats of withholding tuition from frightened N.Y.U. students to calls for violent action from leftist orators. Perhaps the most poignant of all protests was the funeral parade called for April 5, after the city decided to bury the seven remaining unidentified victims in Evergreen Cemetery, East New York (Brooklyn).

Mayor Gaynor decided to bury these unfortunates because he feared that the release of their remains would lead to violence. Nevertheless, the Women's Trade Union League called for a public memorial parade on the same day. Rain drenched the marchers, as if the elements, themselves, mourned the victims. The parade consisted of two processions, one beginning uptown on Fourth Avenue between 19th and 22nd Streets; the other started at Seward Park where East Broadway and Canal Street meet. They joined at Washington Square Park and when the Asch Building was sighted a bone chilling wail was emitted by the marchers. Little Rose Schneiderman, the outspoken enemy of the exploiters, felt queasy in her stomach.

A reporter asked if she was ill. She was, for good reason. "As we marched up Fifth Avenue, there they were. Girls right at the top of hundreds of buildings, looking down on us. The structures were no different from the Asch Building . . . many were . . . worse. . . . There they were, leaning out of the upper windows, watching us. This, not the rain, is making me sick."

On April 11 the grand jury investigating the fire handed up indictments for first and second degree manslaughter against Messrs. Harris and Blanck. Judge O'Sullivan released them on $25,000 bail each. The main evidence against them was a bolted lock attached to a charred piece of wood. It came from the ninth floor of the Asch Building. The owners were charged with the deaths of a girl aged sixteen and a woman of twenty-two whose bodies were found among fifty jammed up at the locked door.

The "Shirtwaist Kings," as they were known in the trade, had made a fortune manufacturing the tops made famous by the illustrator, Charles Dana Gibson. The "Gibson Girl" was the epitome of American womanhood of the time, with her upswept hair, slender figure, long skirt and trim shirtwaist. Harris and Blanck catered to the demands of the American woman through their New York and Philadelphia factories. Now all that they had built up was threatened.

Their trial did not begin until December, 1911. When they entered the New York Criminal Court Building on December 5, a crowd of 300 women surged at them, waving photographs of lost loved ones and crying, "Murderers, murderers! Kill the murderers!" Max D. Steuer, their attorney and some court officers managed to get them to the courtroom. Police cleared the corridors. The next day both men were again mobbed as they entered and left a nearby restaurant at lunch time. The trial dragged on with much contradictory testimony until the embattled owners received a belated holiday gift on December 27. After an hour and three-quarters, the jury found them innocent of the charges. Both the acquitted and the jurors were smuggled out of the courtroom for fear for their lives. Incomprehensibly, the next day's *New York Times* printed the names and addresses of the jurymen!

Nonetheless, reform elements in New York continued to press for measures which would protect factory workers. They were following the admonition pronounced by Rabbi Wise: "The lesson of the hour is that while property is good, life is better, that while possessions are valuable, life is priceless."

New York State authorized a Factory Investigating Commission of nine members during the early summer of 1911. The chairman was Robert F. Wagner, Sr., later U.S. Senator from New York, who sponsored much labor and safety legislation. Vice-Chairman was Alfred E. Smith, later governor of the state and 1928 Democratic candidate for President. Sam Gompers, A.F.L. President, and Mary Dreier were other members. Among the commission's inspectors were Rose Schneiderman and Frances Perkins, who became Franklin D. Roosevelt's Secretary of Labor. Henry Morgenthau provided free top legal counsel in Abram Elkus and Bernard Shientag because the state had not appropriated enough money for legal fees. Within three years, thirty-six new pieces of legislation bolstered the state's labor laws. All were the result of findings by the commission. The sacrifices of the 146 had not been in vain, after all.

Frances Perkins stated later that much of the philosophy and legislation of the New Deal rose, like a phoenix, from the ashes of that hell on a Saturday afternoon almost three quarters of a century ago, the "Great Triangle Fire."

Mary Harris Jones: The Most Dangerous Woman in America

by Joseph Gustaitis

After losing her entire family to yellow fever, Mary Jones found herself working for the labor movement with the Knights of Labor. She would soon be seen across the country trying to organize workers and fighting to improve the conditions in which Americans were forced to labor. In her fight for social justice she would be known by workers as "Mother" Jones and labeled by the supporters of big business as "the most dangerous woman in America."

At forty-one years of age Mary Harris Jones had every reason to believe that she had nothing left in life. Her entire family—a husband and four children—had perished four years before in a yellow fever epidemic. And now, in 1871, just as she was escaping her grief and nearing solvency with her own dress-making business, all her possessions were reduced to ashes in the great Chicago fire.

But for Jones, the conflagration turned out to be a kind of metamorphosis. Throughout the next fifty-nine years, wherever desperate workers went on strike, wherever exploited child laborers cried for help, this querulous, gray-haired, black-bonneted woman with a high-pitched voice and piercing stare appeared to lead them on.

Mary Harris was born near Cork, Ireland, on May 1, 1830. Her father, Richard, sought by authorities for anti-British agitation, fled to the United States in 1835, became a citizen, and sent for his wife and children.

As a child Mary attended school in Toronto, Canada, where her father found work as a railroad laborer. Later she returned to the United States and worked first as a teacher in Monroe, Michigan, and then as a dressmaker in Chicago. In 1861, she was teaching in Memphis when she married George E. Jones, an iron molder. She learned firsthand about the workers' plight from her spouse, a steadfast union man.

While working in Chicago after suffering the loss of her family, Jones witnessed the "Gilded Age" gap between rich and poor. "Often while sewing for the lords and barons who lived in magnificent houses on the Lake Shore Drive," she later recalled, "I would look out of the plate glass windows and see the poor, shivering wretches, jobless and hungry walking alongside the frozen lake front. The contrast of their condition with that of the tropical comfort of the people for whom I served was painful to me. My employers seemed neither to notice nor to care."

After the Great Fire, Mary Jones found solace in attending the meetings of the Knights of Labor, one of the country's first mass labor organizations. With their oratory, ideals, and solidarity, the Knights not only gave Jones the inspiration to rebuild her life but also provided her with a substitute family— a nation of workers who would bestow on her the title "Mother" Jones.

At one Knights meeting, Jones's insightful questions impressed Terence V. Powderly, Grand Master Workman of the Knights from 1879 to 1893. A friendship developed, and Jones became a kind of roving organizer, advocate, and agitator for the nascent labor movement. Everywhere that laborers struggled to obtain better working conditions—in Pittsburgh for the railroad strike of 1877, in Chicago during the Haymarket riot of 1886, and in Birmingham for the 1894 strike of the American Railway Union—Jones could be found. She saw children working twelve-hour days for a dime, strikers murdered in their beds, workers bound to their employers like slaves—forever in debt to the company store.

When asked where she lived, Jones would simply reply, "Well, wherever there is a fight." And she was uncommonly shrewd in the tactics of waging those battles. Her greatest gift, perhaps, lay in planning and executing what are now called "media events." During the Pennsylvania anthracite coal miners' strike of 1900, Jones organized the workers' wives for an all-night march. She had the women "put on their kitchen clothes," as she later said, "and bring their mops and brooms with them and a couple of tin pans. We marched over the mountains fifteen miles, beating on the tin pans as if they were cymbals." Reporters marveled, and Jones became a national figure.

To Jones, child labor was the worst of capitalism's sins, and when textile mill workers around Philadelphia—16,000 of whom were under sixteen years of age—went on strike in 1903, she led about 125 men, women, and children on a 125-mile march across New Jersey, through New York City, and on to President Theodore Roosevelt's home at Oyster Bay, New York. When Jones and her followers finally reached the president's Long Island estate, the Secret Service refused to admit her, and the march ended quietly. But Jones had made her point: child labor was an injustice that had to be corrected.

In 1912, at the age of eighty-two, Jones earned the label "the most dangerous woman in America"—a tag bestowed on her by a prosecutor in West Virginia where Jones had gone in support of a United Mine Workers' strike. A bloody walkout had ensued and the governor declared martial law; Jones was arrested and charged with "conspiracy to murder." "There sits the most dangerous woman in America," thundered the military court prosecutor. "She comes into a state where peace and prosperity reign. She crooks her finger—twenty thousand contented men lay down their tools and walk out." Jones was condemned to twenty years in prison, but, under threat of a Senate investigation, the governor revoked the sentence.

Jones was eight-five when she supported New York City's striking garment and streetcar workers, and eighty-nine when she participated in the nation's first great steel strike (1919). She visited Gary, Indiana, and denounced the capitalist "robbers and political thieves," thundering, "I'll be ninety years old the first of May, but by God if I have to, I'll take ninety guns and shoot hell out of 'em."

A rabblerouser she certainly was. A socialist or communist? Not really. A feminist? Not in the conventional sense—she opposed women's suffrage. And though she helped organize both the Social Democratic Party in 1897 and, in 1905, the Industrial Workers of the World, she was too much an individualist to follow without question, and so she often antagonized union leaders and other allies in the labor movement.

Jones died on November 30, 1930, and was buried in the United Mine Workers' Cemetery at Mount Olive, Illinois. Seven months earlier, on her one-hundredth birthday, among the many congratulations she received was a telegram that read in part, "Your loyalty to your ideals, your fearless adherence to your duty as you have seen it is an inspiration to all who have known you. May you have continued health and happiness as long as life lasts." It was signed by that scion of capitalism, John D. Rockefeller, Jr.

"He's a damn good sport," Mother Jones acknowledged. "I've licked him many times, but now we've made peace."

Two months later, though, after sending Rockefeller, Jr.'s ninety-one-year-old father a goodwill birthday telegram, she added, "I wouldn't trade what I've done for what he's done."

Emmy-Award-winning writer Joseph Gustaitis lives in Brooklyn, New York.

"Politics Is Adjourned!"

by Roy Hoopes

In 1918 the United States was in the midst of World War I and President Woodrow Wilson was calling for peace on the basis of his Fourteen Points. Two years earlier President Wilson had been reelected on the slogan "He kept us out of war." Now with the country in the war, and his seeking a lasting, just peace, Wilson realized the necessity to retain his Democratic Party control of Congress, especially the Senate. In a series of miscalculations and political blunders, the election of 1918 would prove to be a disaster for the president. Roy Hoopes, director of public information at Washington College, tells the story of this election from the special vote in Wisconsin in April, 1918 through the strange campaign of Henry Ford for the senate in Michigan.

Off-year congressional elections are usually decided on local or regional issues and most are soon forgotten, even by historians, who rarely can point to one that proved pivotal or significant to America's history. But most students of government agree that there was at least one exception: the congressional election of 1918 was as significant historically as it was dramatic. Indeed, it has often been said that a bizarre Senate election in one state—Michigan—determined whether or not the United States would join the League of Nations. To add to the drama, that state's defeated "Democrat"—industrialist Henry Ford—was a lifelong Republican.

Democrat Woodrow Wilson was in the White House in 1918, having been reelected two years earlier on the platform, "He Kept Us Out of War." But by April of 1917, America was fully involved in World War I. In a speech to the Congress in January 1918, Wilson had proclaimed his famous "Fourteen Points" formula for peace—point fourteen of which proposed "a general association of nations" to preserve territorial boundaries and enforce the peace. By August 1918 Germany was reeling from battlefield defeats, and the Allies could sense victory. Ex-president Theodore Roosevelt and Senate Republican leader Henry Cabot Lodge were both calling for demands for unconditional surrender by Germany; at the same time there were signs that the Germans might seek a truce based on the president's Fourteen Points.

Wilson, a former historian who had written a book on congressional government, recognized the necessity for Senate support in negotiating the peace treaties that lay ahead. In fact, he had been aware of the need for a Democratic Senate as early as 1917, when it might be said the dramatic election actually began. As historian David Kennedy has pointed out, "the very fates seemed arrayed against the President's party. Death claimed eight Democratic Senators during the 65th Congress, thinning their already sparse majority."

One of the cruelest blows to the Democrats had occurred in the fall of 1917, when Wisconsin Senator Paul O. Hastings was killed in a duck-hunting accident. The following April, Wisconsin held a special election to fill the vacancy created by Hastings' death. The outcome should have served as a lesson to Wilson and his advisors.

Wilson induced Joseph E. Davies, a popular Wisconsin Democrat, to resign his post as chairman of the Federal Trade Commission and run for the empty Senate seat. His opponent was Representative Irvine Lenroot, who had been a steadfast opponent of Wilson's conduct of the war. When Davies left Washington, Wilson wrote him a well-publicized letter congratulating him for having passed the "acid test" of loyalty to the war effort by supporting the Administration (from the Federal Trade Commission where he did not have to vote) on three war measures that Lenroot had opposed in the House. The implication was transparent: unlike Davies, Lenroot lacked "true loyalty and genuine Americanism," as Wilson phrased it.

To doubly insure that the voters got the message, the Democrats dispatched Vice President Thomas Marshall to Wisconsin, where he warned Wisconsinites that their state was "under suspicion" of disloyalty and that the only way to rectify it was to return Davies to Washington as a senator.

The Administration's blatant intervention in the election and the questioning of their loyalty stunned Wisconsin voters. Davies was easily defeated. But rather than learning a lesson from the experience, the Democrats planned a similar intervention in Michigan in the 1918 congressional election, and the president went along with it.

The administration held a ten-seat majority in the Senate going into the election of 1918. Thirty-seven seats were being contested that year, and political experts calculated that if the Republicans were to gain control of the Senate they would have to retain all fourteen of the seats they held and capture at least five more from the Democrats.

The task appeared to be a formidable one for the Republicans, but the Democrats, too, were worried. Secretary of the Navy Josephus Daniels, an ex-North Carolina newspaper editor, was one of the most astute politicians in the

Wilson cabinet. As he saw the situation, "six seats in the Senate were in serious doubt. Five were conceded to the Republicans . . . [but] in Michigan the President saw a glimmer of hope."

And it was Daniels who had first spotted the glimmer. While on a speaking tour in Michigan early in 1918, Daniels had asked the Democratic State Chairman if there was a chance of electing a Michigan Democrat to the Senate. "As much chance as there would be to elect Henry Cabot Lodge from South Carolina," he replied. But there was one Wilson supporter in Michigan, said the chairman, who could get elected—Henry Ford. "He would get the nomination of both the Republicans and Democrats in the primary. He could be elected and his desire for peace and his admiration of Wilson would give the president a senator who would stand by the League of Nations and his other policies." But the chairman said that he did not think Ford was interested in politics, and that the only person who would be able to persuade him to run was the president.

Henry Ford's desire for peace had already been demonstrated in 1915, when he sailed to Europe in the *Oscar II* (the famous "Peace Ship") with the hope of bringing the war to an early end. Once America had entered the conflict, Ford had been a staunch supporter of the president.

Wilson was, in turn, an admirer of Henry Ford. He thought the peace ship effort, although misguided, was a sincere gesture. Moreover, during the closing days of Wilson's presidential campaign in 1916, Ford had made a large contribution that had enabled the Democrats to afford a substantial advertising campaign in California. This had assured victory in that critical state, and, in the opinion of many, had given Wilson his narrow victory over Republican presidential candidate Charles Evans Hughes. The auto manufacturer had also endeared himself to the president by offering to put the Ford Motor Company to work producing war materials without profit. Secretary Daniels summoned Ford to Washington but failed to persuade him to run for the Senate. President Wilson, however, was successful. Ford returned to Michigan and announced his candidacy, saying: "I know nothing about politics . . . and I am not at all concerned about which ticket I am nominated on. I shall not spend a cent nor make a move to get into the United States Senate . . . I would not walk across the street to be elected President of the United States. If I am elected, however, I shall go to Washington and work with President Wilson with everything I possess, first to win the war and then to help the government develop ways of insuring against future wars."

Ford's subsequent campaign was a disaster. It soon came out, of course, that it had been Wilson who had persuaded him to run, and Republicans argued that as in Wisconsin this was a case of the president intervening in a local election.

In the Republican primary Henry Ford was opposed by Truman Newberry, a naval commander who had served in New York during the war and who earlier had been Theodore Roosevelt's Secretary of the Navy. Wilson's plan was for Ford to also run in the Democratic primary unopposed—freeing most Democrats to cross over and vote for Ford in the Republican election. But another Democrat entered the race, forcing many Democrats to vote Democratic to assure Ford's victory there. This, combined with Newberry's acceptability and the large amount of money spent by the Republicans on his behalf in the primary (expenditures that were later found to be illegal), gave the Republican nomination to Newberry. So Ford was forced to run in the subsequent general election as a Democrat, even though he conceded that he was Republican for the same reason that he had two ears—because he was "born that way."

That was not Ford's only problem. His candidacy gave the opposition the opportunity to capitalize on numerous inconsistent and inaccurate statements he had made earlier about Wilson and the war. The industrialist made no public appearances (one of the reasons he had given for not running was that he could not give speeches), but some of his pronouncements to the press were misfires. For example, he recalled going to the polls on his twenty-first birthday to vote for James Garfield—and it did not take the Newberry camp long to point out that Ford was twenty-one in 1884 and that President Garfield was assassinated in 1881.

Another issue that was detrimental to Ford was the question of his son's draft deferment. Edsel Ford had been labeled "indispensable" to the war effort and exempted from the draft in order to run his father's factory. Newberry asked how the senior Ford could be spared for Senate duty if his son could not be spared for military duty?

Newberry, a naval commander who had been in uniform as a recruiting officer, had no trouble establishing his patriotism. But to add a little luster to his military career, just before the election his campaign headquarters released a photograph of Commander Newberry on the bridge of a ship giving orders to his crew. The press release issued with the photo asked: "Where was Edsel Ford . . . while Newberry was baring his breast to the foe in command of a ship of the Navy?" (The fact was that the bridge on which Newberry stood was part of a fake recruiting ship that had been built in Central Park— he had never been to sea, but this was not revealed until after the election.)

The Republican campaign to win control of Congress in 1918 was under the general direction of Will Hays, Republican National Committee Chairman (he would later become head of Hollywood's famous Hays Office of censorship), ex-President Theodore Roosevelt (still bellicose, though in failing health), and Senator Lodge. By now Wilson, not the Republican Right Wing, had become Roosevelt's principal enemy, and he had long since become allied with Lodge against the president. Although Wilson had given his opponents the opportunity to make the war a partisan issue by his actions in the Wisconsin election, the Republicans knew they had to move with care. "The fact is," Lodge wrote a friend early in 1918, "we should run the risk of defeating our own ends if we made the attacks on Wilson that we all want to make. We must give no opening for the charge that we are drawing the party line and the cry that we are not loyal to the war." The objective, as Weeks put it, was to devise "a program which will . . . include supporting the administration in all its war activities but which will give us something to hang party action on when the war is over." In other words, oppose the administration's conduct of the war without opposing the war.

In March Theodore Roosevelt spoke to Maine Republicans, providing what he hoped would be the "keynote on which the congressional campaign can be fought." He argued that President Wilson had allowed the country to be unprepared for war, then had mismanaged mobilization when the war actually began. And even now, he maintained, Wilson was trying to win the war with "kid gloves and fine phrases" when what were needed were "brains and steel." "There is but one way to get a righteous and lasting peace," he argued, "and that is to beat Germany to her knees"—a cry that would intensify as the campaign went to its final weeks and it became public knowledge that Germany was seeking a truce.

As the year drifted toward summer, Congressmen on both sides of the aisle were anxious to get home to campaign, and an adjournment date of July 1 was anticipated. But Wilson's treasury secretary (and son-in-law) William Gibbs McAdoo pressed the president for a revenue bill that was needed to continue financing the war. The president knew this would take all summer, so on May 27 he made a surprise appearance before a joint session of Congress, asking that it delay adjournment long enough to give him a new tax bill based primarily on excess profits—a bill that would be supported by a soon-to-be-released government report revealing wide-spread war-profiteering in American industry.

With this speech a new phrase—"politics is adjourned"—became a hallmark of the 1918 campaign. The 1918 elections, said Wilson, should go to those who gave the least thought to winning them. The press (and Republicans when it suited them) pounded on Wilson's statement, claiming that he had said politics should be adjourned for the campaign.

But Wilson only meant that he was requesting partisan politics be adjourned until he had his tax bill (he was, in fact, destined never to get it) or roughly until the end of the summer, when he assumed the campaign would begin. Wilson certainly did not plan to adjourn politics; in fact, early in June, he requested that his secretary, Joseph Tumulty, work out a tactful, effective plan for asking the country to give him a Democratic Congress without arousing partisan rancor. But Tumulty advised him not to say anything, and so the president refrained. Wilson never completely abandoned the idea, however, which he brought up again with his advisor, Colonel Edward House, in September. House was silent, which students of the peculiar House-Wilson relationship said meant House also opposed it.

Neither did the Republicans have any intention of adjourning from partisan politics for the 1918 election. Only two days after Wilson's speech to Congress, the keynote speaker at the Indiana Republican Convention warned that the election would be concerned with the peace terms given Germany.

"The making of them," he said, "must not be left to the dreamers, the social uplifters, the pacifists and the bolshevists who are now unhappily much in evidence and who appear prominently among the president's chief advisors."

Meanwhile, there was another issue that, in the opinion of many historians, probably hurt Wilson more than the question of support for his war efforts and peace negotiations. People in the western United States were generally incensed by the Administration's insistence in maintaining a wartime ceiling on the price of wheat. It was not the fixed wheat price alone that caused the trouble, but the fact that at the same time Wilson permitted the price of cotton to find its own level—which was very high because of wartime demands.

Cotton, of course, was a Southern staple. Wilson had been born in the South, and the Democrats from the Solid South controlled Congress, facts that angered not only Westerners but also many Northerners. Senator Thomas Gore had sponsored an amendment to the Lever Price Control Act, that if enacted into law, would have raised the price of wheat. The Gore Amendment passed, but Wilson vetoed it in July 1918. The House sustained him, and, as one historian wrote, "the veto proved to be the turning point in Wilson's political fortunes."

Rather than issue his appeal for a Democratic Congress to support him in the postwar period, Wilson decided to go on a nationwide Liberty Bond campaign tour. This would enable him not only to speak on patriotic themes but also to explain to the West why he had chosen to restrict the price of wheat but not cotton. Advisors persuaded him, however, that it would be better if he remained in Washington during the campaign. Theodore Roosevelt, in the meantime, had planned a bond-selling trip to counter Wilson's speeches, and soon he was delivering anti-Wilson speeches that sometimes seemed, because he was selling bonds, to be sanctioned by the government.

Meanwhile, as the campaign went into the late summer and early fall, Republicans across the country were confronted with news from the battlefield telling of German defeats and Allied victories. They may have had some good issues in the failure of the army to supply blankets to the troops, war profiteering, and airplane scandals (growing out of the Administration's failure to send hundreds of planes overseas as had been promised by Wilson's propaganda agency), but with the Americans chasing Germans across the Rhine Valley, who would care? More and more, the key issue became the peace negotiations and the nature of the postwar world.

Lodge had delivered a campaign blast in August warning that Germany was preparing a "poisonous peace campaign" that would enable it to accomplish by negotiations what its armies had failed to achieve in the field. And Roosevelt, on his speaking tour, began to argue that the country's strength would rest on its army, not the League of Nations, and warned people to watch for "quack peace remedies" peddled by the Administration.

On October 5, the country was electrified by the announcement of the first formal peace overtures from the Germans. They had come directly to Wilson, the author of the Fourteen Points, which the Germans hoped would serve as the basis of the truce. This meant that the president spent the entire last month of the campaign preoccupied primarily with peace negotiations.

Since the end of September he had been thinking again of issuing an appeal to the country to give him a Democratic Congress. Now the possibility of imminent surrender heightened his concern. In addition, with the war fading as an issue, Lodge and Roosevelt were intensifying their campaign to discredit the League of Nations idea and discourage anything but an unconditional surrender by the Germans. Politics were no longer "adjourned"—they dominated the campaign.

Wilson responded to the German overture with a cautious note from Secretary of State Robert Lansing, designed to determine the genuineness of the peace overtures and whether the German government actually represented the German people. Despite the noncommittal nature of the note, Republicans in the Senate unleashed a vicious attack on the president for even discussing peace with the Germans before they had been beaten to the ground.

It was not just unconditional surrender and the League of Nations that worried Republicans. Point three of Wilson's Fourteen Points called for the removal of all trade barriers, which Republican Chairman Hays said was an "absolute commitment to the free trade with all the world, thus giving Germany . . . the fruits of a victory."

The Republican response to Lansing's peace note to Germany dispelled any lingering doubts Wilson had about issuing an appeal for a Democratic Congress. The Republicans in the Senate were enough of a problem when they did not have control. Should they achieve control in the Senate, Wilson knew that any treaty that did not totally satisfy Republican hard-liners would never pass.

On October 25, after discussing his decision only with Congressional and National Committee campaign leaders, President Wilson issued a dramatic statement to the press, virtually making it every American's patriotic duty to give him a Democratic Congress to support his peace efforts. "Unity of command," he said, "is as necessary now in civil action as it is upon the field of battle. If the control of the House and Senate should be taken away from the Party now in power, an opposing majority could assume control of legislation and oblige all action to be taken admist contest and obstruction."

A Republican victory, the president said in a remark he would regret the rest of his life, "would certainly be interpreted on the other side of the water as a repudiation of my leadership."

Negative response to Wilson's appeal was immediate and intense; even the Democrats were stunned, with most party leaders (and all of Wilson's cabinet) learning of his statement for the first time when they read the morning newspapers. The Republicans declared emphatically that their patriotism had been impugned (despite the fact that for the past three weeks Republican orators had demonstrated conclusively that they did not support the president in his peace efforts). Now, as GOP Chairman Hays put it, had come this "ungracious . . . wanton . . . mendacious" appeal. The most immediate result, as one historian said, was "to elevate the level of rhetorical violence at which the final few days of the campaign was waged."

When the votes were cast on November 5 (while Wilson was rejoicing with his cabinet because the Allied War Council had just accepted his Fourteen Points and had agreed to the peace terms that he felt certain the Germans would accept) the Republicans gained thirty House seats and six Senate seats, the latter giving them control of the Senate. In Michigan, Truman Newberry had defeated Henry Ford, though by the narrowest of margins.

It quickly became Republican legend and conventional wisdom that Wilson's last-minute appeal had cost him the Senate. But historians have decided that this was probably not the case: the appeal might, in fact, have gained him more votes than he lost. The nation was still essentially Republican, and midterm elections generally go against the incumbent of the White House and favor the party that dominates national politics.

Probably the most damaging factor had been Wilson's veto of the Gore amendment, which was a stroke, said one historian, that "carved apart the fragile political coalition that had carried the Democrats to victory in 1916" The West and Midwest deserted the Democrats in 1918 and would not return to the fold until the Depression.

Following the Michigan election, conclusive evidence was discovered to show that Newberry campaigners had spent money illegally in the primary. Public attention continued to focus on this issue for several years, despite the fact that there was not a chance that the Republican Senate would ever vote to unseat Newberry. Ford hired an army of private detectives to investigate Newberry, and a Grand Rapids court found him guilty and sentenced him to two years in prison. The case was appealed, however, and the Supreme Court eventually declared that the law under which Newberry had been indicted was unconstitutional. In 1922, after the Democrats regained control of the Senate and threatened to reopen the Newberry case, the Senator resigned, although he still had two years left of his term.

The one vote that permitted the Republicans to reorganize the Senate was, indeed, tainted, but it did not matter. The damage had been done, and not just by Newberry and the Michigan Republicans. As a result of the 1918 elections, "the United States," as one historian put it, "for the aftermath of the greatest war that it had ever fought, was to have the sort of Congressional government that had prevailed after the Civil War and that Woodrow Wilson had criticized in his first book [on congressional government] . . . The last act of the tragedy of Woodrow Wilson had begun."

The Real Eliot Ness

by Steven Nickel

The name, Eliot Ness, is well known to modern Americans thanks to a popular television series and later the movie, "The Untouchables." The hero portrayed by Robert Stack on television and Kevin Costner in the movie was a real life figure whose exploits were indeed remarkable. Eliot Ness was a very successful U.S. treasury agent in Chicago in the war against the illegal alcohol empire of Al Capone. Later he would have an adventurous career as public safety director in Cleveland, Ohio. This article gives an intriguing account of this crime fighter from his famous struggle to enforce prohibition at the age of twenty-six to his untimely death.

In the pre-dawn gloom of a frigid March morning in 1942, an automobile with the license plates EN-1 skidded and then slammed into an oncoming vehicle on the Cleveland, Ohio, West Shoreway. By the time Patrolman Joseph Koneval arrived on the scene, the guilty party had fled, leaving the other motorist, Robert Sims of East Cleveland, to be taken to the hospital by a passer-by.

Koneval's investigation of the hit-and-run was not difficult. EN-1 was a familiar license plate in Cleveland. It belonged to the city's director of public safety, Eliot Ness. As a result of the accident, the man who had helped to crush the gangland empire of "Scarface" Al Capone became the object of sensational headlines. Some stories revealed that only hours before the crash the former prohibition agent had been drinking heavily with his wife and friends at the Hollenden Hotel.

Long before Kojack, Columbo, or Crockett and Tubbs, there was Eliot Ness, one of television's most popular and enduring images of the American lawman.

The glorification of Ness actually began shortly after his death in 1957, with the publication of *The Untouchables,* an autobiographical account depicting his two-and-a-half-year crusade against the Capone mob as head of a special Justice Department unit. In April 1959, the Desilu Playhouse presented a two-part dramatization of the book that soon evolved into a weekly series. Through four seasons, television audiences thrilled to the adventures of Ness—played by Robert Stack—in his battle with the underworld forces of Chicago's Prohibition era.

To say that the television image of Ness was exaggerated is an understatement. Faced with the task of creating a new action-packed installment each week, the program's writers plunged into pure fantasy. But the shows had a realistic look and documentary-style narration by Walter Winchell, convincing many viewers that they were watching factual stories. Moreover, the series was fast and exciting, and greatly loved. Had it not been for protests that the show was too violent and promoted a negative stereotype of Italians, it would certainly have run longer than its 114 bullet-riddled episodes.

Twenty-five years of reruns later, Eliot Ness has arrived on the big screen in a film version of *The Untouchables.* (*The Scarface Mob* and *Alcatraz Express,* two movies briefly seen in theaters in 1962, were actually reedited episodes of the television series.) While this most recent account of Ness and his gangbusters contains more gritty realism (and graphic violence), it is not, unfortunately, any more factual than its predecessors.

Certainly a major part of Ness's lasting appeal is the fact that behind the celebrated celluloid image there once actually existed a man who gained fame battling racketeers: a true-life lawman who could not be bought, frightened, or killed off by the criminal underworld he opposed. But for nearly three decades the real Eliot Ness has been eclipsed by his own legend—a legend he helped to create and struggled to equal.

Ness was born in Chicago on April 19, 1903, the son of Norwegian immigrants. His fascination with crime-fighting developed early. When not helping in his father's bakery, Ness could be found reading a Sherlock Holmes mystery, fancying himself following in the footsteps of the fictional master sleuth. His elder sister married a government agent, who enthralled the youngster with stories of law enforcement and taught him to shoot at a firing range.

At age eighteen Ness entered the University of Chicago, majoring in commerce, law, and political science. Quiet and studious in the classroom, he sharpened his athletic skills by becoming an exceptional tennis player on campus and training three nights a week in jujitsu. After graduating in the top third of his class in 1925, Ness signed on as an investigator for the Retail Credit Company. While on the job there he experienced both strenuous legwork and tedious paperwork.

In 1927 Ness entered the Chicago branch of the U.S. Treasury Department, briefly working in a civil assignment before obtaining an appointment as an agent. The following year he was transferred to the Justice Department and assigned to the Prohibition Bureau, becoming one of nearly three hundred agents saddled with the monumental task of drying up the Windy City.

Supplying a thirsty public with bootleg liquor had become a multimillion-dollar business for Chicago criminals, who raked in the profits from an estimated *twenty thousand* local speakeasies. Through the violent, colorful decade of the "Roaring Twenties," Chicagoans witnessed the rise of one mobster above all others—a stocky, cigar-chomping Italian named Alphonse Capone.

By 1929 Capone's infamy had reached Washington, D.C. President Herbert Hoover, outraged by reports of the millionaire ganglord living above the law, instructed his secretary of the treasury, Andrew Mellon, to work on putting the mobster behind bars.

Two of Capone's known criminal activities—income tax evasion and bootlegging—fell under federal jurisdiction. The former was the concern of the Treasury Department, which created a task force led by Agent Frank J. Wilson to work on the Capone case. At the same time, a special unit of Justice Department agents was being formed to combat Capone's alcohol operations.

The task of selecting a team of Justice agents fell to U.S. District Attorney George Emmerson Q. Johnson, and it proved a difficult one because the Prohibition Bureau was riddled with what Ness later called "bad apples." The actual backbone of the Capone empire was its bankroll, enabling the scar-faced mobster and his gangland associates to buy protection and aid from about five hundred Chicago-area policemen, various politicians, and a number of government agents. The federal agents' inability to locate mob-owned breweries or to close speakeasies was sufficient proof that Capone's powerful tentacles had penetrated the Department. Searching for an honest man, Johnson turned his attention to Ness, thanks largely to an enthusiastic recommendation by the young man's brother-in-law.

At the time, Ness was twenty-six years old, single, still living with his parents, and earning $2,800 a year as a Prohibition agent. He had a steady girlfriend, Edna Staley, whom he would marry the following year. Ness stood six feet tall and weighed 180 pounds; his lean frame and slim waistline were offset by broad, powerful shoulders. He had a boyishly handsome face with a ruddy complexion and a wave of freckles across the bridge of his nose, a pleasant smile, wavy brown hair parted in the middle, and sleepy blue-gray eyes that could suddenly turn icy and piercing.

As a Prohibition agent Ness had earned a respectable though unspectacular reputation. Studying his record, Johnson was most impressed by the young man's outspoken jabs at the bureau for "holding back" in its fight against the mob and for not "cleaning house." He exhibited the qualities of honesty and resourcefulness for which Johnson was looking. On September 28, 1929, Johnson summoned Ness to his office and, after a brief interview, informed the young agent he had been chosen to lead the Department's special squad.

Ness was to select his own men, no more than a dozen. They were to be independent of the bureau, accountable to Johnson alone. In addition to destroying gangland breweries, they were to collect evidence connecting Capone and his cronies to violations of federal laws. But most important, Johnson wanted to "dry up" or at least severely impair the mobster's major source of income, an estimated $75,000 annually. If Ness and his small band could cripple Capone financially, the ganglord would lose his powerful web of police and political protection and become vulnerable to the law.

The saga of the "Untouchables" began.

To select his team, Ness probed through the personnel files of active agents in search of men with impressive arrest records and no "Achilles heel in their make-up." From a list of fifty possibles he narrowed his choices to fifteen, finally settling upon nine.

Five—Martin Lahart, Samuel Seager, Lyle Chapman, Barney Cloonan, and Thomas Friel—were Chicago agents with whom Ness had already worked. Four others were outsiders he recruited for their special talents: Paul Robsky, a wire-tapping expert from the New Jersey office; Michael King, a Virginia agent renowned for his ability to tail suspects; William Gardner, an expert at undercover work from the Los Angeles division; and Joseph Leeson, an exceptional driver from Detroit who, at age thirty, was the eldest member of the team.

Like Ness, all nine were single men with at least two years of experience in the Justice Department. Each was an excellent marksman and possessed a spotless record and distinctive background. Seager had been a guard at Sing Sing. Friel was a former Pennsylvania state trooper. Robsky was once an Army officer. Gardner and Chapman had been acclaimed football players.

By mid-October 1929 the special unit was ready to begin its war on Capone's bootlegging empire. Under Ness's spirited leadership, the agents conducted what were basically search-and-destroy operations, locating mob-owned alcohol-producing plants and shutting them down. The majority of their leads came from anonymous phone calls, most probably from rival gangs. Some breweries were discovered only after weeks, sometimes months, of exhaustive legwork and surveillance. Lahart and Gardner, posing as out-of-town criminals, actually managed to briefly infiltrate the ranks of the Capone mob and to pick up leads as they rubbed elbows with some of Capone's chief lieutenants. The agents also made use of paid informants.

Wire taps were another source of information. The most valuable of these bugged the telephones of the Montmartre Cafe, a plush Cicero speakeasy known as the headquarters for Capone's elder brother Ralph.

Ness later described the planting of the Montmartre tap as one of the most harrowing experiences of his career. Four of the agents distracted a small army of gangsters stationed around the building long enough for Ness and Robsky to creep into an alley behind the cafe. Robsky scaled a telephone pole and applied his expertise to the terminal while Ness, his Colt .38 in hand, stood guard in the dark alley below. Though usually cool in the most intense situations, the young lawman found himself jumping at every sound and straining his eyes to detect any movement. When Robsky finally bridged the lines and descended, the pair left the alley unnoticed. Over the next two years the tap on Ralph Capone's private line proved invaluable.

Locating breweries proved an easier task than entering them. Hacking through doorways with axes or battering them down with sledgehammers was a slow, burdensome endeavor that allowed those inside time to destroy evidence or escape through secret exits. Ness realized his unit would have to develop a faster, more efficient means of entry. The solution was a ten-ton flatbed truck equipped with scaling ladders and a giant steel ram that jutted from the front.

Utilizing this device—usually with Leeson at the wheel, Ness riding shotgun, and the other agents in back or covering the exits—the special squad entered marked buildings swiftly and without warning. Ness and his men began to rack up an impressive record of successful raids: a brewery valued at $100,000, discovered in a South State Street warehouse; another $100,000 plant on South Wabash; and a $125,000 operation on North Kilbourn. During its first six months the government team captured a total of nineteen distilleries and six major breweries, costing Capone an estimated $1,000,000.

At this point (the spring of 1930), a young gangster appeared at the squad's headquarters in Chicago's Transportation Building. Claiming he spoke for "the Big Guy," the visitor offered Ness a $2,000 bribe to "lay off," assuring him that another $2,000 would follow each week he behaved. After angrily ejecting the culprit, Ness phoned the press, and that afternoon newsmen crowded into his office. Flashbulbs popped as Ness told of the attempt to buy him and his men, emphatically declaring that bribes and bullets would not deter them from their crusade. A *Chicago Tribune* reporter, in an article printed the next day, first called the tiny band of gangbusters "the Untouchables."

From then on, whenever the agents raided a building, Ness made sure the press was on the scene within moments after the doors were opened.

Fellow lawmen and public officials were openly critical of the unit's publicity, charging that its effectiveness would be impaired and that Ness was seeking personal aggrandizement. Ness, however, defended the press coverage, stressing that both Capone and the public needed to be aware of his group's determination and honesty. He further stated that a tough reputation and positive image would help, rather than hinder, the squad. Ironically, in a way Ness did not then realize, the publicity did help the government's case. Partly due to the attention the "Untouchables" were receiving, the team of Treasury agents was able to operate without detection.

At first Ness's critics seemed correct in blasting the unit for its overexposure in the media. During the next several months Ness and his raiders were miserably ineffective. Capone had tightened security around his bootlegging plants. His lookouts were trained to recognize each of the ten agents; if any were spotted near an establishment, Capone ordered it moved immediately. Other mobsters doggedly tailed the lawmen. Suddenly the "Untouchables" were the ones who were being watched. The unit's phones were even tapped.

The agents soon began to feel the pressure. One evening Ness spotted a Capone crony watching his parents' home. Slipping out the back door and circling behind the gangster, the young agent "roughed him up" (as he later admitted) in an uncharacteristic rage. Fearing for his parents' safety, Ness moved into an apartment the next day. He spent little time there, however, often eating and sleeping in his office along with some of the other "Untouchables."

By feeding the mob false information and evading those tailing them, the agents were able to resume limited operations. One of their few successful raids during this period shut down a $200,000 brewery, the largest catch yet.

Failing to stop Ness with extortion or surveillance, Capone turned to more violent methods of persuasion. A good friend of Ness, an ex-convict who occasionally worked with the agents, abruptly disappeared. A few days later his body turned up in a Chicago Heights ditch. He had been horribly tortured before being shot.

Ness responded to the brutal murder of his friend by staging a bizarre parade past Capone's headquarters at the Lexington Hotel. First he phoned the pudgy ganglord and, after some persistence , managed to get Capone himself on the line. "What's up?" Capone asked.

"Well, Snorky," Ness replied, "I just wanted to tell you that if you look out your front windows at eleven today you'll see something that will interest you."

At the appointed time Capone and his chief henchmen appeared at the windows. Moving along Michigan Avenue at fifteen miles an hour and resembling a funeral procession was a caravan of forty-five trucks the "Untouchables" had seized in their raids on Capone breweries. The confiscated vehicles were on their way to be sold at public auction. Ness later learned from an underworld contact that the sight of the convoy had thrown Capone into a violent rage. Smashing two chairs over a table top he had screamed, "I'll kill 'im, I'll kill 'im with my own bare hands!"

There followed, in quick succession, three attempts on Ness's life. In the first he narrowly escaped a hail of bullets fired from a passing car. Next he was almost run down by a speeding automobile as he crossed a street outside his office. Soon thereafter Ness was climbing into his car when he noticed that the hood latches were unfastened. Examining the motor, he found a dynamite charge wired to the starter.

Ness's "Untouchables," meanwhile, were attempting to locate a super-plant that was rumored to be supplying the Capone empire with most of its alcohol. Another anonymous phone call—this time from a woman—reported a possible location. Ness and Lahart checked out the site, a six-story building on Diversey Avenue. They discovered a legitimate business occupying the first four floors. The top two floors, however, housed a mysterious paint company that, according to the agents investigating, had no past record of business dealings.

After dark the two lawmen crept up a fire escape and managed to find a window through which to peer. Both gasped as they stared at a brightly lit distillery bustling with activity. The center of attention was a colossal forty-foot-high still that rose through a specially cut hole in the fifth-floor ceiling, nearly touching the roof of the building.

Ness and his raiders returned the next night. Unable to use their usual method of smashing down the doors with their ramming truck, Ness and Lahart again ascended the fire escape. At the prearranged moment—exactly midnight—the pair crashed through the windows and aimed their sawed-off shotguns at the startled workers. Seconds later the other "Untouchables" rushed in from a service entrance. The largest Capone bootlegging operation ever uncovered fell without a shot being fired. The giant still was capable of producing an estimated 20,000 gallons of alcohol per day. The distillery was valued at nearly $1,000,000.

From that time on, according to Ness, there were no more major mob-owned breweries left in Chicago—a claim that is unsubstantiated but not unrealistic. By the spring of 1931 the Capone organization had resorted to buying alcohol outside the city and smuggling it in, a more lengthy and costly process. Still on the offensive, the "Untouchables" not only began intercepting shipments but also entered rural areas beyond Cook County to track down the sources. Once they even arrested a small-town police force (a sheriff and his two deputies) that they caught operating a still.

Capone was hurting. A wire tap on the phone of Jake Guzik, the mob's bookkeeper and business manager, revealed how desperate the situation had become. In one conversation, Ness and his men overheard a speakeasy owner pleading frantically for some liquor for his establishment, with Guzik replying that he was unable to supply any. Another time Guzik was contacted by a mob employee who wanted to know how much some local policemen were to be paid. "Nothin'," Guzik answered.

"Whatta ya mean, nothin'?"

"Listen, Hymie," Guzik explained, "you'll have to tell the boys they'll have to take a pass this month."

"They ain't gonna like it."

"Too bad, but we just ain't makin' any dough. And if we ain't got it, we can't pay for it."

With their primary goal of crippling Capone's bootlegging empire completed, the agents began to concentrate on their secondary objective of building a legal case against the mob lord and his associates. Since the start, assembling evidence gathered in the raids had been the job of Lyle Chapman, the tall ex-football player who was also a wizard at paperwork. On June 12, 1931, Ness, armed with Chapman's mass of testimonies and facts, appeared before a federal grand jury and secured indictments against Capone and sixty-eight members of his mob for conspiracy to violate the Volstead Act, citing five thousand separate offenses against Prohibition laws.

As it turned out, however, Capone would never be brought to trial on any of the Prohibition charges. Treasury agents had beaten their Justice Department counterparts by one week, supplying evidence on June 5 to indict Capone for income tax evasion. U.S. District Attorney Johnson chose to prosecute the gangster on the Treasury charges, holding Ness's Prohibition indictments in reserve should Capone evade conviction.

Capone went on trial October 6, 1931. Ness was present in the courtroom each day, not as the star witness, but as a spectator. Two weeks later Alphonse Capone was found guilty. The once-mighty gangster was sentenced to eleven years in a federal penitentiary.

On May 3, 1932, Ness and his "Untouchables" provided the escort for Capone from the Cook County jail to Dearborn Station. After turning their prisoner over to the two U.S. marshalls assigned to deliver him to the federal prison in Atlanta, the agents stood guard until the train departed. It was the last mission for the "Untouchables." The special squad was disbanded and the agents reassigned.

In recognition of his outstanding service with the "Untouchables," Ness was appointed chief investigator of the Chicago Prohibition Bureau. But the Prohibition era was drawing to a close. Late in 1933 the Justice Department transferred Ness to Cincinnati to supervise an entirely different form of alcohol enforcement—tracking down and destroying the thousands of hillbilly stills scattered through the "Moonshine Mountains." Directing operations over a vast territory that included southwest Ohio, most of Kentucky, and parts of Tennessee, he encountered a hostile environment with its own laws and codes of silence.

After less than a year of raiding moonshiners, Ness secured a new post as investigator in charge of the Treasury Department's Alcoholic Tax Unit in northern Ohio. From his office in downtown Cleveland, Ness and thirty-four agents under his command earned a reputation for "hitting a still a day," making hundreds of arrests over the next year.

Cleveland at this time (1935) was America's seventh-largest city, an overcrowded metropolis in dire need of a cleanup from the inside out. Crime and corruption were rampant. The public had lost faith in its police and city officials. Cleveland's newly-elected mayor, Harold Hitz Burton, vowed to restore law and order to the city. He was a sincere, capable statesman, later to become a senator and supreme court justice. A key position in his new administration would be that of public safety director, the person who would personally oversee the entire municipal system of police, firefighting, and traffic control. Burton searched for a man who had a record of unquestionable integrity, a distinguished background in law enforcement, and who was a Republican like himself. Ness qualified on all three counts.

On the morning of December 11, 1935, Burton invited Ness to his office. Their meeting was brief. Ness arrived at City Hall at noon; a half-hour later he was sworn in as director of public safety. At age thirty-two he was the youngest in Cleveland history to hold the post.

The city buzzed over the news of his appointment. As usual, Ness was open and talkative with the newsmen who surrounded him. He stated that his first priority would be that of reorganizing the police force, a job, he said, that would be "tough but lots of fun."

The new safety director made an immediate impact on the city. On the evening of January 10, 1936, County Prosecutor Frank T. Culliton and some constables attempted to raid the Harvard Club, a mob-owned casino in the suburb of Newburgh Heights. The lawmen were refused entrance by gangsters armed with submachine guns. The mobsters threatened to open fire if the raiding party tried to enter. Unable to enlist aid from local police, Culliton phoned Ness.

Although Newburgh Heights was not part of the safety director's jurisdiction, Ness quickly swung into action, gathering recruits from Central Station and arriving outside the Harvard Club with more than forty heavily-armed lawmen. Ness marched alone to the front entrance and coldly told the face at the peephole, "I'm Eliot Ness. I'm coming in with some warrants."

Moments later the door opened and the raid proceeded.

Ness's display of courage and determination won praise from the press and applause from the public. Cleveland had a new hero, one who restored faith in the law. It was the beginning of a bittersweet relationship between the former "Untouchable" and Cleveland, during which Ness would compile one of the most outstanding records of achievement in the city's history.

True to his word, Ness immediately began purging the police department of its "bad apples." He scrutinized the records of everyone in the department suspected of corruption or unfavorable behavior. In the course of his investigation he assembled a file on each suspect—hundreds of them, veterans and rookies alike—containing solid evidence, anonymous tips, and mere rumors. But the undertaking was no witch hunt. Determined to give each individual a fair chance, Ness set out to check every lead, no matter how indisputable or trivial the information appeared.

The task proved enormous. Some legwork was delegated to trusted aides, but for the most part Ness did his own investigating. He reportedly spent almost every night through the summer of 1936 at this work, talking to prostitutes and criminals in bars and back alleys one evening, meeting with prominent, wealthy city figures the next.

Ness took his findings before a grand jury in October, providing sixty-six witnesses who were willing to testify against officers found tainted with corruption. Fifteen of the worst offenders were brought to trial, including a deputy inspector, two captains, two lieutenants, and a sergeant. Two hundred policemen were forced to resign.

Ness also concentrated on modernizing the force and improving police efficiency. He established the Cleveland Police Academy, increased the number of police cars and motorcycles, installed two-way radios in all cars, carefully re-routed their patrols and instituted a system wherein any call could be answered within sixty seconds. Within a year after implementing these and other advancements, Ness was able to report a 38 percent drop in crime overall, and a nearly 50 percent decrease in robberies.

Gradually Ness formed a new band of Cleveland "Untouchables" for difficult assignments and special investigations. With their aid, he brought twenty-three Cleveland mobsters to trial between 1937 and 1941. He supplied the evidence and witnesses, and Prosecutor Culliton—a close friend since the Harvard Club raid—did the rest.

Remarkably, Ness also found time to address the critical problem of juvenile delinquency. He organized a highly successful Boy Scout program, recruiting scoutmasters from the police and fire departments, enlisting sponsorship from local merchants, and providing municipal buildings for meetings. In 1938 he founded the Cleveland Boys town and created a special bureau to handle juvenile cases. Some city officials accused the safety director of "coddling young punks." But statistics, including a 62 percent decrease in juvenile crime, proved the wisdom of his youth program.

Ness's greatest accomplishment, however, was in traffic control. Prior to his appointment, Cleveland was ranked the second-worst American city in traffic-related deaths and injuries, averaging nearly 250 fatalities per year. The entire municipal system of traffic control had broken down.

In 1936 Ness began sweeping reforms in the traffic division, the department formerly called "Siberia," where the least-competent officers had been sent. Ness reversed that policy, cleaning out the undesirable and replacing them with men with favorable records. He created a court handling only traffic cases, and instituted on-the-spot examination of suspected drunk drivers, immediate arrest of those found intoxicated, severe discipline for officers found "fixing" tickets, and a regular program of automobile inspections.

The results of Ness's reforms were spectacular. In 1938 traffic-related deaths dropped by nearly half, to 130. The following year, fatalities further diminished to 115, and the National Safety Council awarded Cleveland the title "safest city in the U.S.A."

Straight-laced, clean-cut, above reproach, and apparently indefatigable, Ness seemed too good to be true. Curiously, although Ness was one of the most visible men in Cleveland, no one knew much about his personal life. He remained an enigma to all, "a mystery man," as one reporter stated.

A few intimate friends of Ness and his wife reported that the crime-fighter relaxed by reading Shakespeare and listening to opera. He was a cat lover, having as many as six at a time. Although labeled a stuffed-shirt by some, Ness confided that he personally had no moral objection to drinking or gambling, the two vices he fought against most vigorously during his career. But as long as these practices were illegal and used by mobsters to build crime empires, it was his duty (some said his passion) to uphold the law. Above all else, Ness believed in the sanctity of the law and despised any form of corruption.

But just when Cleveland became convinced that its safety director was an infallible lawman, a string of unfavorable incidents began to erode his popularity.

In the summer of 1937 a demonstration by striking workers got out of control. Ness sent in an army of police, and they waded into the crowd swinging their nightsticks. The result was chaotic and bloody; more than a hundred strikers were hospitalized. Labor leaders, many still smarting from Ness's investigations, portrayed the former "Untouchable" as a pawn of the companies, attempting to destroy Cleveland's unions.

Then there was the Torso Murderer, a latter-day Jack the Ripper who terrorized Cleveland from the fall of 1935 until 1938, gruesomely dismembering a dozen victims. The failure of police to catch the elusive psychopath triggered a wave of public indignation. While under fire with the rest of the department, Ness attempted to crack the case by leading a raid on a hobo jungle where some believed the killer dwelt. Finding no evidence, he ordered the hapless vagabonds jailed and their makeshift shacks burned.

Instead of praising, the public and press bitterly criticized the safety director and his raiders for venting their frustrations on the shantytown inhabitants. The Torso Murders were never solved, and Ness was one of the principal officials held responsible.

By 1939 Clevelanders noticed their safety director's formerly conservative lifestyle was rapidly changing. That spring he divorced his wife of nearly ten years and began dating Evaline McAndrew, a fashion designer. The two were married in October. Ness and his twenty-eight-year-old bride moved into a fashionable shoreline home in the suburb of Lakewood, where they entertained frequently and lavishly.

In 1940 Ness accepted a post as a consultant with the Federal Social Protection Program, a national public-awareness campaign against venereal disease. The appointment required that he make repeated visits to Washington, D.C., and New York. He also became involved in a number of business ventures. Ness soon came under fire for spending more time pursuing personal interests and less in his role as a safety director. Even press writers, formerly his most ardent supporters, were becoming critical, charging that he had grown complacent in his job.

Ness's alleged shortcomings suddenly become hot topics when, in November 1941, Cleveland elected a new mayor, Democrat Frank J. Lausche. It was no secret Lausche wanted to replace the safety director, and he was not alone. Most prominent Democrats in the city, along with various police officials and labor leaders, were eager to see Ness removed.

Lausche nevertheless proceeded with caution. Although Ness's status had greatly diminished, he was still a powerful figure in Cleveland, with loyal supporters in City Hall, the police and fire departments, and local newspapers.

Four months after Lausche took office, "the accident" occurred. Whatever positive image Ness still enjoyed was now almost ruined. His critics made the most of the situation. The Director of Public Safety a reckless driver? The former Prohibition agent driving while intoxicated?

Looking more serious than usual, Ness faced reporters a few days later and gave his version of the accident. He admitted having had several drinks but insisted that he was not intoxicated, maintaining that the crash had been caused primarily by slippery conditions. He said he had left the scene with the intention of taking his wife—who had the wind knocked out of her—to the hospital. But Evaline soon recovered, asking to be taken home instead. "It was," he stated, "a very unfortunate thing all the way through, but there was no attempt at evasion in any particular."

While Ness may have been guilty merely of bad judgement and simple human error, the damage to his reputation was irreversible. Cleveland's white knight had fallen from his pedestal, and his days as safety director were numbered. Still fearful of public reaction, Lausche and his Democratic colleagues put pressure on the former "Untouchable" to surrender his office. It worked. Less than two months later Ness resigned.

Ness now turned to his advisory post with the federal campaign against social diseases. The Office of Defense appointed him director of the program, a position he held for the next four years. The work kept alive his reputation as a valiant public servant, and won for him, in 1946, the Navy's Meritorious Service Citation.

At the same time, however, Ness's personal affairs kept him at the center of controversy. His myriad business connections occasionally caused him to be linked to scandals and rumors of shady dealings. In the midst of all this, Evaline left Ness and moved to New York.

On January 31, 1946, Ness married for the third time. His new bride was Elizabeth Andersen Seaver, a divorced sculptress. About a year later the couple adopted a son, Robert—Ness's first experience with fatherhood.

In 1947 Ness returned to Cleveland with his family and offered himself as the Republican candidate in that year's mayoral contest. His opponent was the Democratic incumbent, Thomas A. Burke. The labor unions, possessing an immense influence over blue-collar Cleveland, had always despised Ness and threw their support behind Burke. The ex-safety director nevertheless mounted an impressive campaign, raising $150,000.

But Ness was not a politician. Those who recalled the glib, confident young lawman who had attracted hero worship with his dynamic accomplishments were frankly startled by the man now seeking the office of mayor. His once-boyish face was deeply lined, his shoulders were slouched, and a noticeable paunch had appeared at his waist. In public appearances Ness seemed nervous and stiff. His speeches were delivered flatly and failed to address any significant issues. Ness merely relied on his past fame as a crime-fighter and criticized his opponent.

When November arrived Ness won a dismal 85,990 votes—barely half the 168,412 Burke received in a landslide victory. Whatever political aspirations Ness had held perished.

Ten years of obscurity followed. Financially, and perhaps emotionally, Ness never recovered from the defeat. Two divorces, the expenses of his campaign, and a series of unsuccessful business ventures left him in poverty. About a year after the election he returned briefly to Cleveland, inquiring of an old friend about a sixty-dollar-a-week job. A former associate who encountered him recalled later that "he was still a fairly young man, but he simply ran out of gas. He didn't know which way to turn."

In August 1956, Ness and his family moved to Coudersport, Pennsylvania, a small town on the banks of the Allegheny River. While running two small businesses, he began to work on his memoirs, a project that, with the collaboration of journalist Oscar Fraley, would lead to the slam-bang, glorified account of his gangbusting days in Chicago. He hoped the book would be successful enough to relieve his financial plight, as well as recover some of his faded fame.

Ness did not live to see the results. On May 16, 1957, he suffered a fatal heart attack. The former "Untouchable" was dead at forty-four.

At the time of his death, Ness was $8,000 in debt. Listed with his estate was a $200 royalty contract with the publishing company of Julian Messner, Inc., for his manuscript. Only months later *The Untouchables* arrived in bookstores, and soon television propelled Ness into the American public's imagination.

Eliot Ness, whatever his faults, deserves his place in history. Some have dismissed him as a man obsessed with personal pride, interested only in promoting his own public image. But, lest we forget, many of America's most beloved heroes—from Davey Crockett to General Patton—were famous for singing their own praises and were largely responsible for creating their own fame.

Even if the familiar character presented on film is largely unreal, Ness's actual accomplishments were not. In two years Ness and his "Untouchables" had a greater impact in thwarting gangland activities in Chicago than the combined efforts of local, state, and federal authorities had over the course of a decade. As Cleveland's safety director, Ness rejuvenated the city's sagging municipal departments and transformed them into the finest in the nation.

Perhaps more important, however, was the image that Ness projected as a champion of law and order, decency and honesty, integrity and bravery. Like a frontier marshall protecting his town from the forces of lawlessness, he gave to the communities he served a hero to admire.

Ness ultimately fell from public favor only when he failed to live up to his own larger-than-life image. But through *The Untouchables*—the book, television series, and now a motion picture—he has been belatedly immortalized as one of America's great lawmen.

It is an image the real Eliot Ness would have appreciated.

The Causes of the Great Crash

by John Kenneth Galbraith

As illustrated by the conditions in the sweatshops of New York City, industrialization had its human as well as material costs. Yet many Americans living in the mid-1920s might well have looked back over the previous half-century and have been quite satisfied. The nation had emerged as an industrial power and prosperity seemed firmly entrenched. Certainly there had been occasional slumps in the economy, but each time a strong recovery pushed the nation forward.

When the great stock market crash of October, 1929, rocked the country, most people expected the acompanying economic stagnation to be only a temporary downslide in the inexorable march of progress. However, this crash was different, for it was followed by the most serious economic depression in American history. This Great Depression was not just an *economic* turning point in American history, but served as a catalyst for numerous social and political changes as well. Thus, understanding the reasons for the Great Crash and the Great Depression helps make our modern society more comprehensible.

No one does a better job of describing the causes of the crash and the subsequent depression than John Kenneth Galbraith, Professor Emeritus of Economics at Harvard University. Among Galbraith's numerous publications are *American Capitalism, The Affluent Society, The New Industrial State, Economics and the Public Purpose,* and *The Age of Uncertainty.* In all of his writings, the lucid narrative is punctuated with wit and humor. The following essay stands as a classic example of how to present a complex subject in a clear and interesting manner.

The decade of the twenties, or more exactly the eight years between the postwar depression of 1920–21 and the sudden collapse of the stock market in October, 1929, were prosperous ones in the United States. The total output of the economy increased by more than 50 per cent. The preceding decades had brought the automobile; now came many more and also roads on which they could be driven with reasonable reliability and comfort. There was much building. The downtown section of the mid-continent city—Des Moines, Omaha, Minneapolis—dates from these years. It was then, more likely than not, that what is still the leading hotel, the tallest office building, and the biggest department store went up. Radio arrived, as of course did gin and jazz.

These years were also remarkable in another respect, for as time passed it became increasingly evident that the prosperity could not last. Contained within it were the seeds of its own destruction. The country was heading into the gravest kind of trouble. Herein lies the peculiar fascination of the period for a study in the problem of leadership. For almost no steps were taken during these years to arrest the tendencies which were obviously leading, and did lead, to disaster.

At least four things were seriously wrong, and they worsened as the decade passed. And knowledge of them does not depend on the always brilliant assistance of hindsight. At least three of these flaws were highly visible and widely discussed. In ascending order, not of importance but of visibility, they were as follows:

First, income in these prosperous years was being distributed with marked inequality. Although output per worker rose steadily during the period, wages were fairly stable, as also were prices. As a result, business profits increased rapidly and so did incomes of the wealthy and the well-to-do. This tendency was nurtured by assiduous and successful efforts of Secretary of the Treasury Andrew W. Mellon to reduce income taxes with special attention to the higher brackets. In 1929 the 5 per cent of the people with the highest incomes received perhaps a quarter of all personal income. Between 1919 and 1929 the share of the one per cent who received the highest incomes increased by approximately one seventh. This meant that the economy was heavily and increasingly dependent on the luxury consumption of the well-to-do and on their willingness to reinvest what they did not or could not spend on themselves. Anything that shocked the confidence of the rich either in their personal or in their business future would have a bad effect on total spending and hence on the behavior of the economy.

This was the least visible flaw. To be sure, farmers, who were not participating in the general advance, were making themselves heard; and twice during the period the Congress passed far-reaching relief legislation which was vetoed by Coolidge. But other groups were much less vocal. Income distribution in the United States had long been unequal. The inequality of these years did not seem exceptional. The trade-union movement was also far from strong. In the early twenties the steel industry was still working a twelve-hour day and, in some jobs, a seven-day week. (Every two weeks when the shift changed a man worked twice around the clock.) Workers lacked the organization or the power to deal with conditions like this; the twelve-hour day was, in fact, ended as the result of personal pressure by President Harding on the steel companies, particularly on Judge Elbert H. Gary, head of the United States Steel Corporation. Judge Gary's personal acquaintance with these working conditions was thought to be slight, and this gave rise to Benjamin Stolberg's now classic observation that the Judge "never saw a blast furnace until his death." In all these circumstances the increasingly lopsided income distribution did not excite much comment or alarm. Perhaps it would have been surprising if it had.

But the other three flaws in the economy were far less subtle. During World War I the United States ceased to be the world's greatest debtor country and became its greatest creditor. The consequences of this change have so often been described that they have the standing of a cliché. A debtor country could export a greater value of goods than it imported and use the difference for interest and debt repayment. This was what we did before the war. But a creditor must import a greater value than it exports if those who owe it money are to have the wherewithal to pay interest and principal. Otherwise the creditor must either forgive the debts or make new loans to pay off the old.

During the twenties the balance was maintained by making new foreign loans. Their promotion was profitable to domestic investment houses. And when the supply of honest and competent foreign borrowers ran out, dishonest, incompetent, or fanciful borrowers were invited to borrow and, on occasion, bribed to do so. In 1927 Juan Leguia, the son of the then dictator of Peru, was paid $450,000 by the National City Company and J. & W. Seligman for his services in promoting a $50,000,000 loan to Peru which these houses marketed. Americans lost and the Peruvians didn't gain appreciably. Other Latin American republics got equally dubious loans by equally dubious devices. And, for reasons that now tax the imagination, so did a large number of German cities and municipalities. Obviously, once investors awoke to the character of these loans or there was any other shock to confidence, they would no longer be made. There would be nothing with which to pay the old loans. Given this arithmetic, there would be either a sharp reduction in exports or a wholesale default on the outstanding loans, or more likely both. Wheat and cotton farmers and others who depended on exports would suffer. So would those who owned the bonds. The buying power of both would be reduced. These consequences were freely predicted at the time.

The second weakness of the economy was the large-scale corporate thimblerigging that was going on. This took a variety of forms, of which by far the most common was the organization of corporations to hold stock in yet other corporations, which in turn held stock in yet other corporations. In the case of the railroads and the utilities, the purpose of this pyramid of holding companies was to obtain control of a very large number of operating companies with a very small investment in the ultimate holding company. A $100,000,000 electric utility, of which the capitalization was represented half by bonds and half by common stock, could be controlled with an investment of a little over $25,000,000—the value of just over half the common stock. Were a company then formed with the same capital structure to hold *this* $25,000,000 worth of common stock, it could be controlled with an investment of $6,250,000. On the next round the amount required would be less than $2,000,000. That $2,000,000 would still control the entire $100,000,000 edifice. By the end of the twenties, holding-company structures six or eight tiers high were a commonplace. Some of them—the utility pyramids of Insull and Associated Gas & Electric, and the railroad pyramid of the Van Sweringens—were marvelously complex. It is unlikely that anyone fully understood them or could.

In other cases companies were organized to hold securities in other companies in order to manufacture more securities to sell to the public. This was true of the great investment trusts. During 1929 one investment house, Goldman, Sachs & Company, organized and sold nearly a billion dollars' worth of securities in three interconnected investment trusts—Goldman Sachs Trading Corporation; Shenandoah Corporation; and Blue Ridge Corporation. All eventually depreciated virtually to nothing.

This corporate insanity was also highly visible. So was the damage. The pyramids would last only so long as earnings of the company at the bottom were secure. If anything happened to the dividends of the underlying company, there would be trouble, for upstream companies had issued bonds (or in practice sometimes preferred stock) against the dividends on the stock of the downstream companies. Once the earnings stopped, the bonds would go into default or the preferred stock would take over and the pyramid would collapse. Such a collapse would have a bad effect not only on the orderly prosecution of business and investment by the operating companies but also on confidence, investment, and spending by the community at large. The likelihood was increased because in any number of cities—Cleveland, Detroit, and Chicago were notable examples—the banks were deeply committed to these pyramids or had fallen under the control of the pyramiders.

Finally, and most evident of all, there was the stock market boom. Month after month and year after year the great bull market of the twenties roared on. Sometimes there were setbacks, but more often there were fantastic forward surges. In May of 1924 the New York *Times* industrials stood at 106; by the end of the year they were 134; by the end of 1925 they were up to 181. In 1927 the advance began in earnest—to 245 by the end of that year and on to 331 by the end of 1928. There were some setbacks in early 1929, but then came the fantastic summer explosion when in a matter of three months the averages went up another 110 points. This was the most frantic summer in our financial history. By its end, stock prices had nearly quadrupled as compared with four years earlier. Transactions on the New York Stock Exchange regularly ran to 5,000,000 or more shares a day. Radio Corporation of America went to 573¾ (adjusted) without ever having paid a dividend. Only the hopelessly eccentric, so it seemed, held securities for their income. What counted was the increase in capital values.

And since capital gains were what counted, one could vastly increase his opportunities by extending his holdings with borrowed funds—by buying on margin. Margin accounts expanded enormously, and from all over the country—indeed from all over the world—money poured into New York to finance these transactions. During the summer, brokers' loans increased at the rate of $400,000,000 a month. By September they totaled more than $7,000,000,000. The rate of interest on these loans varied from 7 to 12 per cent and went as high as 15.

This boom was also inherently self-liquidating. It could last only so long as new people, or at least new money, were swarming into the market in pursuit of the capital gains. This new demand bid up the stocks and made the capital gains. Once the supply of new customers began to falter, the market would cease to rise. Once the market stopped rising, some, and perhaps a good many, would start to cash in. If you are concerned with capital gains, you must get them while the getting is good. But the getting may start the market down, and this will one day be the signal for much more selling—both by those who are trying to get out and those who are being forced to sell securities that are no longer safely margined. Thus it was certain that the market would one day go down, and far more rapidly than it went up. Down it went with a thunderous crash in October of 1929. In a series of terrible days, of which Thursday, October 24, and Tuesday, October 29, were the most terrifying, billions in values were lost, and thousands of speculators—they had been called investors—were utterly and totally ruined.

This too had far-reaching effects. Economists have always deprecated the tendency to attribute too much to the great stock market collapse of 1929: this was the drama; the causes of the subsequent depression really lay deeper. In fact, the stock market crash was very important. It exposed the other weakness of the economy. The overseas loans on which the payments balance depended came to an end. The jerry-built holding-company structures came tumbling down. The investment-trust stocks collapsed. The crash put a marked crimp on borrowing for investment and therewith on business spending. It also removed from the economy some billions of consumer spending that was either based on, sanctioned by, or encouraged by the fact that the spenders had stock market gains. The crash was an intensely damaging thing.

And this damage, too, was not only foreseeable but foreseen. For months the speculative frenzy had all but dominated American life. Many times before in history—the South Sea Bubble, John Law's speculations, the recurrent real-estate booms of the last century, the great Florida land boom earlier in the same decade—there had been similar frenzy. And the end had always come, not with a whimper but a bang. Many men, including in 1929 the President of the United States, knew it would again be so.

The increasingly perilous trade balance, the corporate buccaneering, and the Wall Street boom—along with the less visible tendencies in income distribution—were all allowed to proceed to the ultimate disaster without effective hindrance. How much blame attaches to the men who occupied the presidency?

Warren G. Harding died on August 2, 1923. This, as only death can do, exonerates him. The disorders that led eventually to such trouble had only started when the fatal blood clot destroyed this now sad and deeply disillusioned man. Some would argue that his legacy was bad. Harding had but a vague perception of the economic processes over which he presided. He died owing his broker $180,000 in a blind account—he had been speculating disastrously while he was President, and no one so inclined would have been a good bet to curb the coming boom. Two of Harding's Cabinet officers, his secretary of the interior and his attorney general, were to plead the Fifth Amendment when faced with questions concerning their official acts, and the first of these went to jail. Harding brought his fellow townsman Daniel R. Crissinger to be his comptroller of the currency, although he was qualified for this task, as Samuel Hopkins Adams has suggested, only by the fact that he and the young Harding had stolen watermelons together. When Crissinger had had an ample opportunity to demonstrate his incompetence in his first post, he was made head of the Federal Reserve System. Here he had the central responsibility for action on the ensuing boom. Jack Dempsey, Paul Whiteman, or F. Scott Fitzgerald would have been at least equally qualified.

Yet it remains that Harding was dead before the real trouble started. And while he left in office some very poor men, he also left some very competent ones. Charles Evans Hughes, his secretary of state; Herbert Hoover, his secretary of commerce; and Henry C. Wallace, his secretary of agriculture, were public servants of vigor and judgment.

The problem of Herbert Hoover's responsibility is more complicated. He became President on March 4, 1929. At first glance this seems far too late for effective action. By then the damage had been done, and while the crash might come a little sooner or a little later, it was now inevitable. Yet Hoover's involvement was deeper than this—and certainly much deeper than Harding's. This he tacitly concedes in his memoirs, for he is at great pains to explain and, in some degree, to excuse himself.

For one thing, Hoover was no newcomer to Washington. He had been secretary of commerce under Harding and Coolidge. He had also been the strongest figure (not entirely excluding the President) in both Administration and party for almost eight years. He had a clear view of what was going on. As early as 1922, in a letter to Hughes, he expressed grave concern over the quality of the foreign loans that were being floated in New York. He returned several times to the subject. He knew about the corporate excesses. In the latter twenties he wrote to his colleagues and fellow officials (including Crissinger) expressing his grave concern over the Wall Street orgy. Yet he was content to express himself—to write letters and memoranda, or at most, as in the case of the foreign loans, to make an occasional speech. He could with propriety have presented his views of the stock market more strongly to the Congress and the public. He could also have maintained a more vigorous and persistent agitation within the Administration. He did neither. His views of the market were so little known that it celebrated his election and inauguration with a great upsurge. Hoover was in the boat and, as he himself tells, he knew where it was headed. But, having warned the man at the tiller, he rode along into the reef.

And even though trouble was inevitable, by March, 1929, a truly committed leader would still have wanted to do something. Nothing else was so important. The resources of the Executive, one might expect, would have been mobilized in a search for some formula to mitigate the current frenzy and to temper the coming crash. The assistance of the bankers, congressional leaders, and the Exchange authorities would have been sought. Nothing of the sort was done. As secretary of commerce, as he subsequently explained, he had thought himself frustrated by Mellon. But he continued Mellon in office. Henry M. Robinson, a sympathetic Los Angeles banker, was commissioned to go to New York to see his colleagues there and report. He returned to say that the New York bankers regarded things as sound. Richard Whitney, the vice-president of the Stock Exchange, was summoned to the White House for a conference on how to curb speculation. Nothing came of this either. Whitney also thought things were sound.

Both Mr. Hoover and his official biographers carefully explained that the primary responsibility for the goings on in New York City rested not with Washington but with the governor of New York State. That was Franklin D. Roosevelt. It was he who failed to rise to his responsibilities. The explanation is far too formal. The future of the whole country was involved. Mr. Hoover was the President of the whole country. If he lacked authority commensurate with this responsibility, he could have requested it. This, at a later date, President Roosevelt did not hesitate to do.

Finally, while by March of 1929 the stock market collapse was inevitable, something could still be done about the other accumulating disorders. The balance of payments is an obvious case. In 1931 Mr. Hoover did request a one-year moratorium on the inter-Allied (war) debts.This was a courageous and constructive step which came directly to grips with the problem. But the year before, Mr. Hoover, though not without reluctance, had signed the Hawley-Smoot tariff. "I shall approve the Tariff Bill. . . . It was undertaken as the result of pledges given by the Republican Party at Kansas City. . . . Platform promises must not be empty gestures." Hundreds of people—from Albert H. Wiggin, the head of the Chase National Bank, to Oswald Garrison Villard, the editor of the *Nation*—felt that no step could have been more directly designed to make things worse. Countries would have even more trouble earning the dollars of which they were so desperately short. But Mr. Hoover signed the bill.

Anyone familiar with this particular race of men knows that a dour, flinty, inscrutable visage such as that of Calvin Coolidge can be the mask for a calm and acutely perceptive intellect. And he knows equally that it can conceal a mind of singular aridity. The difficulty, given the inscrutability, is in knowing which. However, in the case of Coolidge the evidence is in favor of the second. In some sense, he certainly knew what what going on. He would not have been unaware of what was called the Coolidge market. But he connected developments neither with the well-being of the country nor with his own responsibilities. In his memoirs Hoover goes to great lengths to show how closely he was in touch with events and how clearly he foresaw their consequences. In his *Autobiography,* a notably barren document, Coolidge did not refer to the accumulating troubles. He confines himself to such unequivocal truths as "Every day of Presidential life is crowded with activities" (which in his case, indeed, was not true); and "The Congress makes the laws, but it is the President who causes them to be executed."

At various times during his years in office, men called on Coolidge to warn him of the impending trouble. And in 1927, at the instigation of a former White House aide, he sent for William Z. Ripley of Harvard, the most articulate critic of the corporate machinations of the period. The President became so interested that he invited him to stay for lunch, and listened carefully while his guest outlined (as Ripley later related) the "prestidigitation, double-shuffling, honey-fugling, hornswoggling, and skulduggery" that characterized the current Wall Street scene. But Ripley made the mistake of telling Coolidge that regulation was the responsibility of the states (as was then the case). At this intelligence Coolidge's face lit up and he dismissed the entire matter from his mind. Others who warned of the impending disaster got even less far.

And on some occasions Coolidge added fuel to the fire. If the market seemed to be faltering, a timely statement from the White House—or possibly from Secretary Mellon—would often brace it up. William Allen White, by no means an unfriendly observer, noted that after one such comment the market staged a 26-point rise. He went on to say that a careful search "during these halcyon years . . . discloses this fact: Whenever the stock market showed signs of weakness, the President or the Secretary of the Treasury or some important dignitary of the administration . . . issued a statement. The statement invariably declared that business was 'fundamentally sound,' that continued prosperity had arrived, and that the slump of the moment was 'seasonal.' "

Such was the Coolidge role. Coolidge was fond of observing that "if you see ten troubles coming down the road, you can be sure that nine will run into the ditch before they reach you and you have to battle with only one of them." A critic noted that "the trouble with this philosophy was that when the tenth trouble reached him he was wholly unprepared. . . . The outstanding instance was the rising boom and orgy of mad speculation which began in 1927." The critic was Herbert Hoover.

Plainly, in these years, leadership failed. Events whose tragic culmination could be foreseen—and was foreseen—were allowed to work themselves out to the final disaster. The country and the world paid. For a time, indeed, the very reputation of capitalism itself was in the balance. It survived in the years following perhaps less because of its own power or the esteem in which it was held, than because of the absence of an organized and plausible alternative. Yet one important question remains. Would it have been possible even for a strong President to arrest the plunge? Were not the opposing forces too strong? Isn't one asking the impossible?

No one can say for sure. But the answer depends at least partly on the political context in which the Presidency was cast. That of Coolidge and Hoover may well have made decisive leadership impossible. These were conservative Administrations in which, in addition, the influence of the businessman was strong. At the core of the business faith was an intuitive belief in *laissez faire*—the benign tendency of things that are left alone. The man who wanted to intervene was a meddler. Perhaps, indeed, he was a planner. In any case, he was to be regarded with mistrust. And, on the businessman's side, it must be borne in mind that high government office often nurtures a spurious sense of urgency. There is no more important public function than the suppression of proposals for unneeded action. But these should have been distinguished from action necessary to economic survival.

A bitterly criticized figure of the Harding-Coolidge-Hoover era was Secretary of the Treasury Andrew W. Mellon. He opposed all action to curb the boom, although once in 1929 he was persuaded to say that bonds (as distinct from stocks) were a good buy. And when the depression came, he was against doing anything about that. Even Mr. Hoover was shocked by his insistence that the only remedy was (as Mr. Hoover characterized it) to "liquidate labor, liquidate stocks, liquidate the farmers, liquidate real estate." Yet Mellon reflected only in extreme form the conviction that things would work out, that the real enemies were those who interfered.

Outside of Washington in the twenties, the business and banking community, or at least the articulate part of it, was overwhelmingly opposed to any public intervention. The tentative and ineffective steps which the Federal Reserve did take were strongly criticized. In the spring of 1929 when the Reserve system seemed to be on the verge of taking more decisive action, there was an anticipatory tightening of money rates and a sharp drop in the market. On his own initiative Charles E. Mitchell, the head of the National City Bank, poured in new funds. He had an obligation, he said, that was "paramount to any Federal Reserve warning, or anything else" to avert a crisis in the money market. In brief, he was determined, whatever the government thought, to keep the boom going. In that same spring Paul M. Warburg, a distinguished and respected Wall Street leader, warned of the dangers of the boom and called for action to restrain it. He was deluged with criticism and even abuse and later said that the subsequent days were the most difficult of his life. There were some businessmen and bankers—like Mitchell and Albert Wiggin of the Chase National Bank—who may have vaguely sensed that the end of the boom would mean their own business demise. Many more had persuaded themselves that the dream would last. But we should not complicate things. Many others were making money and took a short-run view—or no view—either of their own survival or of the system of which they were a part. They merely wanted to be left alone to get a few more dollars.

And the opposition to government intervention would have been nonpartisan. In 1929 one of the very largest of the Wall Street operators was John J. Raskob. Raskob was also chairman of the Democratic National Committee. So far from calling for preventive measures, Raskob in 1929 was explaining how, through stock market speculation, literally anyone could be a millionaire. Nor would the press have been enthusiastic about, say, legislation to control holding companies and investment trusts or to give authority to regulate margin trading. The financial pages of many of the papers were riding the boom. And even from the speculating public, which was dreaming dreams of riches and had yet to learn that it had been fleeced, there would have been no thanks. Perhaps a President of phenomenal power and determination might have overcome the Coolidge-Hoover environment. But it is easier to argue that this context made inaction inevitable for almost any President. There were too many people who, given a choice between disaster and the measures that would have prevented it, opted for disaster without either a second or even a first thought.

On the other hand, in a different context a strong President might have taken effective preventive action. Congress in these years was becoming increasingly critical of the Wall Street speculation and corporate piggery-pokery. The liberal Republicans—the men whom Senator George H. Moses called the Sons of the Wild Jackass—were especially vehement. But conservatives like Carter Glass were also critical. These men correctly sensed that things were going wrong. A President such as Wilson or either of the Roosevelts (the case of Theodore is perhaps less certain than that of Franklin) who was surrounded in his Cabinet by such men would have been sensitive to this criticism. As a leader he could both have reinforced and drawn strength from the contemporary criticism. Thus he might have been able to arrest the destructive madness as it became recognizable. The American government works far better— perhaps it only works—when the Executive, the business power, and the press are in some degree at odds. Only then can we be sure that abuse or neglect, either private or public, will be given the notoriety that is needed.

Perhaps it is too much to hope that by effective and timely criticism and action the Great Depression might have been avoided. A lot was required in those days to make the United States in any degree depression-proof. But perhaps by preventive action the ensuing depression might have been made less severe. And certainly in the ensuing years the travail of bankers and businessmen before congressional committees, in the courts, and before the bar of public opinion would have been less severe. Here is the paradox. In the full perspective of history, American businessmen never had enemies as damaging as the men who grouped themselves around Calvin Coolidge and supported and applauded him in what William Allen White called "that masterly inactivity for which he was so splendidly equipped."

FDR: A Practical Magician

by John Kenneth Galbraith

On March 4, 1983, the United States marked the fiftieth anniversary of Franklin Delano Roosevelt's first inauguration. The perspective of more than fifty years allows us to make some reasonably safe assessments regarding FDR's politics and policies.

That he was "the dominant political figure of this century," as Professor Galbraith writes, is beyond question. His leadership during the severe crises of the Great Depression and World War II have assured his place among America's greatest presidents. The "Roosevelt Revolution," whether viewed as liberal or as essentially conservative, certainly has left a lasting legacy.

Thus, *what* Franklin D. Roosevelt accomplished is settled. *How* he was able to accomplish it is more difficult to discern. Professor Galbraith, who reminds us of his own affection for the man, is nonetheless perceptive in his analysis. By understanding the qualities of great presidential leadership, perhaps the nation and its future leaders can build upon those legacies which FDR left us a half-century ago.

That Franklin D. Roosevelt was, and preeminently so, the dominant political figure of this century—that he stood astride its first half like the Colossus itself—will not be in doubt. Nor are the reasons subject to serious dispute. It was his fate and fortune to face the two great tragedies of the time and to guide its greatest social achievement. The tragedies were, of course, the Second World War and the Great Depression, and few will quarrel as to the bearing of these two events on the Roosevelt transcendence. The world emerged better and in many ways stronger from both. We will never know, in either case, the disasters, even catastrophes, that might have been.

There can be equally little disagreement on Roosevelt's part in the most significant achievement of the age. It was Franklin D. Roosevelt who led the great transition in modern capitalism in the United States—the transition from an economic and social system in which participants were expected to bear the cost of their own helplessness or misfortune, earned or unearned, to one in which a compassionate protection tempered the inherent hardships and cruelties of the economy. Unemployment compensation, old-age pensions, lower-cost housing, varied support to agriculture, employment opportunity, and much more came together to compose this change that has earned the name the Roosevelt Revolution.

The revolution that Roosevelt brought about is both celebrated and not quite forgiven to this day. The poor are still thought by the stern to be unduly favored, with moral damage resulting. Under free enterprise, men, women, and children are meant to suffer; that suffering, like more income to the affluent, is essential as an incentive. No one would be more pleased than FDR at the success of the Roosevelt Revolution or less surprised at the deeply theological resistance it continues to engender.

There is general agreement, then, that the Depression, the war, and the great economic and social transformation of the first half of the twentieth century were central to the making of the Age of Roosevelt. Historians can often unite even on the obvious. What remains sharply in debate are the qualities of mind and personality that brought FDR, faced with such tragedy and such challenge, to such eminence. Never did history have so dense a pace as between 1932 and 1945. There was enough in those years to have overthrown a lesser man a dozen times. What allowed one leader so completely to dominate such a time?

Because love and loyalty have a blinding effect, the testimony of anyone who was there is somewhat flawed. The word of FDR's death, which reached me on that April evening in 1945, brought a sense of trauma I had never previously experienced in my life. I had felt a faith, affection, and commitment that, it seemed, would last forever. Not in the preceding twelve years had it occurred to me that a President might be wrong. Were a Roosevelt decision or action in conflict with my earlier views, I was always able to make the requisite adjustment and promptly did so. And it was the same for the others who proudly called themselves Roosevelt men. Thus my warning against too easily accepting us as witnesses. We are, needless to say, far, far better in our judgment of modern Presidents.

The ability to inspire loyalty and the compelling sweep of his personality were certainly important in the Roosevelt achievement. But important too was his enormous joy in combat. There are politicians who evade battle; there are those who invite it. The one who invites it, as did FDR, earns a loyalty from his followers not given to those political leaders whose instinct is to accommodation, appeasement, and retreat. Partly this is because there is pleasure for all participants in the contest, but it is also because there is no danger for the soldiers that retreat or surrender will leave them leaderless and exposed. This is not to say, of course, that Roosevelt never yielded; he was a master, as of much else, of the tactical withdrawal. But he never retreated because he was averse to the conflict; he never gave in because he sought to be loved by his enemies.

From this enjoyment of battle came the adversary tradition in American social and economic policy—the feeling of American business that government is inherently and intrinsically inimical or wrong. And in lesser measure the reverse. Not everyone will think this a good legacy. On more matters than not, government and business interests have a complementary role. Nor, in the longer, deeper view, is the conflict real.

Most of the Roosevelt Revolution, properly viewed, was conservative. It was intended to preserve the social tranquility and sense of belonging without which capitalism could not have survived—and still will not survive. It protected values and institutions that were at risk. But the softening of the edges of capitalism and the transition to the welfare state were accomplished far more harmoniously in the other industrial lands than in the United States. They might, perhaps, have come more peacefully here too, with less enduring strain on the political fabric, but for the Roosevelt delight in his enemies—his commitment to the ancient Pulitzer injunction that one should not only comfort the afflicted but afflict the comfortable. Certainly this attitude added to the joy of all of us who were there. With what pleasure we made the President's enemies our own. How deeply we scorned those among us who were thought to have an instinct to appease. How unpleasant, on occasion, we must have been as people with whom to do business.

There is a myth, cultivated by Walter Lippmann among others, that Roosevelt was a man of words and not thought. That it was his practice to air ideas liberally, to test them on audiences casual and otherwise, is certainly true. Many, in consequence, came away in deep alarm as to the direction in which the President's mind seemed to be running. But the Roosevelt performance was distinctly different; there, ideas were linked to intensely practical, powerfully relevant action. The farm crisis in 1933 was thought to have many causes; his solution was to provide the farmers with cheap loans and organize them to produce less for higher prices. Whatever the reasons for unemployment, the obvious answer was for the government to provide jobs through the Public and Civil Works Administrations. The National Recovery Act (NRA), much belabored by economists then and since, recognized a basic characteristic of modern capitalism: wages and prices interact in the modern economy; prices can shove down wages, and lower wages and reduced purchasing power can allow and force further price reductions—deflation. The opposing dynamic—wages pressing up prices, prices pulling up wages—is a cause of inflation, as we know today—or should know. Then as now there was a strong practical case for direct intervention to arrest this malign process; there was a strong practical case for the NRA.

Unemployment compensation, old-age pensions, and public housing were eminently relevant to the problems they addressed. The mobilization of the American economy in World War II was the most successful exercise in economic management of modern times—a huge increase in production, no net reduction in aggregate civilian consumption, and all with no appreciable inflation. On none of these matters did the President fail to get alternative proposals—elaborate designs that substituted pretense and rhetoric for real solutions.

I do not suggest that FDR's ability to link ideas to effective action and to link initiative to desired result was infallible. In 1933, like our recent Presidents, he was briefly attracted to the magic of the monetarists—to the notion that the economy could be regulated in all its complexity by monetary witchcraft. But here, in brilliant contrast to his successors, he quickly repented. Roosevelt was, indeed, a man of many ideas, but it was his genius to select those that were most relevant to a firm and useful result.

Those who agree, at least in part, on the effectiveness of individual Roosevelt measures have another criticism of the President. They concede that these measures, or some of them, were a necessary response to diverse needs; they insist, however, that FDR was incapable of envisaging and embracing a comprehensive and internally consistent design. He had no all-inclusive theory of the state, the economy, and the social order. This is true; and it is something, I suggest, that no one can regret. Those scholars and politicians who have an overall plan are almost always more impressive in oratory than in action, and they can be callous as they pursue their plan relentlessly or await its effects. Coolidge and Hoover had such a design—and left the economy in all its complexity to the ultimately benign operation of laissez-faire. Those who suffered in the interim were the natural cost of the larger benefit. There is a similar plan in the minds of those who now speak so confidently of the "miracle of the market," of the pervasive wickedness of public regulation and the generally inimical character of the modern welfare state. The twentieth century has no more powerful lesson than the suffering that can be imposed by those, on both the right and the left, who are captured by a comprehensive design for social and economic policy. We remember and celebrate Roosevelt because, mercifully, he was exempt from cruel and confining theory. He moved from the needed result to the relevant action precisely because he was unencumbered by ideological constraint. That, no doubt, is another way of saying that Franklin D. Roosevelt was a superbly practical man.

This willingness to adapt, to change, and to act was at the basis of the Roosevelt success as a political leader, of his hold on the American people and through them directly on the Congress as well. No one can doubt his virtuosity in speech, in dealing with the press, and, above all, on the radio. But none of this talent would have survived and served for those twelve intense years had it not been associated with concrete action and visible result. We hear so much these days of the compelling television personality—the politician who has "mastered" this medium, allowing him to persuade workers, women, blacks, and the poor contrary to the viewers' need, interest, or fortune. I doubt that such a triumph of personality over underlying purpose is truly possible; certainly FDR's mastery of radio and the fireside chat would not have been effective had it been discovered that those stirring words were a disguise for social neglect and inaction.

The Roosevelt magic had yet another source. This was his ability to extend a sense of community, a community not confined by national frontiers and one to which all men and women of goodwill and good purpose could believe that they belonged.

When the President spoke of his commitment to economic betterment and social justice, of his resistance to the regressive world of the dictators and of his hope for a future in which the young would not face periodic slaughter—in which death would not be a statistic—he did not speak as a leader to followers, not even as a President to his people. He spoke as one involved in an effort in which all had a part, as a participant to fellow participants. It was this sense of a common effort with the President, membership in a common community, to which people responded.

The feeling was strongest in the United States, and it was made stronger by those who stood outside and saw it as a threat to the economic and social eminence that had once been their more or less exclusive possession. They could not resist, but they would not belong. Once again one sees Roosevelt's debt to his opposition. But this sense of community went far beyond national boundaries. He extended it to Latin America, where it was the essence of his avowal of the Good Neighbor policy. And to Britain, most notably in the months when she stood alone. And on to distant India with the commitment to Indian nationhood, which causes his name to be revered there to this day. But most of all this sense of community reached out to our immediate neighbor, Canada.

Recently, to illustrate this point, Thomas H. Eliot, a leading architect of the Social Security Act in the 1930s and a Roosevelt congressman from Massachusetts in the early forties, sent me a quotation I had not previously seen from the President's response to a welcoming speech made on his arrival in Canada for a visit. Roosevelt said: "While I was on my cruise last week, I read in a newspaper that I was to be received with all the honors customarily rendered to a foreign ruler. Your Excellency, I am grateful for the honors; but something within me rebelled at that word 'foreign.' I say this because when I have been in Canada I have never heard a Canadian refer to an American as a 'foreigner.' He is just an 'American.' And in the same way, across the border in the United States, Canadians are not 'foreigners.' They are 'Canadians.' I think that that simple little distinction illustrates to me, better than anything else, the relationship between the two countries."

It is one of the many legacies that we have from Franklin D. Roosevelt that we all belong, without exception, to a yet larger commonwealth. In this larger community there is a general concern for the economic well-being of all people and for the reality of social participation and social justice. Above all, there is a commitment to the negotiation, conciliation, and peaceful resolution of national differences on which, as another and somber legacy of the Roosevelt years, our very survival now depends.

Prelude in the Pacific

by Edward Oxford

On November 26, 1941 a Japanese naval task force, including six aircraft carriers, left the remote Kurile Islands. Their destination was the United States naval base at Pearl Harbor, Hawaii. The American military commanders in Hawaii had no knowledge of this movement, despite the fact that U.S. intelligence officials had been decoding Japanese messages for over a year. But the Japanese had begun to use a new code, which had not been broken. In the fall, 1941, there was concern in the United States and in the British empire that the Japanese would attack somewhere. Codebreakers tried desperately to discover the Japanese plans. These tense days in November, 1941 are detailed in this article, as author Edward Oxford shows the events leading to the fateful attack on December 7.

A hazy tropical moon floated above the green palms and white beaches of the Hawaiian Islands during the last, languorous hours of December 6, 1941.

Saturday evening on Oahu was, this close to payday, a time of lights and laughter for thousands of the U.S. soldiers, sailors, and airmen stationed across the island. At the Navy's recreation center at Pearl Harbor, enlisted men cheered as bands from warships of the U.S. Pacific Fleet competed in "The Battle of Music." A mile to the south, at the Hickam Field post theater, off-duty personnel watched Clark Gable in *Honky Tonk*. And ten miles inland, on the quadrangle greens of Schofield Barracks, soldiers took their ease with "3.2" beer.

Men who remained in their quarters tuned in "Songs of the Islands" on Honolulu radio station KGMB. It was, in fact, a very good night to hear Hawaiian music. Whenever the Army Air Corps flew new bombers in from the mainland, the radio station played records all night long—to serve as a homing beacon for the aircraft. A flight of twelve B-17s would be reaching Oahu early on Sunday morning.

That same evening, in the Japanese Consulate on Nuuanu Avenue, a fourth-level consul known as Tadashi Morimura worked late at his desk. This was a rather unusual place for Morimura to be found on a Saturday night. After sundown, the dashing young diplomat habitually circulated among the bars, hotels, and teahouses of Honolulu's beguiling demimond.

But this was not a usual night. And Tadashi Morimura was not an ordinary consular official. His real name was Takeo Yoshikawa. He was an officer in Japanese naval intelligence. For the past eight months, posing as a diplomat, he had served as Japan's key spy in Pearl Harbor.

During that time, Ensign Yoshikawa had watched the U.S. Pacific Fleet at dawn and at noon and at dusk, observing its comings and goings from vantage points in Pearl City and on Aiea Heights and Tantalus Mountain.

He had, riding day after day in the trusty "Royal Taxi Company" cab driven by "Johnny" Mikami, taken note of Hickam Field, Wheeler Field, Kaneohe Bay Naval Air Station, Bellows Field, and Schofield Barracks.

Some two hundred of his coded espionage messages had streamed back to Tokyo: BATTLESHIPS LEAVING ON TUESDAY RETURN ON FRIDAY . . . ALL SHIPS REMAIN IN PORT FOR ABOUT ONE WEEK . . . BATTLESHIPS ARE OFTEN MOORED IN PAIRS IN BATTLESHIP ROW . . . DESTINATIONS OF CARRIERS NOT KNOWN . . .

Now, at his desk Yoshikawa gathered papers. He leafed through files. Then he pulled together some sketches and maps. Orders had come from Tokyo. Tomorrow he was to burn his most secret documents.

For the Hawaiian Islands, resplendent beneath the December moon—as well as for Japan and the United States—this gentle night marked the end of the beginning.

A day of wrath had been in the making for decades. Ever since Japan began to emerge as a world power at the turn of the century, the mysterious island-nation and the mighty mainland nation had watched one another warily and with growing enmity across the vast Pacific Ocean.

Time and again during the waning months of 1941, Japanese and American diplomats had made ritualistic peace proposals and counterproposals. But the diplomats, perhaps as much as the nations for whom they spoke, seemed to be under the power of forces beyond their strength to control. The warmakers of Japan intended to pursue their own course, regardless of what the Americans—or even their own nation's "peace party"—wanted.

In early November, the Japanese Army and Navy had set forth a "Central Agreement"—their orchestration for wide-scale war. They would strike southward into Thailand, the Philippines, and Malaya. They would sweep across the Dutch East Indies. They would set up a defense perimeter in the mid-Pacific Ocean. And they would smash the U.S. Pacific Fleet at Pearl Harbor.

The official *Japan Times and Advertiser* had affirmed its nation's resolve: "Japan is master of its own fate. It has a free hand to proceed as it wills for the safeguarding of its own State. If it is necessary to fight America for that purpose, awful though the thought of such a holocaust, Japan will not hesitate to defend its people and its interests. It has the power, the purpose and the plan. . . ."

Now, even as Honolulu dreamed away the hours of a soft-breezed Saturday night, something quite like fate was abroad on the moon-glinting waters of the Pacific Ocean. In seas north of the Hawaiian Islands, the phantom shapes of a Japanese attack fleet were churning their way toward Oahu.

In mid-November thirty-one Japanese warships, tankers, and submarines had quietly assembled at desolate Hitokappu Bay in the remote Kurile Islands northeast of Hokkaido. These were the ships of Vice-Admiral Chuichi Nagumo's *Kido Butai* (Striking Force). Their target: Pearl Harbor. The designated time of attack: soon after dawn on the morning of December 7, Hawaiian time.

At six o-clock on the cloudy morning of November 26, the task force, its preparations complete, weighed anchor and sailed into the mists of the North Pacific Ocean. Six aircraft carriers—*Akagi, Kaga, Soryu, Hiryu, Shokaku,* and *Zuikaku*—moved in paired columns; they carried some four hundred aircraft. The battleships *Kirishima* and *Hiei* followed behind. Three cruisers, nine destroyers, and three submarines screened the formation. And eight accompanying oil tankers lumbered along at their top speed—about fourteen knots. For most of its perilous, eleven-day voyage, *Kido Butai* had to hold to that pace.

Diving deep by day, running on the surface at night, twenty-five other submarines moved well in advance of *Kido Butai,* reconnoitering the wide seas. On the morning of December 7 this auxiliary strike force was to be positioned around Oahu; after the air attack its units would torpedo any U.S. warships that tried to flee the harbor. Five of the submarines carried two-man midget submarines clamped to their hulls. Released ten miles off Oahu's shore, the midgets would attempt to slip into Pearl Harbor. Still other submarines between the Hawaiian Islands and the U.S. mainland would sink any American ships they intercepted. Keeping precisely to its charted course, the task force followed the track that had been surveyed by the liner *Taiyo Maru* in October. Passing between the Aleutian Islands and Midway Island on a course that would keep it beyond the range of U.S. air patrols, the fleet moved steadily through the "Vacant Sea"—that part of the ocean between the great southern routes connecting Hawaii and Japan and China, and the northern routes to the Aleutians. Few ships were ever seen in these remote waters.

The tankers refueled the warships at intervals along the way. Rolling seas made the fuelings dangerous. Several sailors were swept into the ocean.

The Japanese Navy took pains to cloak the passage of *Kido Butai* in total secrecy. During the first days of December, hundreds of sailors back in the home islands were sent on leave to Tokyo, so that foreign eyes might not notice a sudden diminution in the numbers of navy men seen there. High command ordered the fleet to move in strict radio silence.* No telltale waste was thrown from the ships, and blackout conditions applied at night.

Kido Butai could not speak, but it listened—for the transmissions of the Number 1 station of the Tokyo intelligence signals unit. The signals would tell Admiral Nagumo either to turn back or to continue on to Pearl Harbor.

The plans that Fleet Admiral Isoroku Yamamoto and his staff had carefully formulated for the operation provided for every contingency. If an American, British, or Dutch ship sighted the task force, the unfortunate vessel was to be sunk. If a ship of any other nation hove into view, boarding parties were to prevent its sending a radio message.** Should American naval forces sight *Kido Butai* before its carriers began their final run-in on December 6, the Japanese fleet was to turn back toward the home islands. If the Americans detected the fleet in the last hours before the scheduled hour of attack, Nagumo himself was to decide on the course of action. If the last-gasp negotiations with America came to a sudden settlement, Nagumo's force was to await further orders. And if, by some chance, the ships of the U.S. Pacific Fleet were not in Pearl Harbor as expected, Nagumo was to send out search planes—as far as one hundred and fifty miles south of Oahu—to locate and sink them.

Gentlemen do not read each other's mail. Or so stated a rule of the well-bred. But in the not-so-polite world of intelligence work, such niceties did not apply. Although the United States and Japan were still at peace in late 1941, U.S. intelligence experts and their Japanese counterparts were already waging a silent war, each adversary seeking vital information about the other's tactics, strategy, and operations.

For the United States in the Pacific, much of this effort centered not on the use of spies but on radio intelligence—the gathering of information on Japanese military movements and intentions through radio direction finding, traffic analysis, and most importantly, decrypting intercepted messages.

---

*Japanese and American officials and naval historians have steadfastly held that *Kido Butai* kept to strict radio silence as the attack fleet headed across the North Pacific toward Pearl Harbor. Recent research in formerly classified materials, however, indicates that ships of *Kido Butai* did, in fact, break radio silence during their furtive voyage. Author Robert Stinnett, in his recently published book *George Bush: His World War II Years,* draws upon U.S. Naval Security Group Command records to prove the point. According to Stinnett, U.S. Navy radio listening posts on the island of Oahu and at Dutch Harbor in the Aleutian Islands intercepted signals from the Japanese attack force in late November and early December. These broadcasts were also heard on the West Coast, according to Robert Ogg, a special intelligence agent of the Twelfth Naval District in San Francisco at the time. As well, the Oahu intercept post picked up signals of the advance Japanese submarine force while it was on its southerly course to Pearl Harbor. These startling intelligence reports were dutifully forwarded to Station U.S., the U.S. naval intelligence center in Washington, D.C. Presumably, they were then passed on to President Franklin D. Roosevelt at the White House. Some of the most troubling questions that still loom over the Pearl Harbor event have to do with the intelligence reports of the intercepted signals.

**On December 5 the Soviet freighter *Uritsky,* en route from the U.S. West Coast to Vladivostok, passed within viewing range of the attack force. Inexplicably, the ship was allowed to continue—and equally puzzling, it radioed no reports of having sighted the warships.

Ever since the early 1920s, U.S. Army and Navy cryptanalysts had repeatedly succeeded in penetrating many of the more than fifty code and cipher systems that served Japan's respective diplomatic, army, naval, air force, and general security needs.

Unknown to the Japanese, American codebreakers had even cracked what they termed "Purple"—the most complex of Japan's score of diplomatic ciphers. In 1939 Tokyo had begun using the "Purple" system for transmitting its highest-level dispatches to and from embassies in Washington, D.C., Berlin, Rome, London, Shanghai, and other cities. By September 1940, after eighteen months of excruciating effort, a team of brilliant U.S. Army Signal Corps cryptanalysts working under William F. Friedman had succeeded in analyzing the key elements of the "Purple" cipher and constructed a remarkable duplicate of the Japanese electromechanical "Type B" cipher machine—a device they had never even seen. Incredibly, their intricate, improvised box of plug wires and sparking telephone relays unscrambled the most secret Japanese diplomatic messages in minutes.

It all seemed like magic. Indeed, the code-name "MAGIC" was given to the messages that U.S. intelligence specialists using this machine so unerringly unraveled.*

Station U.S., the Navy's radio intelligence center, was located in the low, rambling Navy Building near the Mall in Washington, D.C. Some four hundred specialists worked here, striving to decrypt, translate, and evaluate the hundreds of messages intercepted each day from nations throughout the world. Members of the Signal Intelligence Service, Army counterparts who performed similar duties and shared the task of deciphering MAGIC intercepts, occupied offices in the adjacent Munitions Building.

To monitor and record Japanese radio traffic, Navy personnel manned listening posts on Oahu, in the Philippines, and in Washington, Maryland, Maine, and Florida. Army monitoring posts in the Hawaiian Islands and the Philippines, as well as in the Canal Zone, California, Texas, and New Jersey also picked up Japanese signals.

The Navy's MAGIC group at Station U.S. rated a special, locked-door inner-sanctum. Their prized "Purple" machine, a wooden box about the size of a milk crate, rested on a long table between two electric typewriters. Above the maze of wires and switches, clocks on the wall showed the time around the world.

Hidden behind a wall panel was a list of "the twelve apostles"—the names of persons permitted to receive MAGIC messages: the president, the secretaries of State, War, and Navy; four high-ranking Navy officers; and four high-ranking Army officers. At times these men were reading MAGIC "gist sheets" (summaries) even before code clerks in the Japanese Embassy a few blocks away deciphered receivings on their machine.

---

*The British scored a counterpart coup in the European theater. They used Enigma, a captured German coding machine, to decipher secret German messages. The code-name "Ultra" referred to these intercepts.

No overseas commanders were to receive MAGIC.

By mid-1941 President Franklin D. Roosevelt had learned, through MAGIC messages, three momentous facts. Japan was not planning to attack Russia, as Adolf Hitler had hoped she would. Rather, Japan would strike southward. And, Japan would arm for war against Britain and the U.S.

Washington saw a Japanese drive southward as a virtual certainty, an attack upon the Hawaiian Islands unlikely. It was in accordance with this strategic view that the eight "Purple" machines were apportioned. Washington retained four. Three went to the British in Southeast Asia. One was assigned to Station Cast at Cavite in the Philippines.

No "Purple" machine was granted to the Hawaiian Islands. Admiral Husband E. Kimmel, commander of the U.S. Pacific Fleet at Pearl Harbor, was not privy to the MAGIC messages. Neither, for that matter, was General Walter C. Short, who commanded U.S. Army forces in the Hawaiian Islands.

Kimmel had to depend on letters from Admiral Harold Stark, chief of naval operations, for glimpses into happenings on the diplomatic front. These took more than a week to reach Pearl Harbor. Often they were bland, reassuring, and vague. In late October, for example, Stark wrote to Kimmel: "Personally I do not think the Japs are going to sail into us." Washington, it seemed, was working "to maintain the status quo in the Pacific."

It was not until December that Kimmel even encountered the code word "Purple." The notation appeared by mistake on a dispatch sent to him from Washington. Kimmel asked fleet intelligence officer Lieutenant Commander Edwin T. Layton what "Purple" meant. Layton had never heard of the term.

Washington, so felt Washington, knew best.

The defense of Pearl Harbor, in the minds of certain of Washington's highest-level leaders, apparently seemed an academic matter. The big show was going to be in Southeast Asia. Everybody knew it. Everybody said so.

The MAGIC intercepts had become a trusted—perhaps too well trusted—source of intelligence. Historian Ladislas Farago, in *The Broken Seal,* contends: "Mr. Roosevelt and his associates assumed that thanks to the 'MAGICS,' they could learn well in advance everything the Japanese were planning, enabling them to apply whatever preventative or counter measures they deemed advisable or necessary. This reliance on 'MAGIC' as the instrument of warning became partly responsible for the complacency with which the American authorities approached the final crises in November and December 1941."

Ironically, Tokyo withheld the sophisticated "Type 2" cipher machine from her Honolulu consulate. Thus, instead of being sent by "Purple," espionage messages from Japan's Pearl Harbor spy went by way of less complex, medium-grade consular ciphers. But this apparent weakness in security proved to be a fortuitous masterstroke; the fact that the messages were sent by an easily-compromised cipher lulled American intelligence experts into assuming they were ordinary dispatches and of no strategic consequence. That the messages were signed by the consul general instead of Ensign Yoshikawa and addressed to the foreign ministry in Tokyo instead of Japanese naval intelligence further reinforced this impression.

Some fifty espionage messages were to flash back and forth between the Honolulu consulate and Tokyo during the twenty-four days from November 12 to December 7. All were intercepted and forwarded to Station U.S. Eighteen were decoded by the time of the attack. Almost all of these were of crucial importance. They supplied increasingly clear clues—for those willing to give them a careful reading—that the Japanese had targeted Pearl Harbor for a massive attack.

Washington, fatefully, paid little heed.*

Even what later became known as Tokyo's "bomb-plot" message, sent to Yoshikawa on September 24, stirred but slight excitement in the corridors of command. The message asked for a "grid" of Pearl Harbor—a clear inference that the base was being targeted for attack. The intercept made the highest-level rounds in Washington, even reaching the White House. The message spurred no call to action. And neither the director of naval intelligence, nor the chief of war plans, nor even the chief of naval operations saw fit to tell Admiral Kimmel of the ominous message. Any more than their Army counterparts told General Short of it.

In his book *Deadly Magic,* former U.S. Navy cryptographic officer Edward Van Der Rhoer points out: "It might have been thought that Honolulu merited special attention in view of the fact that the U.S. Pacific Fleet was based at Pearl Harbor. But the Office of Naval Intelligence considered [Yoshikawa's] reports to be of no more than low-level intelligence, and this rather scornful appraisal found its reflection in the low priority assigned to the intercepts."

In irony upon irony, Washington withheld from Station Hypo—the Navy's cryptographic center at Pearl Harbor—the decrypt-keys to reading the Honolulu messages. Typically, these messages (transmitted by commerical cable companies) were intercepted by listening stations in Puget Sound and San Francisco. But they were also picked up by the Navy's own listening station at Heeia, just twelve miles from Pearl Harbor. A courier regularly delivered the intercepts to cryptanalysts at Station Hypo. As ordered, they simply placed the dispatches into a pouch and sent them to the mainland via the next Pan American Clipper to the West Coast.

Up to a week passed before the intercepts finally reached their destination at Station U.S., five thousand miles from Pearl Harbor. There the messages piled up—along with hundreds of other medium-grade dispatches—waiting their turn to be examined, deciphered, and translated.

Here, for example, is how the processing of four intercepts of messages sent to and from Japan's Pearl Harbor spy was handled:

A report by Yoshikawa on the disposition the U.S. Fleet at Pearl Harbor, sent out and intercepted on November 24, was deciphered and translated at Station U.S. twenty-two days later—on December 16.

*Intimations of a possible attck on Hawaii had come as early as January 1941, when the Peruvian charge d'affaires in Tokyo told the U.S. Embassy of rumors that the "Japanese planned, in the event of trouble with the United States, to attempt a surprise mass attack on Pearl Harbor using all of their military facilities." The warning was relayed to the State Department in Washington, and then to the Navy—but was discounted as baseless.

Tokyo's order to Yoshikawa to report on U.S. ships, dated November 25, was processed on December 8.

Yoshikawa's report about the fleet's schedule, sent on December 1, was deciphered on December 10.

Tokyo's request for daily ship movements, intercepted on December 2, was processed on December 30.

As of Saturday, December 6, 1941, Station U.S. had a full set of the more than two hundred messages that Yoshikawa sent to Tokyo. For all the good this did Americans, the station might just as well have had none of them.

As Commander Joseph Rochefort, who headed Station Hypo, remembered those doubt-filled days: "We seemed to have a freezing of the mind. If the Japanese attacked Pearl Harbor, this means war. War with the United States is going to be won by the United States. So why should the Japanese attack Pearl Harbor? The answer is, 'They don't.'"

Observed *Codebreakers* author David Kahn, "While the world gazed with tunnel vision toward Southeast Asia, and American radio intelligence envisioned the Japanese carriers in home waters, six of them . . . were in fact butting eastward through the . . . vacant sea. . . . Temporarily oblivious to the possibility of a surprise attack on Pearl Harbor, [American military intelligence] watched the [Japanese] forces moving against Malaya as hypnotically as a conjurer's audience stares at the empty right hand while the left is pulling the ace out of a sleeve."

What American intelligence officers needed most during the nerve-rending fall of 1941 was the substance of messages sent to and from the Japanese fleet itself. But the frightening fact was that these were the very transmissions they could not decipher.

For years in the past, American cryptanalysts had cracked variation after variation of Japan's more than twenty naval codes. But beginning in about November 1940, baffling new versions of the top-level naval ciphers began to appear. The U.S. Navy Codebreakers were stunned by them—much as immunologists might be confused by a strange new virus—and were able to recover only bits and pieces.

More than four decades later, in his book . . . *And I Was There,* Layton was to declare: "Never in history had a nation steered into a confrontation with a rival power with more information about the general intentions of the potential enemy than the United States had about Japan on the eve of the Pacific war. But our leaders in Washington gambled on the assumption that our eavesdropping in Tokyo's diplomatic traffic would provide an early warning of their moves—even though we had lost our ability to tap into their naval communications."

It was roughly equivalent to a boxer's knowing just about all there was to know about his opponent at the start of their fight—except that his enemy would hit him even before the opening bell sounded.

The Japanese had a saying that covered such a situation: "Win first, fight later."

In Station Hypo's subeterranean chamber at Pearl Harbor, a bitter drama unfolded. "The dungeon," as it was called, had an armed guard at its entrance. Inside, some of the best codebreakers in the world desperately strove to crack the new cipher variations. But try as they might, they could barely make dents in them. Rather than simply introducing changes that kept the old system basically intact, the Japanese had created an entirely new one.

The U.S. intelligence experts were thus forced to divine Japanese fleet movements and intentions through less precise methods. Navy signalmen manning a network of radio direction-finders in the Philippines, Samoa, Midway, Hawaii, and Dutch Harbor in the Aleutian Islands helped them pinpoint the sources of Japanese warship signals. As well, the anlaysts studied the volume and traffic patterns on the Japanese fleet's hundreds of radio circuits. More and more messages were being routed southward—to Southeast Asia.

This was to be expected. But the intelligence officers at Station Hypo, like those back in Washington, were uncertain as to how—or whether—the Hawaiian Islands figured into Japan's grand scheme of things.

Station Hypo's cryptanalysts had scant sense of the MAGIC decrypts that were in the possession of Washington. And they had even less sense of just where the Japanese fleet was. "This meant," Layton wrote, "that the Pacific Fleet, the principal instrument of our military power in the Pacific, was not equipped to monitor the enemy beyond its harbor wall."

Station Hypo was trying to track six Japanese aircraft carriers in particular: *Akagi, Kaga, Hiryu, Soryu, Shokaku,* and *Zuikaku*. But by the middle of November, the vessels seemed to have vanished. U.S. listening stations picked up no ship-to-aircraft communications. Station Hypo hoped that the carriers remained in their home waters, but feared that they were not.

On the morning of December 2, an alarmed Layton held an intelligence briefing for Kimmel. "You mean," asked the incredulous admiral, "that the carriers could be coming around Diamond Head, and you wouldn't know it?" "I hope," replied Layton lamely, "they would be sighted before then."

In fact, the "lost" carriers were in the middle of the Pacific Ocean, heading straight toward Station Hypo.

That very day, just after *Kido Butai* crossed the International Date Line, Admiral Nagumo received one of the briefest, most fateful messages in the annals of naval warfare: "NIITAKA-YAMA NOBORE (CLIMB MOUNT NIITAKA)." The code words meant that Nagumo was to proceed with the attack on Pearl Harbor.

During the first week of December, Yoshikawa had the sure sense that time was running out. On December 2, the consulate received word from Tokyo to begin destroying some of its most sensitive documents. To avoid attracting outside attention, staff members burned the papers in a bathtub.

The next day Yoshikawa flashed to Tokyo a long, rather peculiar message that would later become known to U.S. codebreakers as the "lights message." This dispatch detailed a plan for sending signals to the Japanese about U.S. fleet movements.

Yoshikawa did not originate the message. Rather, he had received the plan from Bernard Julius Otto Kuehn, Japan's "sleeper-spy" in the Hawaiian Islands. The former Nazi had been under well-paid espionage contract to the Japanese since 1935.

As ordered by Tokyo, Kuehn had come up with a scheme to report on American warships. Using an eight-unit code, he was to flash lights in windows of his Oahu beachside house by night, and hang sheets in patterns on his clothesline by day. Paid advertisements would be placed on radio station KGMB—using certain phrases to convey ship movements.

On Saturday, December 6, Yoshikawa rose at 7 A.M. At about 11 A.M. he set off in the usual "Royal Taxi Company" cab for Pearl Harbor. For nearly three hours the spy proceeded from one observation point to another. He then returned to the consulate to send a crucial message to Tokyo. He reported that the U.S. battleships moored in the harbor were unprotected by torpedo nets. He noted that there were no signs of barrage balloons. And, almost exultantly, he offered the unasked-for opinion that there was opportunity "to take advantage for a surprise attack."

The "surprise attack" phrase should have been enough to alert officers at Station U.S.—even at this late point in time—to take action. Such, however, was not meant to be. The message was not processed until December 8.

Throughout the afternoon, Yoshikawa continued his observations of Pearl Harbor. The two U.S. carriers—*Enterprise* and *Lexington*—were gone.* But the rest of the fleet was in. Scores of warships rode at anchor. Their crews were ashore. And tomorrow was Sunday.

Late in the day, Yoshikawa headed back to the consulate. He had made his last espionage journey.

By midday on December 6, Nagumo turned his task force south toward Hawaii. Leaving the tankers behind, *Kido Butai* upped its speed to twenty knots. Then the carrier *Akagi* broke out the historic "Z" flag that Admiral Togo had hoisted at Tsushima, Japan's famed naval victory over Russia in 1905.

If events back at Station U.S. in Washington, meanwhile, during the "lost weekend" of December 6–7 struck one as something from an improbable motion-picture melodrama, the "lights message" sequence would seem to fit the unlikely script.

On Saturday, the code specialists there were to work a half-day. Among them was a new civilian translator, Dorothy Edgers. An American who had lived in Japan for thirty years, she had an excellent command of the Japanese language.

---

*In late November, concerned that the Japanese might attack Wake and Midway islands from their own mid-Pacific islands, Washington had ordered the *Enterprise* to Wake and the *Lexington* to Midway. Both carried fighter planes to reinforce the islands' defenses.

That morning, digging through the lower-priority intercepts, Edgers came across an intriguing dispatch. It happened to be the Honolulu consulate's three-day-old "lights message." The more she studied it, the more concerned she became.

"It was about a set of signals," Mrs. Edgers later recalled. "Signals about the U.S. Fleet in Oahu. There were to be lights in windows or bonfires on peaks." Puzzled by the odd message, she continued to work on its translation until late into the afternoon. She felt that the strange, detailed signal instructions boded danger.

Then Edgers resolutely sought out Lieutenant Commander Alwin Kramer, who was in charge of the naval intelligence translation section. In keeping with the tragedy of errors that prevailed that weekend, she couldn't have chosen a worse moment to make known her misgivings.

Kramer, an erudite, brutally overworked officer, on that relentless day was in the throes of unraveling a message of overwhelming importance. The first intercepts of a fourteen-part dispatch—a diplomatic note in English being sent from Tokyo to its ambassador in Washington, D.C., for presentation to the U.S. secretary of state the following day—were coming in on the "Purple" machine.

Edgers caught Kramer in mid-stride and thrust the "lights" message into his hands. Kramer, very much preoccupied, glanced at it.

"What shall I do with it?" she asked.

Kramer seemed barely to sense the meaning of the message. Rather, he picked out what he felt were a few flaws in Edger's interpretation of the Japanese wordage.

"Commander," she insisted, "don't you think this intercept ought to be distributed right away?"

Kramer handed the translation back to her. "You just go home, Mrs. Edgers. We'll get back to this piece on Monday," he said, and went on his way.

The evening cold of December 6 pressed in upon Washington. At about 8 P.M., President Roosevelt summoned Grace Tully, his personal secretary, to whom he dictated a triple-priority message to Emperor Hirohito. In it, FDR sought peace "for the sake of humanity." A little later he mentioned to a visitor: "This son of man has just sent his final message to the Son of God."

Barely an hour later, a courier arrived with a jolting MAGIC intercept containing the first thirteen parts of the fourteen-part message that Tokyo had sent to the Japanese Embassy in Washington. The fourteenth part, tantalizingly, had not yet been sent.

President Roosevelt read the intercept in a second-floor study. For ten minutes, his aide, Harry Hopkins, paced about the room while the president studied the message. The dispatch, in effect, seemed to reject America's conditions for peace. The finishing touch—the "peace or no peace" of it all—remained unexpressed.

Roosevelt said to Hopkins, "This means war." Hopkins remarked that it was too bad the United States could not strike the first blow. "No," Roosevelt said, "we can't do that. We are a democracy and a peaceful people."

Station U.S. kept fitful watch for the fourteenth part of Japan's message.

In Honolulu, sometime after five o-clock that Saturday afternoon, Yoshikawa buzzed for the consulate code clerk. He handed the clerk the last espionage message the spy would be sending to Tokyo. It read: VESSELS MOORED IN HARBOR: NINE BATTLESHIPS; THREE CLASS-B CRUISERS; THREE SEAPLANE TENDERS; SEVENTEEN DESTROYERS. ENTERING HARBOR ARE FOUR CLASS-B CRUISERS; THREE DESTROYERS. ALL AIRCRAFT CARRIERS AND HEAVY CRUISERS HAVE DEPARTED HARBOR. NO INDICATION OF ANY CHANGES IN U.S. FLEET. "ENTERPRISE" AND "LEXINGTON" HAVE SAILED FROM PEARL HARBOR. NO AIR RECONNAISSANCE IS BEING CONDUCTED.

The message was enciphered, then sent by RCA radiogram to Tokyo. It cost a mere $6.82 to transmit. And it was the death warrant for the Pearl Harbor fleet.

Part of that evening, Yoshikawa rested and read books. He looked out into the consulate garden. Communications specialists were burning their code books in a fiery pit.

Later Yoshikawa strolled about the consulate grounds, alone in the night. A bright haze, ten miles or so to the west, meant that the lights were on at Pearl Harbor. He could hear no aircraft patrolling aloft. All was quiet on the Pacific front.

He went to bed before midnight, but had difficulty falling asleep.

Honolulu was crowded this night with swarms of "swabbies" and "gyrenes" and "dogfaces" on pass. Many tested their marksmanship at shooting galleries, had their pictures taken, got tattooed, or wandered the side streets of Chinatown. Scores crowded the upstairs tables of Wo Fat's restaurant. Seamen, gunnery sergeants, and buck privates drank hard and long at tough-knuckled places such as the Mint, the Two Jackets, and Bill Leader's bar. More than a few servicemen pursued what passed for brief romantic interludes in rooms at such "hotels" as the Rex, the Pensacola, and the New Senate.

Tomorrow, of course, would be Sunday, a day when officer and enlisted man alike—save for those on watch, guard, or kitchen police duties—would be free to rest. And to wonder why, if Saturday night had been so good, how come he felt so bad? The best thing about Saturday night was that a man always had time for one more drink. Tomorrow was tomorrow. It would take care of itself.

At midnight, the dancing at the decorous Royal Hawaiian Hotel stopped. The band played "The Star Spangled Banner." It was time for the revelers to leave.

A few miles offshore, a Japanese submarine rose slowly from the sea. Its commander peered through binoculars at the hotel's pink storybook towers. They were bathed in soft light—the picture of peace in paradise.

At 1:50 A.M. on Sunday, December 7, the aircraft carrier *Akagi* received Yoshikawa's message, relayed from Tokyo. It was the last word Nagumo needed in order to do the mighty deed. He stepped over to the navigator's plotting table and stared at the "fix" mark. The attack fleet was a little less than four hundred miles north of Honolulu. By dawn's early light, he would unleash the Japanese air attack on Pearl Harbor.

Reading Notes: Gordon W. Prange's *At Dawn We Slept: The Untold Story of Pearl Harbor* (McGraw-Hill, 1981) contains an in-depth overview of the weeks leading up to the attack. Michael Slackman's *Target: Pearl Harbor* (University of Hawaii Press, 1990) provides a more concise summary. Edwin T. Layton's *"And I Was There": Pearl Harbor and Midway—Breaking the Secrets* (William Morrow, 1985) describes these events as seen by the U.S. command at Pearl Harbor. Ladislas Farago's *The Broken Seal: "Operation Magic" and the Secret Road to Pearl Harbor* (Random House, 1967), Edward Van Der Rhoer's *Deadly Magic* (Scribner's, 1978), and David Kahn's *The Codebreakers* (Macmillan, 1967) contain material on radio intelligence operations prior to the attack.

We Are Americans, Too: War and Minorities in the Twentieth Century

by William F. Mugleston

Because the United States is a nation of minorities (or, as Walt Whitman put it, a "nation of nations"), it faces special problems in wartime unique to no other country. Whoever the foreign enemy may be, that nationality will be represented in the populace of the home front. The following essay examines the experiences of German-Americans in World War I, Japanese-Americans in World War II, and Arab-Americans in more recent times. Minorities with ethnic affiliations to a foe abroad are often the objects of unreasoning fear, suspicion, and hatred. Americans exhibit a disturbing readiness to suspend traditional civil liberties in wartime, ironic behavior for a country that wages its battles in support of freedom and democracy abroad.

"Evidently we are the most reactionary country in the world right now," Felix Frankfurter exclaimed in the spring of 1919. Frankfurter, a Harvard law professor and later U.S. Supreme Court Justice, was commenting on the anti-German, anti-Bolshevik hysteria that had swept over the United States during and after World War I. Once the U.S. finally entered the Great War, the quest for one-hundred percent conformity and patriotism knew no limits.

The government's Committee on Public Information, under the zealous leadership of journalist George Creel, did a masterful job of whipping up civilian opinion in support of the war effort. It published some thirty pamphlets in many languages explaining to the world America's role in the war. It encouraged citizens to report critics of the war to the Justice Department, dispatched an army of "Four-Minute Men" to give patriotic pep talks to women's clubs, movie audiences, lodges, and anyone else who would listen, and produced films that praised the American fighting man and portrayed his German enemy as bestial Huns raping and pillaging their way across Europe, with the

Western Hemisphere their next target. The CPI recruited professional historians to pin the blame for the outbreak of the war squarely on Germany, a gross distortion of the historical record. Billboards encouraging citizen loyalty blanketed the land. Creel even planted stories in hundreds of foreign newspapers extolling the American version of the war's origin and goals.

Across the country, the fury of anti-German sentiment ran rampant. Perfectly loyal citizens of German extraction found yellow paint splashed on their homes. Schoolchildren with German surnames were beaten up by classmates. Near St. Louis, Missouri in April, 1918, a mob of 500 seized young German-born Robert Prager, who had attempted to join the American Navy but been rejected for medical reasons. Stripped and wrapped in an American flag, he was dragged through the streets and then lynched. After a trial that acquitted the mob leaders, one jury member shouted, "Well, I guess nobody can say we aren't loyal now."

The Governor of Iowa urged that no public conversations be allowed in German. Sauerkraut became "liberty cabbage," dachshunds "liberty pups," the frankfurter became a "hot dog," German measles "liberty measles," hamburger "liberty steak," and Berlin Street in New Orleans General Pershing Street. Orchestras stopped playing German music; librarians pulled books about Germany from the shelves (and sometimes burned them, shades of a later Nazi Germany). Public schools banned the teaching of the German language, and some universities abolished their entire German departments, apparently reversing the old advice to "know your enemy."

Two pieces of federal legislation, the June 1917 Espionage Act and the more extreme Sedition Act of May 1918, gave a gloss of legality to this crusade. Under this legislation persons who opposed the draft or the sale of government bonds, discouraged recruiting by the military, or who would "wilfully utter, print, write or publish any disloyal, profane, scurrilous or abusive langauge about the form of government of the United States, or the Constitution or the flag, or the uniform of the Army or Navy, or bring the form of government . . . or the Constitution . . . into contempt . . . or advocate any curtailment of production of anything necessary to the prosecution of the war" were subject to imprisonment up to twenty years and fines up to $10,000.

Under these laws the government banned Socialist newspapers from the mails, jailed some 400 conscientious objectors, and prosecuted those who cited the pacifistic teachings of Christianity. Eugene V. Debs, veteran labor organizer and leader of the Socialist Party, was sentenced to twenty years in a federal prison for speaking out against the war. (As Socialist candidate for President in 1920, he polled over 900,000 votes while behind bars. President Warren G. Harding pardoned him in 1921 after the wartime hysteria had subsided.) Victor Berger, editor of the socialist Milwaukee *Leader* and a U.S. Congressman from that city, received a similar sentence for antiwar editorials in his paper. Congress twice refused him a seat to which he had been duly elected.

If it was any comfort to them, German-Americans were not the only targets of militant patriotism and intolerance. Normal American freedoms of expression to criticize the government, its leaders and taxes went by the board for all citizens in a frenzy of conformity and suppression of free speech that Americans would have found intolerable in more placid times. One woman received a ten-year jail term for saying, "I am for the people, and the government is for the profiteers." Normal lunchtime conversation between workers, in which one might innocently complain about taxes or express war weariness, could bring a knock on the door from agents of the Justice Department concerning one's loyalty. Moreover, the efforts of the Committee on Public Information and other federal authorities spawned amateur spy chasers and local witch hunts around the country. In Butte, Montana in August, 1917, Frank Little, a union organizer for the antiwar Industrial Workers of the World, was tied to the rear of an automobile, dragged through the streets, and hanged.

Although over 2100 persons were prosecuted under the Espionage and Sedition Acts, fewer than half of those were convicted, and only ten for actual sabotage. It hardly excuses what was done that most of those convicted unjustly were released at war's end as passions subsided. All in all, the vast majority of Americans in World War I paid their taxes, bought their liberty bonds, supported their country, and went about their daily lives and work as they usually do in peace and war. The crusades of federal authorities, federal and state courts, and assorted lynch mobs and "committees of public safety" seemed a classic exercise in overkill against exaggerated threats. Every wartime government necessarily engages in propaganda to keep up the spirits of its citizenry, but in a society such as the United States, with a tradition of human rights and civil liberties, World War I sorely tested the boundaries of those rights. While engaged in a war to save democracy abroad, Americans came perilously close to losing it at home.

* * * * *

President Franklin Roosevelt promised Americans, shortly after Pearl Harbor, "We will not, under any threat, or in the face of any danger, surrender the guarantees of liberty our forefathers framed for us in our Bill of Rights." Indeed, the climate for German-Americans was considerably better in the Second World War. The shock of the Pearl Harbor attack pulled Americans together in the war effort, and there was little public dissent. Even American Communists supported the war against Hitler. German-Americans made it clear they were pro-American and dissociated themselves from the horrors of Nazi Germany. Moreover, they were now large enough in numbers and strong enough politically to fend off abuses. Pro-Nazi fringe groups such as the Khaki Shirts and Silver Shirts were poorly led, small in membership, and impotent politically. Even the larger German-American Bund, which staged some impressive rallies in the late thirties, feeding on anti-Semitic and isolationist sentiment, was well-infiltrated by the FBI, which determined that the organization's leaders were all talk and little action. The FBI effectively neutralized the few genuine Nazi espionage rings in the United States during the war that were aiming at sabotage and intelligence gathering.

But Roosevelt's promise was not upheld for everyone. Japanese-Americans were the victims of the grossest violation of civil liberties in American wartime history. Their numbers, about 127,000 in 1940, represented only one-tenth of one percent of the American population. Thus there was no political payoff to be gained by any public official in defending them, even if any could be found who felt sympathy for them, an unlikely proposition given the panicky climate immediately after Pearl Harbor.

The Nisei, the majority of the Japanese-Americans, some 80,000, were born in the United States and were as much citizens as those who jailed them. Their elders, the Issei, 47,000 strong, had been born in Japan and immigrated to the U.S., but were declared enemy aliens as soon as the war began, even though some were American veterans of World War I. Those most affected were the 112,000 living on the West Coast. This notably quiet and inoffensive group of people worked in agriculture and small retail businesses, or as fishermen or maids. Few had been able to enter professional occupations; all endured racial prejudice and legalized discrimination of various sorts. They occupied a social and racial niche on the West Coast roughly equivalent to that of blacks elsewhere in the country.

Their dismay over Pearl Harbor and affirmations of loyalty to the United States fell on deaf ears, except to the tiny number of Caucasians who knew them personally. For a time officials feared a Japanese attack on the U.S. mainland, and the assumption was that Japanese living here must be in on it. A lack of evidence of such collusion, confirmed by the FBI, did nothing to calm fears. "The fact that no sabotage has taken place to date is a disturbing and confirming indication that such action will be taken," announced Lieutenant General John L. DeWitt, commander of Army forces in the west.

President Roosevelt signed a proclamation aimed at "enemy aliens." After a virulent campaign by western politicians and newspapers, the Japanese-Americans were ordered to sell their homes and businesses as rapidly as possible and report to temporary holding areas. ". . . To hell with habeas corpus," cried the polemical columnist Westbrook Pegler. More disturbing were the ideas of Walter Lippmann, one of the most respected newspapermen in the country. Since the coastal areas of the West had been officially declared a combat zone, no one without good cause, Lippmann contended, had any business being there. "There is plenty of room elsewhere for him to exercise his rights," although Lippmann failed to explain why other Americans not of Japanese extraction could remain in the combat zone.

The War Relocation Authority established ten major relocation centers in desolate areas of six western states and Arkansas. Here some 112,000 detainees languished for four years behind barbed wire and armed guards. It was difficult but not impossible to leave the camps legally; some 35,000 Japanese-Americans managed to do so. They had to pledge their loyalty to the country and show they had a job waiting or a spot in a college class. Given the widespread animosity and suspicion on the part of the American public, it was unlikely that many camp residents would be welcomed anywhere. Only the American Civil Liberties Union and a few similar organizations vigorously protested the treatment of the Japanese or tried to improve conditions in the camps.

When the Army finally realized that it had able-bodied citizens of military age locked up, it offered them the opportunity to put on the uniform and fight for their country. Amazingly, considering the shabby and unconstitutional treatment they had endured, only 28% refused to swear loyalty to the United States. From the remainder was formed the 442nd Regimental Combat Team, which, along with another battalion of Japanese-Hawaiians, performed battle in Europe with astounding valor and without a single desertion.

Most depressing, perhaps, the Supreme Court in a series of cases upheld the evacuation of the Japanese from their homes, deferring to military necessity. Justice Harlan Fiske Stone, while deploring "distinctions between citizens solely because of their ancestry," concluded nonetheless that "in a time of war residents having ethnic affiliations with an invading enemy may be a greater source of danger than those of a different ancestry," a sentiment German-Americans in an earlier conflict would have understood well. In truth, not one camp detainee was ever accused of sabotage, much less found guilty. As one fisherman remembered, "We hadn't done anything wrong. We obeyed the laws. I lost everything." Then he added, with remarkable charity, "But I don't blame anyone. It was a war."

Litigation over the right of internees to sue the federal government for property losses slowly made its way through the court system in the postwar years. In 1986 a federal court of appeals ruled in favor of the surviving detainees, and two years later President Ronald Reagan signed the Civil Liberties Act of 1988. Congress officially apologized for the wartime treatment of Japanese-Americans, and each survivor (an estimated 60,000) won a one-time tax-free payment of $20,000. Yet while signing the Act, President Reagan stated that it was "not for us today to pass judgement upon those who may have made mistakes while engaged in that great [wartime] struggle." Some questioned that conclusion. If those living could not pass judgement on or learn from the mistakes of their forebears, then history is a poor tool for understanding the present or avoiding similar tragedies in the future. Indeed, even the Japanese-American community itself was divided over the wisdom of financial reparations to survivors. Some argued that it was more critical to turn some of the camps into memorials to a great American injustice, and, said Senator Daniel Inouye of Hawaii, a veteran of the 442nd, to "awaken this experience enough to haunt the conscience of this nation."

* * * * *

Apparently the lessons of two world wars were not well learned. In recent times, as the United States has periodically experienced stormy relations with certain Middle Eastern countries, the same outcroppings of bigotry and distrust toward minorities have surfaced again. Following the seizure of 58

American hostages in Teheran, Iran in November 1979, persons living in the United States who "looked Iranian" felt the sting of suspicion. The American bombing of Libya in April 1986, hostage-taking in Lebanon, and terrorism directed against American overseas military personnel and international airline passengers added to domestic tensions. Any residents of the United States who spoke with an accent and looked like they were from the Middle East or North Africa could be objects of fear, mistrust, and hatred. The need for such an organization as the American-Arab Anti-Discrimination Committee was a testimony to the depth of the problem. Some Americans indicted all Iranians and all Libyans (like all Japanese-Americans earlier), or made no distinctions between Middle Eastern nationalities and cultures ("They're all the same"), lumping Iraqis, Iranians, Libyans, Egyptians, Palestinians, Jordanians, Lebanese and Saudi Arabians into one homogeneous whole, as was earlier done with Chinese, Japanese, and other Asians.

The 1991 Persian Gulf war against Saddam Hussein's Iraq continued the pattern. Although the conflict ended quickly and decisively, there was still time for probes of dubious legality against U.S. residents with ethnic ties to the Middle East. In clear violation of First Amendment rights, the FBI questioned Arab-Americans about their political beliefs, associations, and knowledge of terrorist plots, as if any random Arab-American was necessarily an expert on terrorism. In February a major American airline denied access to its flights to all passengers with Iraqi passports, and backed off only under pressure of a lawsuit. Yet discriminatory practices against Arab-American travelers continued. In Missouri, a telephone caller told an Arab-American, "You belong to Iraq or Iran. I don't care where you go but get out of this country. You don't belong here." A Texas pastor announced that Arabs "are the way they are because they worship the Devil." Arab-Americans were physically assaulted in stores and malls, had their lives threatened, and their homes and businesses vandalized and sometimes burned. Arabs who bore the common surname Hussein faced special problems and were often urged to change their names (as some German-Americans did in World War I). T-shirts denigrating Arabs were big sellers during the Gulf war; some radio talk show hosts told crude anti-Arab jokes. Movies and television sometimes stereotyped Arabs as crazed terrorists or oil-rich profiteers. Even when newspapers ran serious stories on the Mideast conflict, Arab interviewees were sometimes threatened. "I will kill you if the Americans in Kuwait are hurt," a caller warned an Arab-American newspaper reporter in Michigan. A teenager from Iraq living in the United States expressed the fear of many of his peers: "A lot of my elders have spoken about how, if Americans become paranoid, they may decide to place [Arabs] in internment camps like the Japanese in World War II. It is a really scary situation."

* * * * *

"If the war didn't happen to kill you, it was bound to start you thinking," commented one of George Orwell's characters on the First World War. Such a statement could apply to America's wars as well. From the Revolutionary

War, that won independence for a slave-holding nation, to the War of 1812, that confirmed that independence, to the Mexican War, that ripped open the scar of slavery, to the Civil War, the bloodiest of them all, that vindicated the union, to the Spanish-American War, that introduced the United States to the world, to two world wars, that established America's world superpower status, to the unjustly forgotten Korean War, to the agony of Vietnam, that finally circumscribed the limits of American empire, war has dramatically enlarged the economy of the United States, magnified its power in world affairs, redefined relations between the races, and enhanced the roles of women. It has brought untold grief but also boundless pride to millions of families. Most worrisome, however, has been the ease with which Americans have been willing to suspend their traditional freedoms in the frenzied pursuit of foreign enemies. In times of peace and feelings of national security, rights of free speech, dissent, and nonconformity are more easily tolerated. Wartime, however, is the supreme test of a nation's commitment to civil liberties, when not only national security but national existence itself may seem threatened. But can the Bill of Rights be turned on and off so easily?

The greatest of all American Presidents saw the problem long before the wars of modern times. Early in 1864, contemplating the bleak Union prospects on the battlefield, calls for postponement of the Republican nominating convention, and the unlikelihood of his own re-election that fall, Abraham Lincoln wrote, "We cannot have free government without elections; and if the [southern] rebellion could force us to forego or postpone a national election, it might fairly claim to have already conquered and ruined us." Twentieth-century Americans might well have asked themselves if their generations's wars had also forced them to forsake basic national values and institutions.

Since 1945, the American people, like those who lived in earlier eras, have experienced both good times and bad. During the immediate post-World War II years, most Americans were anxious to resume a normal life after the hardships of the war and the prededing Great Depression. In fact, the 1950's were years characterized by general prosperity and political consensus. At the same time, the African American minority resumed serious challenges to the established order. The demand for change expanded in the years since 1960, as American Indians, Hispanics, women, and recent immigrants sought their portion of the enduring American Dream.

Political unrest accompanied the social turmoil and the divisive war in Vietnam during the 1960's and early 1970's. From the time of the assassination of President John F. Kennedy to the resignation of President Richard M. Nixon, the political order was often stretched to its limits. Increasingly in recent years, Americans have become disillusioned and chose to treat politics as a spectator sport that they preferred to watch on television.

In foreign policy, the tragedy of the Vietnam War was balanced to some extent by the apparent triumph of the United States in the Cold War. Placing these developments in perspective provides another opportunity to learn from our collective experience. As students and products of our history, we must continue to draw upon the strengths of our heritage to deal more effectively with the global and domestic challenges which lie ahead.

1945-Present

The Fifties: A New Perspective

by William L. O'Neill

The decade of the 1950s has often been derided by historians and social critics alike as a period of mindless consumerism in an anesthetizing suburban environment, where babies, Buicks and backyard barbecues were the highest civic priorities, all presided over by a popular though out-of-touch and uninvolved president. This is a commonplace but inaccurate view of the fifties, asserts William L. O'Neill, Professor of History at Rutgers University, in the following interview. The desire for the suburban lifestyle was not unique to the fifties, O'Neill maintains, but has been the norm for much of the modern American history. White Americans of the period enjoyed strong family ties, low divorce and crime rates, stable employment, high educational levels, and healthy cities, things Americans of later times could only envy. While minorities certainly did not share equally in this abundance and suffered shameful segregation and discrimination, even their family structures were more intact than in the 1980s and 90s. National leadership fostered low inflation, "sensible national economic policies," and a continuation of popular New Deal programs. O'Neill is the author of *American High* (1986) and numerous other works.

Interview: William O'Neill

Q. Professor O'Neill, in general, what sort of American dream was envisioned in post World War II domestic life? How was this dream defined by and for whom?

A. Well, the stereotype everyone is familiar with is the "Leave it to Beaver" sort of thing or "Happy Days." The family in the suburbs living the good life, and that stereotype actually reflects the desires that people had at the time. There was a tremendous desire on the part of Americans to get into the new suburban home and experience all the things that we associate with the stereotype. It was genuinely wanted and an extraordinarily large number of people were able to get it. There are obvious exceptions. Minorities don't figure in this and for blacks the 50s was not a great period of upward growth and suburban mobility. But a surprisingly large number of white families achieved their dream.

Q. What explains that at that particular time so many people seemed to buy into that?

A. Well, people had always wanted to do it, this desire to get out of the city and to have grass and your own house and so on. That goes very far back. If you read the histories of suburbanization, they talk about the suburban dream that people had even before the Civil War. The problems was, it wasn't technically doable. People didn't make enough money. World War II is what really made it possible for such large numbers to own suburban homes. There were 16 million, mostly men, who served in World War II and were eligible for the GI Bill. After the war, the GI Bill enabled you [to] buy a house for nothing down and with interest payments of around four or five percent. You could buy a house for less than you could rent an apartment, and thanks to the improvement in the highways and the great flood of motor cars that were being produced and sold, it was now possible to get from your ideal suburban home to a job some distance away. And income levels were higher on a broader level as well.

Q. Why did so many people buy into what appears to be the conformity of the era of the 1950s?

A. Well, my belief is that this whole notion of there being an unusual level of conformity and herd-mindedness in the fifties is a myth that was invented by disappointed social critics at the time. The people who developed this thesis had been radicalized in the 1930s, had been Marxists or Trotskyists or whatever, and [while] the thirties had been from an economic standpoint disastrous for many Americans, it had been terrific for politically minded people, especially those on the left. It was the thirties that were unusual, not the fifties. The fifties were typical in that historically, most Americans have been interested primarily in getting a good job and raising their families and educating them as well as they can. That's the normal thing. So books like *The Lonely Crowd* and the like I think simply falsified reality. People were doing what they had always done, or what they had always wanted to do but couldn't afford. And it had a positive side to it too. I mean, when we look back now on the fifties, you look at this criticism on the one hand of it being a period of mindless conformity and so on and so on. On the other hand, what you see are stable family structures, the divorce rate was extremely low, and the educational level was higher than it had ever been before. This was the time when intact family structure and a highly successful national infrastructure and sensible national economic policies combined to bring a better life to more people than had ever been the case before.

Q. Let's go back and pick up on that point you were making in terms of who was excluded from the "American dream" in the late forties into the 1950s? What groups were left out in particular?

A. Blacks, the largest minority, are conspicuous because segregation continued throughout the period. The fight against it of course begins with *Brown v. Board of Education* in '54 that started desegregating the schools, and then in '55 you've got Martin Luther King and [the] bus boycott in Montgomery. So, the fight that's going to be successful in the sixties gets started in the fifties. It doesn't have very much effect at first, and America remained a very segregated society, north and south. The north [was] not legally bound by statutes like in the south. But the north was just as segregated, in some ways more segregated than the south. So blacks are really left out and they aspire by and large to the same things. I mean black dreams were not really any different than those of whites, but discrimination and segregation really left them out of it at that point. Feminists disliked the fifties a lot. One always hears about the feminine mystique, the way that women were supposed to lack independence, and Betty Friedan's *The Feminine Mystique* spoke to an audience that suffered from the prejudice against women having careers and the like. When I entered graduate school in the late 1950s, a professor gave a speech to the incoming graduate students and he said to us literally in so many words, if you're married or female, get out. There's no room for people who are not serious in this program. That was a very widespread attitude at the time. So, feminists rightly complain about the opportunities that women were denied. On the plus side, there was a traditional social contract involved which was still being kept, in which the wives agreed to raise the family and take care of the home and so on, and husbands agreed to support them. The men did in fact support them. The divorce rate was low. So although it's a traditional arrangement and one that feminists rightly complain about because of the lack of opportunity, it also made for a very healthy family structure. It was a good way to bring up children.

Q. Focusing in specifically on labor-management relations, although there was a period of severe strikes in '46 as we made the transition to a peacetime economy, it seems as though there did develop in this era management's willingness to go along with unions. To what extent was there a fundamental change in labor-management relations in the late 40s and into the 1950s?

A. It took place primarily during the war. The thirties had been a period of great union organization and intense confrontation and fabulous strikes that sometimes literally went on for years in the case of the little steel companies. The last labor massacre took place in 1937 when Republic Steel guards fired into a crowd of 100 men, women and children and killed ten or twelve. That was traditional labor-management relations. During the war, the government prevented that. The unions gave a no-strike pledge and the government in return insisted that management grant unions certain kinds of security and job guarantees and work force rules and the like. So, corporations had to negotiate with union leaders whether they liked it or not because otherwise they would lose their government contracts. What they discovered was that this was not nearly as difficult a relationship as they had supposed. That in fact the union leaders were not revolutionaries, they weren't out to break the company, and that if you had a good working relationship with union leaders you would have fewer wildcat strikes and a more dependable work force. So there were advantages which many employers had failed to realize, plus it didn't cost anything because in the postwar period, whatever you had to pay out to workers in terms of extra benefits and pay you could make back by raising the prices of your goods. There was no foreign competition. Nobody buys Japanese cars. The Japanese aren't even making cars at this point. So the American market is one in which you don't need protection because there are no competitors, and manufacturers could simply pass the costs along to the consumers. And it worked wonderfully for everyone because consumers were making more money and could afford the higher costs of the automobile or whatever. So, [in] the fifties there were strikes, but on the whole labor-management relations smoothed out a lot and there was a nice reciprocal back-scratching arrangement established that lasted for several decades.

Q. Just a brief follow up on that. How confident were Americans in this new economic stability of the 1950s?

A. During the war, and immediately afterwards, there was a lot of apprehension, and many predictions that once this great wave of government spending stopped as a result of the war, you'd probably go back to the thirties again. There was a great fear that the depression was going to come back or at least some aspects of the depression. And I think the first few years after the war, particularly among older people whose memory of it was most vivid, there were worries about this. By the 1950s these had pretty much disappeared. The strength of the economy turned out not to be a flash in the pan as everybody had supposed.

Q. Why was there a GI Bill for World War II veterans and, first of all, what were the short-term effects of that?

A. The GI Bill is one of the greatest pieces of legislation Congress ever passed, and the reason they did it was because there was a tradition after previous wars of paying cash bonuses to veterans. There had been a Civil War bonus and a First World War bonus and these had inevitably led to all kinds of political fighting and struggling because the veterans were always complaining about the terms of the bonus and when was it going to be paid, and during the Depression there had been bonus marches on Washington in which World War I veterans wanted their cash early, now, when they needed it, not twenty years later. So Congress for once gave the problem a lot of thought and concluded that what they ought to do was not just hand out a packet of cash. It didn't seem to do much good anyway and it was politically complicated, so they worked [out] a program by which the government would support you, not completely, but would offer considerable support if you wanted to buy a house, if you wanted to go to school, if you wanted to start your own business. Well, it was a great [success]. I wish we had something like this today and not just for veterans. It was helped also by the fact [that] when you talk about the life of the fifties, you're talking about people who went through World War II as young men and young women. The typical man spent three years in the service and that meant that their wives if they were married, or their fiancees, were separated from their loved ones for three years and often trying to keep homes and raise children under very difficult wartime circumstances. This generation had been through a tough experience, more than most American generations, and the result had been, interestingly enough, to make them extraordinarily enthusiastic and motivated about fitting into civilian life and really making a go of it. They were unlike the poor veterans of the Vietnam war who often came back so demoralized and felt rejected by society. World War II veterans had had a terrible time if they'd been in combat. I mean, the war was much bigger and more dreadful and many more Americans were killed in it than in Vietnam. But it took place in a positive context, where people appreciated them and where their accomplishments were recognized. So, when they got back to being civilians, they were going to be 200% civilians and they were going to work harder and study more and get a better house, than any generation before them. Their common experience and their motivation, together with the GI Bill, created this tremendous start for the period.

Q. Long term, what were the effects of that GI Bill?

A. Well, the long term, I think, was to create a class of Americans who were better educated and more prosperous than had ever been the case before, and the success of the United States in the fifties and sixties has a lot to do with the emergence of this generation. I mean, it worked, the long term effects I think were very great. They had some ideas that were difficult to deal with later on, their sense of patriotism and respect for order and so on. It was hard for many of them to sympathize with the sort of values that developed in the sixties and later on. But on the whole they've done a pretty good job it seems to me.

Q. Would you comment very briefly on the effects of the GI Bill on the black veteran?

A. I said earlier that blacks were left out of the American dream in certain respects, but this was not true of the black veteran. Blacks were discriminated against in the armed services during the war, and they served in segregated units for the most part. But a recent study by several historians discovered that black ex-servicemen in the post-war period did much better than blacks who did not go into the army because, like their white counterparts, they had the same energy and ambition and desire to be 200% civilians and they too got the GI Bill of rights and the associated benefits did apply to black Americans and other minorities.

Q. Under President Eisenhower, the Republicans seemed to accept the basic tenets of the New Deal. How and why did this political consensus come about?

A. Yes, you're right. And one of the best things that Eisenhower did was to make it clear that the New Deal was here to stay. The right wing of the Republican Party was very reactionary in this period and still cherished the belief that you could undo the New Deal and take away Social Security and the Securities and Exchange Commission and the T.V.A. and all those things that the New Deal had created. Eisenhower was a very moderate individual and one of the reasons why he went into politics was to nullify that wing of the Republican Party. Although he was a Republican, he could see that by and large these New Deal things had worked. They had great popular support and if the Republican Party spent its time trying to tear them down, it wasn't going to get anywhere. [Eisenhower] says in his memoirs and all his actions are consistent in this regard, that he wanted to reform the Republican Party, to make it an internationalist party and not one that was constantly trying to prevent the United States from having allies, and to make it a party that accepted the realities of American life in the 1950s, one of which was that the New Deal had come here to stay.

Q. How important were presidents Truman and Eisenhower and the federal government in general in maintaining prosperity in the forties and fifties?

A. Under Truman, the federal government was not very helpful. Truman not only knew nothing about economics, he had almost no interest in it and he tended to respond to it in terms of what pressure group was giving him the most heat. So he would go both ways on issues. Inflation was the one where he often took the most flack. When inflation started up after the war, when the wartime controls diminished, first he tried to get inflation controls established, and then when Congress wouldn't go for his bill and passed another bill, he vetoed their bill and then inflation got out of control. Truman had no consistent philosophy and as a result, his management of the economy was not very successful. Fortunately, there were all these savings that were going into the economy, and it was growing, but government policies were not very consistent. Under Eisenhower, you've got a period of very solid economic growth with most of the problems squeezed out. Eisenhower, though he was not very well trained in economics, had a couple of very clear principles in mind. He believed that inflation had to be avoided at all costs and that stable prices were the foundation of prosperity. He also believed that government spending to that end had to be kept out, and he understood that the only way you could really save in government spending was in the military. You couldn't cut back Social Security or the post office, and the Department of Agriculture was too powerful and had too big a constituency. Most areas of the federal budget you couldn't do anything with. But he regarded the military budget as really bloated and he cut it down sharply and then resisted immense political pressure throughout the rest of his administration to enlarge the military. So, he held the line on military spending. He held the line on inflation. He wouldn't cut taxes because taxes are what is keeping the budget balanced. And although like all Republicans, he thought it would be nice if you could find a government that didn't cost anything, he understood that in the real world, you have to pay for what you get. So, more than most presidents, Eisenhower was directly responsible. The United States had other advantages. Again, we didn't have the foreign competition and we had full employment. But he maximized our advantages and was a good shepherd of the economy.

Q. Why did America "need a breathing spell" at this time? Was this to be expected after the stress of the Depression and World War II?

A. Well, I think of the fifteen years after the war as a kind of period of reconstruction. Not exactly in the sense as after the Civil War, but the American people had been through a lot. They'd been through the Great Depression, which had been the most horrifying experience in modern times for most of them, and it was one that almost everybody in the country had experienced in one way or another. It was followed immediately by this tremendous world war which had caused all these upheavals in the country. It had led sixteen million men and women into uniform and about 400,000 of them had been killed in the process and people had to do without everything for four or five years. And there had been the very intense politics of the 1930s, the struggle over the New Deal, and then struggle during the war of what kind of a post-war world it was going to be and what the country was going to do in it. So, by the end of the war, people were really politically exhausted. I think under those circumstances, to have supposed that they would then become deeply involved in crusades for reform and social justice and progress and all that was unreasonable. You cannot keep people up to these high pitches indefinitely. And there was a very large backlog of things that had to be done. There had been almost no residential housing constructed for fifteen years. The housing market collapsed in 1930 and then, during the war, you couldn't get materials. A huge part of the population needed to be rehoused. During the war, most infrastructure work had come to an end. Roads, schools, things like that. Schools were running double shifts, triple shifts at the end of the war. The GIs had to be absorbed and educated and housed and churched and all these things. The low level of political activity is exactly what you would expect under the circumstances, and it was extremely unreasonable of the social and political critics of the time to resent this. I understand why they did, but it's like complaining about the tide. People can only do so much.

Q. What happens during this—as you call it—reconstruction? Do we Americans tend to get regenerated? Do we get the batteries revved up again? Is what goes on during these sorts of periods similar to other such times in our history?

A. Well, there are cycles in American history politically. Arthur Schlesinger, Sr., wrote an article years ago on the cycles of reform, pointing out that reform presidents seem to come along every twenty years or so. And there really does seem to be a cycle in American politics in which you get periods of reform and renewal and then after that reaction and the need to rest and consolidate. So, the 1950s fits into that pattern very well. The thirties had been the great era of reform and then the war had been very demanding in a different kind of way. In the fifties you got a period of consolidation, as it were. The gains of the New Deal were preserved, the economy was built up, people got a chance to recover from their political excitement and expand the physical plant of the country. But, in the course of doing so, most social problems were ignored. Civil rights got very little attention, as did poverty. It's a prosperous period, but you know, there's never a time when there isn't poverty. It had been brought down to some extent, but there was still a lot of it. By the end of the 1950s, this necessary period, I think, of rest and renewal and reconstruction was over. It was time now to deal with the social problems, that's why you needed a change. Eisenhower had been a very fine president in many ways and a much more successful one than most of his critics had expected that he would be before he came into office. But he was a moderate president. A president of the status quo. He was interested in protecting what the country had, and he did a good job of that. But these problems, the race problems and so on were building up. You needed a change and of course, that's what we got in the 60s. We got the right kind of government in the fifties and to a considerable extent in the sixties when we needed it. But it was a different kind of government because the times were different.

Q. What were the long-term effects of the apparent political consensus on the role of government in American life?

A. Well, in my view, the effects of the fifties were not long-term enough. In the sixties there was a lot of political pressure to undo the worst aspects of the 1950s the segregation and the racism and the lack of social services.

And under Lyndon Johnson in particular, much of this was done and you've got the Civil Rights bill and the Voting Rights Act and Medicare and Medicaid and a whole lot of things that the country had really needed which you couldn't get given the politics of the 1950s. That was the positive thing. The negative thing, however, is that in getting rid of what was bad about the fifties we've also managed to get rid of an awful lot that was good about it, the strong family structure, the low divorce rate, the low crime rate, the safe cities. The country as a whole was in many ways a much healthier place in the fifties. Even for blacks, for example, who were so clearly disadvantaged and discriminated against, the fifties were beneficial. The illegitimacy rate among black families in the 1950s was something like 15%. Today it's 65%. The divorce rate generally was about a third of what it is today. The social chaos, the violence, the crime, the disintegrating family structure, these are things we have now that didn't exist in the fifties to anything like the same degree. So, I feel that the fifties has been obliterated to a very large extent and the good has gone down along with the bad.

Q. With Eisenhower's acceptance, like you said, of the continuation of the New Deal, did that mean then that long term, the Republicans, even into the Reagan era, [kept] the basic [belief] that [there was a] legitimate role of the federal government in American economic and social life?

A. The Republican right changed as a result of these experiences. Eisenhower had been, of course, absolutely correct that if the right-wingers persisted they would ruin the GOP as they tended to be racist as well as isolationists and opposed to social programs. They always liked programs that benefitted special business interests. Eisenhower understood that that wing had to go, and in fact it did go. Barry Goldwater's campaign in 1964 was the last attempt of a Republican presidential candidate to undo the New Deal. He criticized Social Security and he was absolutely destroyed at the polls. But, all the same, Goldwater marks the transition because he was not a racist unlike previous conservatives. He was not an isolationist who felt that we shouldn't have a foreign policy. And after his terrific beating, particularly over Social Security, those who felt like him understood that while they would try to prevent future social programs from being instituted, the ones that existed were pretty much sacred so far as the American public was concerned. Nixon I don't think you can call a conservative. I don't know what you could call him exactly. I don't think he had a center. Nixon was the complete political man and totally expedient. But under Reagan, you get this new kind of conservatism that really comes into its own and it's not racist, it is internationalist. It's willing to maintain existing social programs and even make modest expansions in certain ways. So, it's very different from the 50s.

Q. If you would, comment on the positive and perhaps the negative long-range effects of the 1950s on the American psyche or the American mindset. Did it become a significant point of reference for whites as well as minorities?

A. Well, for whites, I would say it's a lost golden age, it really is. This is one of those stereotypes, but this is a period in which a working man and his wife could buy a very nice modern house for twice their normal income in a nice clean suburb where their children would go to school. They could anticipate regular increases in their income as they got older and that they would be living in an essentially drug-free, crime-free environment. That was true not just for middle class people, it was true for a large part of the working class as well. If you worked for Ford or GM, you were in the progressive United Auto Workers with its high benefits and wonderful pension program and the like. So, it is a lost golden age for white Americans in particular, and in many ways more so for white working class Americans even than for middle class Americans. Middle class Americans have survived the economic deterioration of the country that's been going on the last twenty years much better than working class people have because the whole category of well paid union jobs in heavy industry that made the fifties and the sixties so affluent has just virtually disappeared. On the other hand, for feminists and for some blacks, the fifties is the dark age from which the country was fortunate it emerged.

Trumpet of Conscience: A Portrait of Martin Luther King, Jr.

by Stephen B. Oates

Martin Luther King, Jr., was the preeminent figure of the mid-twentieth century civil rights movement in the United States. No one more eloquently articulated the goals and philosophy of the movement or was more persuasive in arguing that non-violence was more effective than violence in overcoming oppression. No other black leader had greater credibility with the nation's white power structure. To the world at large this Nobel Prize winner bestrode his times with selfless devotion and supreme confidence.

But the private King had had to overcome his own legacy of hate, enjoyed the material comforts of life and the company of men of wealth, had a weakness for women, and doubted his own right to lead the masses. In this article Stephen B. Oates paints a sensitive and appreciative portrait of the civil rights leader. Oates, a Professor of History at the University of Massachusetts at Amherst, has written biographies of King, Abraham Lincoln, John Brown, Nat Turner, and William Faulkner.

He was M. L. to his parents, Martin to his wife and friends, Doc to his aides, Reverend to his male parishioners, Little Lord Jesus to adoring churchwomen, De Lawd to his young critics in the Student Nonviolent Coordinating Committee, and Martin Luther King, Jr., to the world. At his pulpit or a public rostrum, he seemed too small for his incomparable oratory and international fame as a civil rights leader and spokesman for world peace. He stood only five feet seven, and had round cheeks, a trim mustache, and sad, glistening eyes—eyes that revealed both his inner strength and his vulnerability.

He was born in Atlanta on January 15, 1929, and grew up in the relative comfort of the black middle class. Thus he never suffered the want and privation that plagued the majority of American blacks of his time. His father, a gruff, self-made man, was pastor of Ebenezer Baptist Church and an outspoken member of Atlanta's black leadership. M. L. joined his father's church when he was five and came to regard it as his second home. The church defined his world, gave it order and balance, taught him how to "get along with people." Here M. L. knew who he was—"Reverend King's boy," somebody special.

At home, his parents and maternal grandmother reinforced his self-esteem, praising him for his precocious ways, telling him repeatedly that he was *somebody.* By age five, he spoke like an adult and had such a prodigious memory that he could recite whole Biblical passages and entire hymns without a mistake. He was acutely sensitive, too, so much so that he worried about all the blacks he saw in Atlanta's breadlines during the Depression, fearful that their children did not have enough to eat. When his maternal grandmother died, twelve-year-old M. L. thought it was his fault. Without telling anyone, he had slipped away from home to watch a parade, only to find out when he returned that she had died. He was terrified that God had taken her away as punishment for his "sin." Guilt-stricken, he tried to kill himself by leaping out of his second-story window.

He had a great deal of anger in him. Growing up a black in segregated Atlanta, he felt the full range of southern racial discrimination. He discovered that he had to attend separate, inferior schools, which he sailed through with a modicum of effort, skipping grades as he went. He found out that he—a preacher's boy—could not sit at lunch counters in Atlanta's downtown stores. He had to drink from a "colored" water fountain, relieve himself in a rancid "colored" restroom, and ride a rickety "colored" elevator. If he rode a city bus, he had to sit in the back as though he were contaminated. If he wanted to see a movie in a downtown theater, he had to enter through a side door and sit in the "colored" section in the balcony. He discovered that whites referred to blacks as "boys" and "girls" regardless of age. He saw "WHITES ONLY" signs staring back at him in the windows of barber shops and all the good restaurants and hotels, at the YMCA, the city parks, golf courses, swimming pools, and in the waiting rooms of the train and bus stations. He learned that there were even white and black sections of the city and that he resided in "nigger town."

Segregation caused a tension in the boy, a tension between his parents' injunction ("Remember, you are *somebody*") and a system that constantly demeaned and insulted him. He struggled with the pain and rage he felt when a white woman in a downtown store slapped him and called him "a little nigger" . . . when a bus driver called him "a black son-of-a-bitch" and made him surrender his seat to a white . . . when he stood on the very spot in Atlanta where whites had lynched a black man . . . when he witnessed nightriding Klansmen beating blacks in the streets. How, he asked defiantly, could he heed the Christian injunction and love a race of people who hated him? In retaliation, he determined "to hate every white person."

Yes, he was angry. In sandlot games, he competed so fiercely that friends could not tell whether he was playing or fighting. He had his share of playground combat, too, and could outwrestle any of his peers. He even rebelled against his father, vowing never to become a preacher like him. Yet he liked the way Daddy King stood up to whites: he told them never to call him a boy and vowed to fight this system until he died.

Still, there was another side to M. L., a calmer, senuous side. He played the violin, enjoyed opera, and relished soul food—fried chicken, cornbread, and collard greens with ham hocks and bacon drippings. By his mid-teens, his voice was the most memorable thing about him. It had changed into a rich and resonant baritone that commanded attention whenever he held forth. A natty dresser, nicknamed "Tweed" because of his fondness for tweed suits, he became a connoisseur of lovely young women. His little brother A. D. remembered how Martin "kept flitting from chick to chick" and was "just about the best jitterbug in town."

At age fifteen, he entered Morehouse College in Atlanta, wanting somehow to help his people. He thought about becoming a lawyer and even practiced giving trial speeches before a mirror in his room. But thanks largely to Morehouse President Benjamin Mays, who showed him that the ministry could be a respectable forum for ideas, even for social protest, King decided to become a Baptist preacher after all. By the time he was ordained in 1947, his resentment toward whites had softened some, thanks to positive contact with white students on an intercollegiate council. But he hated his segregated world more than ever.

Once he had his bachelor's degree, he went north to study at Crozer Seminary near Philadelphia. In this mostly white school, with its polished corridors and quiet solemnity, King continued to ponder the plight of blacks in America. How, by what method and means, were blacks to improve their lot in a white-dominated country? His study of history, especially of Nat Turner's slave insurrection, convinced him that it was suicidal for a minority to strike back against a heavily armed majority. For him, voluntary segregation was equally unacceptable, as was accommodation to the status quo. King shuddered at such negative approaches to the race problem. How indeed were blacks to combat discrimination in a country ruled by the white majority?

As some other blacks had done, he found his answer in the teachings of Mohandas Gandhi—for young King, the discovery had the force of a conversion experience. Nonviolent resistance, Gandhi taught, meant noncooperation with evil, an idea he got from Henry David Thoreau's essay "On Civil Disobedience." In India, Gandhi gave Thoreau's theory practical application in the form of strikes, boycotts, and protest marches, all conducted nonviolently and all predicated on love for the oppressor and a belief in divine justice. In gaining Indian independence, Gandhi sought not to defeat the British, but to redeem them through love, so as to avoid a legacy of bitterness. Gandhi's term for this—*Satyagraha*—reconciled love and force in a single, powerful concept.

As King discovered from his studies, Gandhi had embraced nonviolence in part to subdue his own violent nature. This was a profound revelation for King, who had felt much hatred in his life, especially toward whites. Now Gandhi showed him a means of harnessing his anger and channeling it into a positive and creative force for social change.

At this juncture, King found mostly theoretical satisfaction in Gandhian nonviolence; he had no plans to become a radical activist in the segregated South. Indeed, he seemed destined to a life of the mind, not of social protest. In 1951, he graduated from Crozer and went on to earn a Ph.D. in theology from Boston University, where his adviser pronounced him "a scholar's scholar" of great intellectual potential. By 1955, a year after the school desegregation decision, King had married comely Coretta Scott and assumed the pastorship of Dexter Avenue Baptist Church in Montgomery, Alabama. Immensely happy in the world of ideas, he hoped eventually to teach theology at a major university or seminary.

But, as King liked to say, the *Zeitgist,* or spirit of the age, had other plans for him. In December 1955, Montgomery blacks launched a boycott of the city's segregated buses and chose the articulate twenty-six-year-old minister as their spokesman. As it turned out, he was unusually well prepared to assume the kind of leadership thrust on him. Drawing on Gandhi's teachings and example, plus the tenets of his own Christian faith, King directed a nonviolent boycott designed both to end an injustice and redeem his white adversaries through love. When he exhorted blacks to love their enemies, King did not mean to love them as friends or intimates. No, he said, he meant a disinterested love in all humankind, a love that saw the neighbor in everyone it met, a love that sought to restore the beloved community. Such love not only avoided the internal violence of the spirit, but severed the eternal chain of hatred that only produced more hatred in an endless spiral. If American blacks could break the chain of hatred, King said, true brotherhood could begin. Then posterity would have to say that there had lived a race of people, of black people, who "injected a new meaning into the veins of history and civilization."

During the boycott King imparted his philosophy at twice-weekly mass meetings in the black churches, where overflow crowds clapped and cried as his mellifluous voice swept over them. In these mass meetings King discovered his extraordinary power as an orator. His rich religious imagery reached deep into the black psyche, for religion had been the black people's main source of strength and survival since slavery days. His delivery was "like a narrative poem," said a woman journalist who heard him. His voice had such depths of sincerity and empathy that it could "charm your heart right out of your body." Because he appealed to the best in his people, articulating their deepest hurts and aspirations, black folk began to idolize him; he was their Gandhi.

Under his leadership, they stood up to white Montgomery in a remarkable display of solidarity. Pitted against an obdurate city government that blamed the boycott on Communist agitation and resorted to psychological and legal warfare to break it, the blacks stayed off the buses month after month, and walked or rode in a black-operated carpool. When an elderly woman refused the offer of a ride, King asked her, "But don't your feet hurt?" "Yes," she replied, "my feet is tired but my soul is rested." For King, her irrepressible spirit was proof that "a new Negro" was emerging in the South, a Negro with "a new sense of dignity and destiny."

That "new Negro" menaced white supremacists, especially the Ku Klux Klan, and they persecuted King with a vengeance. They made obscene phone calls to his home, sent him abusive, sickening letters, and once even dynamited the front of his house. Nobody was hurt, but King, fearing a race war, had to dissuade angry blacks from violent retaliation. Finally, on November 13, 1956, the U.S. Supreme Court nullified the Alabama laws that enforced segregated buses, and handed King and his boycotters a resounding moral victory. Their protest had captured the imagination of progressive people all over the world and marked the beginning of a southern black movement that would shake the segregated South to its foundations. At the forefront of that movement was a new organization, the Southern Christian Leadership Conference (SCLC), which King and other black ministers formed in 1957, with King serving as its president and guiding spirit. Operating through the southern black church, SCLC sought to enlist the black masses in the freedom struggle by expanding "the Montgomery way" across the South.

The "Miracle of Montgomery" changed King's life, catapulting him into international prominence as an inspiring new moral voice for civil rights. Across the country, blacks and whites alike wrote him letters of encouragement; *Time* magazine pictured him on its cover; the National Association for the Advancement of Colored People (NAACP) and scores of church and civil organizations vied for his services as a speaker. "I am really disturbed how fast all this has happened to me," King told his wife. "People will expect me to perform miracles for the rest of my life."

But fame had its evil side, too. When King visited New York in 1958, a deranged black woman stabbed him in the chest with a letter opener. The weapon was lodged so close to King's aorta, the main artery from the heart, that he would have died had he sneezed. To extract the blade, an interracial surgical team had to remove a rib and part of his breastbone; in a burst of inspiration, the lead surgeon made the incision over King's heart in the shape of a cross.

That he had not died convinced King that God was preparing him for some larger work in the segregated South. To gain perspective on what was happening there, he made a pilgrimage to India to visit Gandhi's shrine and the sites of his "War for Independence." He returned home with an even deeper commitment to nonviolence and a vow to be more humble and ascetic like Gandhi. Yet he was a man of manifold contradictions, this American Gandhi. While renouncing material things and giving nearly all of his extensive honorariums to SCLC, he liked posh hotels and zesty meals with wine, and he was always immaculately dressed in a gray or black suit, white shirt, and tie.

While caring passionately for the poor, the downtrodden, and the disinherited, he had a fascination with men of affluence and enjoyed the company of wealthy SCLC benefactors. While trumpeting the glories of nonviolence and redemptive love, he could feel the most terrible anger when whites murdered a black or bombed a black church; he could contemplate giving up, turning America over to the haters of both races, only to dedicate himself anew to his nonviolent faith and his determination to redeem his country.

In 1960, he moved his family to Atlanta so that he could devote himself fulltime to SCLC, which was trying to register black voters for the upcoming federal elections. That same year, southern black students launched the sit-in movement against segregated lunch counters, and King not only helped them form the Student Nonviolent Coordinating Committee (SNCC) but raised money on their behalf. In October he even joined a sit-in protest at an Atlanta department store and went to jail with several students on a trespassing charge. Like Thoreau, King considered jail "a badge of honor." To redeem the nation and arouse the conscience of the opponent, King explained, you go to jail and stay there. "You have broken a law which is out of line with the moral law and you are willing to suffer the consequences by serving the time."

He did not reckon, however, on the tyranny of racist officials, who clamped him in a malevolent state penitentiary, in a cell for hardened criminals. But state authorities released him when Democratic presidential nominee John F. Kennedy and his brother Robert interceded on King's behalf. According to many analysts, the episode won critical black votes for Kennedy and gave him the election in November. For King, the election demonstrated what he had long said: that one of the most significant steps a black could take was the short walk to the voting booth.

The trouble was that most blacks in Dixie, especially in the Deep South, could not vote even if they so desired. For decades, state and local authorities had kept the mass of black folk off the voting rolls by a welter of devious obstacles and outright intimidation. Through 1961 and 1962, King exhorted President Kennedy to sponsor tough new civil rights legislation that would enfranchise southern blacks and end segregated public accommodations as well. When Kennedy shied away from a strong civil rights commitment, King and his lieutenants took matters into their own hands, orchestrating a series of southern demonstrations to show the world the brutality of segregation. At the same time, King stumped the country, drawing on all his powers of oratory to enlist the black masses and win white opinion to his cause.

Everywhere he went his message was the same. *The civil rights issue,* he said, *is an eternal moral issue that will determine the destiny of our nation and our world. As we seek our full rights, we hope to redeem the soul of our country. For it is our country, too, and we will win our freedom because the sacred heritage of America and the eternal will of God are embodied in our echoing demands. We do not intend to humiliate the white man, but to win him over through the strength of our love. Ultimately, we are trying to free all of us in America—Negroes from the bonds of segregation and shame, whites from the bonds of bigotry and fear.*

We stand today between two worlds—the dying old order and the emerging new. With men of ill-will greeting this change with cries of violence, of interposition and nullification, some of us may get beaten. Some of us may even get killed. But if you are cut down in a movement designed to save the soul of a nation, no other death could be more redemptive. We must realize that change does not roll in "on the wheels of inevitability," but comes through struggle. So "let us be those creative dissenters who will call our beloved nation to a higher destiny, to a new plateau of compassion, to a more noble expression of humaneness."

That message worked like magic among America's long-suffering blacks. Across the South, across America, they rose in unprecedented numbers to march and demonstrate with Martin Luther King. His singular achievement was that he brought the black masses into the freedom struggle for the first time. He rallied the strength of broken men and women, 'helping them overcome a lifetime of fear and feelings of inferiority. After segregation had taught them all their lives that they were *nobody,* King taught them that they were *somebody.* Because he made them believe in themselves and in the beauty of chosen suffering, he taught them how to straighten their backs ("a man can't ride you unless your back is bent") and confront those who oppressed them. Through the technique of nonviolent resistance, he furnished them something no previous black leader had been able to provide. He showed them a way of controlling their pent-up anger, as he had controlled his own, and using it to bring about constructive change.

The mass demonstrations King and SCLC choreographed in the South produced the strongest civil rights legislation in American history. This was the goal of King's major southern campaigns from 1963 to 1965. He would single out some notoriously segregated city with white officials prone to violence, mobilize the local blacks with songs, scripture readings, and rousing oratory in black churches, and then lead them on protest marches conspicuous for their grace and moral purpose. Then he and his aides would escalate the marches, increase their demands, even fill up the jails, until they brought about a moment of "creative tension," when whites would either agree to negotiate or resort to violence. If they did the latter, King would thus expose the brutality inherent in segregation and so stab the national conscience so that the federal government would be forced to intervene with corrective measures.

The technique succeeded brilliantly in Birmingham, Alabama, in 1963. Here Police Commissioner Eugene "Bull" Connor, in full view of reporters and television cameras, turned firehoses and police dogs on the marching protestors. Revolted by such ghastly scenes, stricken by King's own searching eloquence and the bravery of his unarmed followers, Washington eventually produced the 1964 Civil Rights Act, which desegregated public facilities— the thing King had demanded all along from Birmingham. Across the South, the "WHITES ONLY" signs that had hurt and enraged him since boyhood now came down.

Although SNCC and others complained that King had a Messiah complex and was trying to monopolize the civil rights movement, his technique worked with equal success in Selma, Alabama, in 1965. Building on a local movement there, King and his staff launched a drive to gain southern blacks the unobstructed right to vote. The violence he exposed in Selma—the beating of black marchers by state troopers and deputized possemen, the killing of a young black deacon and a white Unitarian minister—horrified the country. When King called for support, thousands of ministers, rabbis, priests, nuns, students, lay leaders, and ordinary people—black and white alike—rushed to Selma from all over the country and stood with King in the name of human liberty. Never in the history of the movement had so many people of all faiths and classes come to the southern battleground. The Selma campaign culminated in a dramatic march over the Jefferson Davis Highway to the state capital of Montgomery. Along the way, impoverished local blacks stared incredulously at the marching, singing, flag-waving spectacle moving by. When the column reached one dusty crossroads, an elderly black woman ran out from a group of old folk, kissed King breathlessly, and ran back crying, "I done kissed him! The Martin Luther King! I done kissed the Martin Luther King!"

In Montgomery, first capital and much-heralded "cradle" of the Confederacy, King led an interracial throng of 25,000—the largest civil rights demonstration the South had ever witnessed—up Dexter Avenue with banners waving overhead. The pageant was as ironic as it was extraordinary, for it was up Dexter Avenue that Jefferson Davis's first inaugural parade had marched, and in the portico of the capital Davis had taken his oath of office as president of the slave-based Confederacy. Now, in the spring of 1965, Alabama blacks—most of them descendants of slaves—stood massed at the same statehouse, singing a new rendition of "We Shall Overcome," the anthem of the civil rights movement. They sang, "Deep in my heart, I do believe, We have overcome—*today*."

Then, within view of the statute of Jefferson Davis, and watched by cordons of state troopers and television cameras, King mounted a trailer. His vast audience listened, transfixed, as his words rolled and thundered over the loudspeaker: "My people, my people listen. The battle is in our hands. . . . We must come to see that the end we seek is a society at peace with itself, a society that can live with its conscience. That day will be a day not of the white man, not of the black man. That will be the day of man as man." And that day was not long in coming, King said, whereupon he launched into the immortal refrains of "The Battle Hymn of the Republic," crying out, "Our God is marching on! Glory, glory hallelujah!"

Aroused by the events in Alabama, Washington produced the 1965 Voting Rights Act, which outlawed impediments to black voting and empowered the attorney general to supervise federal elections in seven southern states where blacks were kept off the rolls. At the time, political analysts almost unanimously attributed the act to King's Selma campaign. Once federal examiners were supervising voter registration in all troublesome southern areas, blacks were able to get on the rolls and vote by the hundreds of thousands, permanently altering the pattern of southern and national policies.

In the end, the powerful civil rights legislation generated by King and his tramping legions wiped out statutory racism in America and realized at least the social and political promise of emancipation a century before. But King was under no illusion that legislation alone could bring on the brave new America he so ardently championed. Yes, he said, laws and their vigorous enforcement were necessary to regulate destructive habits and actions, and to protect blacks and their rights. But laws could not eliminate the "fears, prejudice, pride, and irrationality" that were barriers to a truly integrated society, to peaceful intergroup and interpersonal living. Such a society could be achieved only when people accepted that inner, invisible law that etched on their hearts the conviction "that all men are brothers and that love is mankind's most potent weapon for personal and social transformation. True integration will be achieved by true neighbors who are willingly obedient to unenforceable obligations."

Even so, the Selma campaign was the movement's finest hour, and the Voting Rights Act the high point of a broad civil rights coalition that included the federal government, various white groups, and all the other civil rights organizations in addition to SCLC. King himself had best expressed the spirit and aspirations of that coalition when, on August 28, 1963, standing before the Lincoln Memorial, he electrified an interracial crowd of 250,000 with perhaps his greatest speech, "I Have A Dream," in which he described in rhythmic, hypnotic cadences his vision of an integrated America. Because of his achievements and moral vision, he won the 1964 Nobel Peace Prize, at thirty-four the youngest recipient in Nobel history.

Still, King paid a high price for his fame and his cause. He suffered from stomachaches and insomnia, and even felt guilty about all the tributes he received, all the popularity he enjoyed. Born in relative material comfort and given a superior education, he did not think he had earned the right to lead the impoverished black masses. He complained, too, that he no longer had a personal self and that sometimes he did not recognize the Martin Luther King people talked about. Lonely, away from home for protracted periods, beset with temptation, he slept with other women, for some of whom he had real feeling. His sexual transgressions only added to his guilt, for he knew he was imperiling his cause and hurting himself and those he loved.

Alas for King, FBI Director J. Edgar Hoover found out about the black leader's infidelities. The director already abhorred King, certain that Communist spies influenced him and masterminded his demonstrations. Hoover did not think blacks capable of organizing such things, so Communists had to be behind them and King as well. As it turned out, a lawyer in King's inner circle and a man in SCLC's New York office did have Communist backgrounds, a fact that only reinforced Hoover's suspicions about King. Under Hoover's orders, FBI agents conducted a ruthless crusade to destroy King's public life. Hoover's men tapped King's phones and bugged his hotel rooms; they compiled a prurient monograph about his private life and showed it to various editors, public officials, and religious and civil leaders; they spread the word, Hoover's word, that King was not only a reprobate but a dangerous subversive with Communist associations.

King was scandalized and frightened by the FBI's revelations of his extramarital affairs. Luckily for him, no editor, not even a racist one in the South, would touch the FBI's salacious materials. Public officials such as Robert Kennedy were shocked, but argued that King's personal life did not affect his probity as a civil rights leader. Many blacks, too, declared that what he did in private was his own business. Even so, King vowed to refrain from further affairs—only to succumb again to his own human frailties.

As for the Communist charge, King retorted that he did not need any Russians to tell him when someone was standing on his neck; he could figure that out by himself. To mollify his political friends, however, King did banish from SCLC the two men with Communist backgrounds (later he resumed his ties with the lawyer, a loyal friend, and let Hoover be damned). He also denounced Communism in no uncertain terms. It was, he believed, profoundly and fundamentally evil, an atheistic doctrine no true Christian could ever embrace. He hated the dictatorial Soviet state, too, whose "crippling totalitarianism" subordinated everything—religion, art, music, science, and the individual—to its terrible yoke. True, Communism started with men like Karl Marx who were "aflame with a passion for social justice." Yet King faulted Marx for rejecting God and the spiritual in human life. "The great weakness in Karl Marx is right here," King once told his staff, and he went on to describe his ideal Christian commonwealth in Hegelian terms: "Capitalism fails to realize that life is social. Marxism fails to realize that life is individual. Truth is found neither in the rugged individualism of capitalism nor in the impersonal collectivism of Communism. The kingdom of God is found in a synthesis that combines the truths of these two opposites. Now there is where I leave brother Marx and move on toward the kingdom."

But how to move on after Selma was a perplexing question King never successfully answered. After the devastating Watts riot in August 1965, he took his movement into the racially troubled urban North, seeking to help the suffering black poor in the ghettos. In 1966, over the fierce opposition of some of his own staff, he launched a campaign to end the black slums in Chicago and forestall rioting there. But the campaign foundered because King seemed unable to devise a coherent anti-slum strategy, because Mayor Richard Daley and his black acolytes opposed him bitterly, and because white America did not seem to care. King did lead open-housing marches into segregated neighborhoods in Chicago, only to encounter furious mobs who waved Nazi banners, threw bottles and bricks, and screamed, "We hate niggers!" "Kill the niggers!" "We want Martin Luther Coon!" King was shocked. "I've been in many demonstrations all across the South," he told reporters, "but I can say that I have never seen—even in Mississippi and Alabama—mobs as hostile and as hate-filled as I've seen in Chicago." Although King prevented a major riot there and wrung important concessions from City Hall, the slums remained, as wretched and seemingly unsolvable as ever.

That same year, angry young militants in SNCC and the Congress of Racial Equality (CORE) renounced King's teachings—they were sick and tired of "De Lawd" telling them to love white people and work for integration. Now they advocated "Black Power," black separatism, even violent resistance to liberate blacks in America. SNCC even banished whites from its ranks and went on to drop "nonviolent" from its name and to lobby against civil rights legislation.

Black Power repelled the older, more conservative black organizations such as the NAACP and the Urban League, and fragmented the civil rights movement beyond repair. King, too, argued that black separatism was chimerical, even suicidal, and that nonviolence remained the only workable way for black people. "Darkness cannot drive out darkness," he reasoned: "only light can do that. Hate cannot drive out hate: only love can do that." If every other black in America turned to violence, King warned, then he would still remain the lone voice preaching that it was wrong. Nor was SCLC going to reject whites as SNCC had done. "There have been too many hymns of hope," King said, "too many anthems of expectation, too many deaths, too many dark days of standing over graves of those who fought for integration for us to turn back now. We must still sing 'Black and White Together, We Shall Overcome.' "

In 1967, King himself broke with the older black organizations over the ever-widening war in Vietnam. He had first objected to American escalation in the summer of 1965, arguing that the Nobel Peace Prize and his role as a Christian minister compelled him to speak out for peace. Two years later, with almost a half million Americans—a disproportionate number of them poor blacks—fighting in Vietnam, King devoted whole speeches to America's "immoral" war against a tiny country on the other side of the globe. His stance provoked a fusillade of criticism from all directions—from the NAACP, the Urban League, white and black political leaders, *Newsweek, Life, Time,* and the *New York Times,* all telling him to stick to civil rights. Such criticism hurt him deeply. When he read the *Time's* editorial against him, he broke down and cried. But he did not back down. "I've fought too long and too hard now against segregated accommodations to end up segregating my moral concerns," he told his critics. "Injustice *any*where is a threat to justice everywhere."

That summer, with the ghettos ablaze with riots, King warned that American cities would explode if funds used for war purposes were not diverted to emergency antipoverty programs. By then, the Johnson administration, determined to gain a military victory in Vietnam, had written King off as an antiwar agitator, and was now cooperating with the FBI in its efforts to defame him.

The fall of 1967 was a terrible time for King, the lowest ebb in his civil rights career. Everybody seemed to be attacking him—young black militants for his stubborn adherence to nonviolence, moderate and conservative blacks, labor leaders, liberal white politicians, the White House, and the FBI for his stand on Vietnam. Two years had passed since King had produced a nonviolent victory, and contributions to SCLC had fallen off sharply. Black spokesman Adam Clayton Powell, who had once called King the greatest Negro in America, now derided him as Martin Loser King. The incessant attacks began to irritate him, creating such anxiety and depression that his friends worried about his emotional health.

Worse still, the country seemed dangerously polarized. On one side, backlashing whites argued that the ghetto explosions had "cremated" nonviolence and that white people had better arm themselves against black rioters. On the other side, angry blacks urged their people to "kill the Honkies" and burn the cities down. All around King, the country was coming apart in a cacophony of hate and reaction. Had Americans lost the will and moral power to save itself? he wondered. There was such rage in the ghetto and such bigotry among whites that he feared a race war was about to break out. He felt he had to do something to pull America back from the brink. He and his staff had to mount a new campaign that would halt the drift to violence in the black world and combat stiffening white resistance, a nonviolent action that would "transmute the deep rage of the ghetto into a constructive and creative force."

Out of his deliberations sprang a bold and daring project called the poor people's campaign. The master plan, worked out by February 1968, called for SCLC to bring an interracial army of poor people to Washington, D.C., to dramatize poverty before the federal government. For King, just turned thirty-nine, the time had come to employ civil disobedience against the national government itself. Ultimately, he was projecting a genuine class movement that he hoped would bring about meaningful changes in American society—changes that would redistribute economic and political power and end poverty, racism, "the madness of militarism," and war.

In the midst of his preparations, King went to Memphis, Tennessee, to help black sanitation workers there who were striking for the right to unionize. On the night of April 3, with a storm thundering outside, he told a black audience that he had been to the mountaintop and had seen what lay ahead. "I may not get there with you. But I want you to know tonight that we as a people *will* get to the promised land."

The next afternoon, when King stepped out on the balcony of the Lorraine Motel, an escaped white convict named James Earl Ray, stationed in a nearby building, took aim with a high-powered rifle and blasted King into eternity. Subsequent evidence linked Ray to white men in the St. Louis area who had offered "hit" money for King's life.

For weeks after the shooting, King's stricken country convulsed in grief, contrition, and rage. While there were those who cheered his death, the *New York Times* called it a disaster to the nation, the *London Times* an enormous loss to the world. In Tanzania, Reverend Trevor Huddleston, expelled from South Africa for standing against apartheid, declared King's death the greatest single tragedy since the assassination of Gandhi in 1948, and said it challenged the complacency of Christian Church all over the globe.

On April 9, with 120 million Americans watching on television, thousands of mourners—black and white alike—gathered in Atlanta for the funeral of a man who had never given up his dream of creating a symphony of brotherhood on these shores. As a black man born and raised in segregation, he had had every reason to hate America and to grow up preaching cynicism and retaliation. Instead, he had loved the country passionately and had sung of her promise and glory more eloquently than anyone of his generation.

They buried him in Atlanta's South View Cemetery, then blooming with dogwood and fresh green boughs of spring. On his crypt, hewn into the marble, were the words of an old Negro spiritual he had often quoted: "Free at Last, Free at Last, Thank God Almighty I'm Free at Last."

Kennedy as President: A Perspective

by Robert James Maddox

The tragically short administration of President John F. Kennedy makes it impossible to determine just what he would have done in certain critical areas, such as the Vietnam War. Kennedy's many admirers have praised his domestic politics and his handling of foreign affairs, especially the unnerving Cuban Missile Crisis, and they have credited his administration with reinvigorating a nation grown complacent in the 1950s. Kennedy's detractors, who have increased over the years, point to his flawed personal life, a reluctance to take a leadership role in crucial areas such as the civil rights movement, and inept and dangerous handling of foreign crises. Overall, they see an administration long on show and short on substance.

In the following essay, Robert James Maddox, Professor of History at Pennsylvania State University, traces Kennedy's early life, the significant role of his family and his wealth, his unpromising early political career, and the major highlights of his thousand days in office. The author concludes with a sensitive and balanced assessment of the strengths and weaknesses of his presidency. How the future will judge the martyred Kennedy is still unclear, Maddox admits, but he closes with a cogent observation by a Kennedy aide: "Some politicians get elected by playing upon a society's fears and prejudices, others by appealing to its strengths and hopes. Kennedy called upon the best the United States had to offer." Maddox is author of *The New Left and the Origins of the Cold War* (1973), *The Unknown War with Russia: Wilson's Siberian Intervention* (1977), and other works.

Most Americans over a certain age will remember for the rest of their lives exactly where they were and what they were doing when they heard the news on November 22, 1963. "President Kennedy has been shot." People began clustering everywhere, talking, speculating, praying. At first there was great confusion over what had actually happened. Some reports had it that Kennedy's wounds were not mortal, others that they were. There were stories that

Vice President Lyndon Johnson had been killed, and others that he had suffered a fatal heart attack. Finally the uncertainty ended: President Kennedy was dead. Then followed, through several days of almost paralyzed attention, those vivid scenes run over and over again on television: the motorcade in Dallas; the President's wife beside the coffin in her bloodstained dress; Lyndon Johnson's short speech at the airport, "This is a sad time for all people . . . ," the funeral.

It would be difficult, after such a brief interval, to assess anyone's presidency with very much objectivity. The manner of Kennedy's death renders the problem all but insoluble. Not only is it impossible to predict with accuracy what he would have accomplished had he lived out his term (let alone had he been reelected) but the assassination itself created an aura which shapes every perception. What was said of the dead Lincoln might fairly be said of Kennedy, "Now he belongs to the ages." Any evaluation of his presidency must be tentative until a longer perspective develops.

John Fitzgerald Kennedy was born into wealth. His father, Joseph Kennedy, Sr., had had a meteoric career in the business world, with interests running from real estate and the stock market to liquor and motion pictures. A loner of consuming ambition, Joe had trod on many toes, driven many shrewd deals, and made a host of enemies along the way. Having grown up in Boston where the elite of old New England families looked with disdain upon sharp-trading Irishmen, Kennedy carried a chip on both shoulders. He raised his large number of children as though they were some sort of team, whose goal it was to win every honor and distinction that could be won. "I don't think much of people who have it in them to be first, but finish second," as he put it, "If you've got a second choice, then you haven't got a first choice." Jack's mother, Rose Kennedy, provided a moderating influence. She too was descended from Boston Irish (her father was John F. "Honey Fitz" Fitzgerald, a colorful if somewhat roguish politician), and she was in her own way as tough as old Joe.

Jack was the second son in the family, the first being Joseph, Jr., a handsome, engaging young man who seemed destined for success in whatever he attempted. Though the matter can be exaggerated, and has, it must have been difficult for Jack to defer to the older boy as each Kennedy in turn was expected to do. While Joe seemed to stand out in everything, Jack's accomplishments came less easily. He was a capable student and athlete but excelled as neither. Through most of his early years, John F. Kennedy was an attractive, bright young man who, considering his father's wealth and connections, might have been expected to make a modest mark in the world or business or in public affairs. He scarcely seemed touched by greatness.

World War II marked a turning point in young Jack's life. Shortly after the fighting broke out in Europe he set himself to work on an honors' thesis at Harvard which later was published with some fanfare as *Why England Slept*. Whether the manuscript would have been published on its merits without the elder Kennedy's intercession is debatable, but it was an unexpected capstone to an otherwise undistinguished academic career. When the United States entered the war Jack enlisted in the Navy and ultimately commanded a patrol torpedo boat in the South Pacific. The story of his boat's collision with a Japanese destroyer and Jack's heroism in the days following is too well known to be retold here, but it revealed something of the tough core beneath the surface of the casual, easygoing young man. The war also brought to the Kennedys the first of a series of disasters to strike this successful but star-crossed family. Joe Jr., so obviously groomed for leadership, was killed while flying a mission against the Germans. Jack was now the oldest boy, and it fell to him to achieve the triumphs his father sought. "I got Jack into politics," Joe Sr. boasted, "I told him Joe was dead and therefore it was his responsibility to run for Congress."

At first Jack did not fit very well the role his father had assigned him. Moderately ambitious, shrewd enough, and backed with almost limitless resources, he seemed unwilling to make the total commitment Joe Jr. most likely would have made. Speaking to a friend about his father's ambitions, Jack once complained that the elder Kennedy wanted to "parlay a lost PT boat and a bad back into a political advantage." Jack was a natural in politics. He had charm, he was photogenic, a war hero, a Kennedy of Boston. He trod easily up the ladder: six years in the House of Representatives, two well-organized victories when he ran for Senate. Yet, when one considers Kennedy's career in Congress, one is struck by how little he did other than to hold office. No important legislation bears his name, he was neither a reformer nor a member of the inner clubs where power is wielded. He was on the periphery of national events, apparently content pretty much to be what he was. The presidential bug had not yet bitten.

In view of the fact that Kennedy later ran for the presidency as a liberal, there has been much discussion of his politics during his years in Congress. His performance there never ranked very highly on liberal scales, and many people remembered that he had been conspicuously absent during the battle against McCarthyism during the 1950's. Kennedy admirers, and Kennedy himself, explained this conversion as the result of growth and maturity. "Some people have their liberalism 'made' by the time they reach their late twenties," he once said, "I didn't. I was caught in crosscurrents and eddies. It was only later that I got into the stream of things." Kennedy detractors take a different view, and attribute his metamorphosis to political experience. They see Kennedy a pragmatic, not to say cynical, politician who was willing to ride whichever horse he thought would win the prize.

Jack first attained some national recognition when he made a bid for the vice presidential nomination at the Democratic convention in 1956. He lost, but the experience seems to have whetted his appetite and pointed him towards seeking the presidency in 1960. At last he was willing to commit himself to the grueling rigors the ambitious politician has to endure. In addition to his personal assets, he had going for him enormous wealth and a hard-driving organization with the immediate family as its hub and radiating outward via family ties and personal friendships. The Kennedys had no difficulty in attracting to their cause bright, dedicated men and women.

Jack's thrust for the Democratic nomination bothered many liberals. His credentials were suspect to them, and he appeared to be usurping a place rightfully held by Adlai Stevenson. Stevenson, whose devotion to liberal causes was both deeper and of longer duration than Jack's, to many people "deserved" the nomination. Twice before he had run for the presidency against Dwight Eisenhower's enormous popularity, and had been snowed under. Now, his supporters reasoned, Stevenson should be given the opportunity to run when there was a chance of winning. There were other contenders as well: notably the ebullient Hubert Humphrey, a seasoned campaigner, and Lyndon Johnson of Texas, a powerful figure in the Senate and a man who commanded considerable support in the South and West. Jack's task was not going to be easy.

The Kennedy organization, which hitherto had operated within the state of Massachusetts, now expanded to function on a national level. At its head stood Jack's younger brother Bobby, whose tousled hair and lop-sided grin made him look like someone from an Andy Hardy movie. In fact Bobby was a hard-driving, at times ruthless campaigner, completely dedicated to his brother's cause. "Gentlemen," he once told a group of politicians, "I don't give a damn if the state and city organizations survive after November, and I don't give a damn if *you* survive. I want to elect John F. Kennedy." Bobby raised many hackles. He was a bratty upstart to some of the professionals, but he worked tirelessly, ran a tight ship, and acted as a lightning rod for some animosities which otherwise might have been directed against Jack. And not the least ingredient in the Kennedy drive was the money, the ever-present money. In a crucial primary in West Virginia, for instance, the Kennedy machine overwhelmed Hubert Humphrey with campaign spending. Kennedy had "bought" the primary. Humphrey men complained, and they were not far wrong. Jack himself commented wryly on the situation later. "I got a wire from my father that said 'Dear Jack: Don't buy one vote more than necessary. I'll be damned if I'll pay for a landslide.'"

By the time the Democratic convention opened in July 1960, Jack occupied a powerful position. He had knocked Humphrey out of contention in the primaries, and he was far more efficiently organized than either Stevenson or Johnson. Stevenson was a demonstrable loser, the Kennedy people argued, while their man had never lost a campaign. Johnson they dismissed as a purely sectional candidate, one who could not appeal to the party's liberal wing. Many liberals gagged a bit at accepting this recent convert, but they, too, wanted to win. They gagged a bit more when, after securing the nomination, Kennedy promptly offered the vice presidential nomination to Johnson in a blatant move to attract Western and Southern support.

The campaign of 1960 was run against the background of the two Eisenhower administrations. "Ike" had retained his popularity throughout the eight years, though there were deep stresses within the society which would explode during the 1960's. But Ike's popularity was purely personal, an asset that cannot be transferred. And the overall impression the Eisenhower administration gave was that it was run by faceless men, most of whom were a bit long in the tooth (Eisenhower himself had suffered two heart attacks while in office). Even Vice President Nixon, scarcely older than Jack, could at most hope to attract support because people believed he would be competent, not because he possessed any personal magnetism. The entire Kennedy campaign, therefore, was run on the theme of the vigorous young innovator who would "get the country moving again" after eight years of Republican lethargy.

The election of 1960 was neither better nor worse than most presidential races. Some of the tactics used by Kennedy strategists were questionable to say the least. As part of the effort to depict the Eisenhower administration (of which Nixon was a part) as inert, the Kennedy people called attention to what they referred to as a "missile gap" between the United States and the Soviet Union. When Harry S. Truman left office, it was proclaimed, the United States enjoyed an impregnable position by virtue of its vast superiority in nuclear strength. That superiority had been squandered during the Eisenhower years, thus endangering the nation's security. The "missile gap" was an invention which had no basis in fact. A second instance applied to Cuba, which during the Eisenhower years had seen Fidel Castro overthrow the corrupt Batista regime. Kennedy flailed away at the Republicans for having allowed "communism" to take over a country only ninety miles from American shores, and for sitting by ever since. What he did not reveal was that he had been briefed by administration officials that rebel forces at that very time were being financed and trained to overthrow Castro. Thus, as Nixon complained, he had to remain silent (he could not very well explain what was being done) in the face of a charge Kennedy knew to be false.

The climax of the campaign was the famous television debates between the two candidates. Kennedy, as the lesser-known man, stood to profit from the exposure, provided he held his own in the exchanges. This he did and more. Appearing cool and collected, Kennedy came off impressively as he fielded questions with ease. He showed an impressive grasp of detail, and an appealing wit. Nixon fared less well. Makeup problems, mechanical gestures, a tendency to perspire easily, and a certain artificial piousness (he promised not to curse if elected, but made no promises about his language if he lost), helped him not at all. The debates were unedifying in substance, as both candidates hedged and trimmed shamelessly. Yet Kennedy's performance, and it was just that, may have won him the presidency in what turned out to be a very tight election.

How close it was! Out of almost 69 million votes cast, Kennedy's popular margin was only 119,450. Pundits delighted in pointing out how a few thousand votes here, a few thousand there, could have swung the election to Nixon. And practically every group large enough—and some that were not—instantly proclaimed it was their contribution that put Kennedy over the top. This, coupled with strong charges (not without substance) of corruption in some of the larger Democratic cities, tarnished Kennedy's victory. He had won, but he had received no clear mandate from the people and Congress was still controlled by a coalition of Republicans and conservative Democrats.

Despite its shaky origins, the Kennedy administration got under way with bright hopes. Though a fierce snowstorm had raged the day before, the swearing-in ceremony was conducted in bright, chill sunshine. The aged poet Robert Frost struggled through electronic difficulties (smoke began issuing from one of the microphone cables) and a glaring sun which prevented him from reading his prepared address, but he nonetheless proclaimed the dawn of a new era. Kennedy himself delivered a ringing speech in which he declared that a new generation had taken over the nation's destinies. Alternately militant ("We shall pay any price, bear any burden, meet any hardship . . . to assure the survival and the success of liberty") and conciliatory ("Let us never negotiate out of fear. But let us never fear to negotiate"), Kennedy called upon the American people to join a crusade at home and abroad. "And so, my fellow Americans, ask not what your country can do for you; ask what you can do for your country." It was inspiring rhetoric to some, unsettling to others.

The promises of the inauguration seemed to be unfolding in fact as the Kennedy administration began. A host of talented people descended upon Washington, a disproportionate number (malcontents were heard to mutter) from Kennedy's *alma mater,* Harvard. The chauffeur-driven Cadillacs, as one put it, were being replaced by swarms of Volkswagens piloted by college professors. In any event Washington's tempo perceptibly quickened. Throughout the Kennedy administration there was a pronounced emphasis upon energy and movement rather than deliberation. Kennedy and his subordinates, as often as not, were praised for the long hours they worked, their "tough" mentalities, the number of words per minute they could read, and the vigorous physical activities they pursued. A generally favorable press, more than anything else, helped to create the impression that a new era was at hand. The touch football games, the fifty-mile hikes, and the gowns Jackie wore, provided far better copy than Ike's golf scores. There were complaints, of course, but Jack's ready wit often defused even the most valid criticisms. When asked about the propriety of naming the inexperienced Bobby as Attorney General, for instance, Kennedy replied that he could not see where "it's wrong to give him a little legal experience before he goes out to practice law."

The approximately 1000 days Jack Kennedy was to spend in office will always be remembered more for foreign policy issues than for domestic legislative achievement. And the opening chapter was an unmitigated disaster. Kennedy had inherited the Cuban insurrection program left over from his predecessor. The "armies" being trained were small and unimpressive, and were driven by internal factionalism. What led Kennedy to proceed were two considerations: First, had he disbanded the program he would have created instantly an angry, vociferous group which would have denounced his act as a surrender to the forces of communism. As a Democrat, Kennedy was only too well aware of the use certain Republicans would have made of this to discredit his administration before it got under way. Second, the Central Intelligence Agency, which had conceived and directed the operation, advised him that Cuba was a pressure cooker of discontent, with Castro uneasily sitting on the lid. The real purpose of the invasion force would be to act as a detonator for the popular explosion that was sure to follow. Besides, it was argued, even if by some chance the scheme failed, the landing forces could make their way to nearby mountain ranges, there to develop insurgency operations much in the manner that Castro himself had done.

The "Bay of Pigs" affair, as it became known, was a fiasco from start to dismal finish. Operations went awry, cover stories were exposed almost from the beginning. Most important, the assumptions upon which the plan was based proved groundless. There was no popular uprising against Castro, no defections of his armed forces. And there was no opportunity for the landing forces to escape to the mountains which in fact were far away. It quickly became known that the United States had financed, trained, and mounted the expedition, an act which violated numerous agreements to which this nation was party.

President Kennedy emerged from this affair a chastened man. Criticized by some for having failed to use American air power to save the situation, by others for having permitted it to go forward at all, he accepted full responsibility. "Victory has a hundred fathers," he noted ruefully, "and defeat is an orphan." He had learned something valuable, he claimed, which was that never again would he trust those "experts" with their charts and pointers and glib sales pitches. Yet it was a grim situation for an avowedly 'iberal administration, and there is no evidence to show that Kennedy considered the operation in terms other than whether it would work.

Foreign policy crises plagued the Kennedy administration until the time of his death. There was his personal confrontation with the Soviet leader Khruschev in the summer of 1961, in which Kennedy admittedly came off badly against the tough, cagey Russian. There were several clashes over Berlin, during one of which Kennedy placed the United States military on a standby alert. There were recurring problems in Africa, South America, and especially in southeast Asia. Vietnam was not at that time the major preoccupation it became during the administration of Lyndon Johnson, but it *was* Kennedy who first sent to Vietnam American combat troops in large numbers.

The most dangerous event of the Kennedy years once again involved Cuba. For reasons which can only be guessed, Premier Khruschev decided to install in Cuba missiles capable of handling atomic warheads. Preparations for the missile sites were already well under way before the Kennedy administration received hard evidence that this was so. Though such a development did not really alter the existing balance of nuclear terror (the United States had missile bases around the periphery of the Soviet Union), Kennedy felt he could under no circumstances stand by passively. There were a number of considerations involved: Acceptance of such a move by the United States might embolden the Russians to move aggressively elsewhere, the United States would suffer in terms of prestige with its allies, and not least the American people would not tolerate a do-nothing policy—particularly from a man who had criticized his predecessor for having permitted Castro to take power in the first place. Kennedy has been quoted as having stated that he would have been impeached had he allowed the Soviet gambit to go unopposed.

For a period of almost two weeks in October 1962 the world teetered on the lip of nuclear war. The few advisers who suggested that the United States could permit the installations rather than run the risk of war were not taken seriously. The others were divided between those who wished to attack the installations ("surgical strikes" was the euphemism employed) and those who wished to impose what would amount to a blockade of Cuban waters in order to intercept Soviet ships en route with missiles abroad. This show of determination, they argued, would cause Khruschev to back down without bloodshed. Kennedy chose this "middle" course, dangerous though it was. And it worked. The Russian ships did halt in the face of the blockade, but the possibilities for disaster—another Russian step in the game of "chicken," a communications failure, a trigger-happy American commander—are horrifying to contemplate, even from this distance. In the end an agreement was worked out whereby the Russians agreed to abandon the missile installations in return for an American pledge not to try again to overthrow Castro. Throughout the crisis Kennedy remained unflappable and, when it was over, remarked with typical understatement that he and the other participants had "earned their pay" that month.

Although crisis situations quite naturally received most attention during Kennedy years, other matters deserve mention. Kennedy, like Eisenhower before him, thought his greatest accomplishment would be to modify the potentially dangerous relationship between the United States and the Soviet Union. His record is mixed in this regard, but the situation was promising by the time of his death. The Nuclear Test Ban Treaty, for instance, has been regarded by many as a significant step towards ending the "cold war." In other areas of foreign relations Kennedy put forward such innovative programs as the Peace Corps and the Alliance for Progress, the latter an effort to tie American aid to social reform in Latin America.

Kennedy fared badly in the field of domestic legislation. In some areas—civil rights, tax reform, medical care for the aged, etc.—the administration was defeated outright, and in others had to accept watered-down versions of original measures. Kennedy himself was partly responsible for the failures as he devoted so much of himself to foreign affairs, and neglected to cultivate the really powerful figures in Congress. There were also complaints that he did little to swing public opinion behind his proposals. Given the structure of Congress at the time, however, he may not have been able to accomplish much more no matter what he did.

Civil rights had become a major issue even before Kennedy took office. Here the matter involved not only legislative proposals but the administration's willingness to enforce existing laws. Kennedy moved too quickly in this area to suit some, and not quickly enough to suit others. Certainly he and his brother Robert, as Attorney General, pursued the matter more vigorously than had Eisenhower, yet they avoided confrontations where possible. By the time of his death, some black leaders had become disillusioned with the gap between Kennedy's rhetoric and the actual accomplishments of his administration. Always the pragmatist, Kennedy tended to move where he thought he could prevail and to hold back when he could not.

Foreign affairs, domestic legislation, civil rights, the list of issues which can be discussed with reference to Kennedy is endless. What overall conclusions about his presidency can one draw? Perhaps the best way to approach the problem is to state the best possible construction of his impact as claimed by Kennedy admirers, and then to put forward the version offered by his critics.

Kennedy's greatest quality, according to those who supported him, was his intellectual and moral growth over the years. While few defended his early mistakes such as the Bay of Pigs affair, they have argued that Kennedy profited from his failures as well as his successes and had a sure grasp of foreign policy at the time of his death. Kennedy never would have embarked upon that dreadful escalation in Vietnam which destroyed his successor's presidency. Indeed, several people close to him have reported, Kennedy intended to remove the combat troops already there following the 1964 election (providing, of course, he won). Furthermore, it has been pointed out, much of the discontent and violence which marred the later years of the 1960's can be traced directly to revulsion against that war. As to domestic matters, pro-Kennedy writers have contended that he *was* learning to use the levers of the system effectively and would have been far more successful had he lived. Besides, they argue, innovative legislation often is defeated when first put forward and that the mere passage of time would have served Kennedy's interests.

Finally, according to Kennedy admirers, the measure of an administration consists of more than a balance sheet of victories and defeats on specific issues. Kennedy, they say, called upon the nation for a standard of excellence which was inspiring to young and old alike. He used the presidency as Theodore Roosevelt urged using it, as a "bully pulpit." He exuded an air of activism and dedication that gave people confidence that the national government was responsive and responsible. Kennedy's death, therefore, shattered a mood which, if allowed to continue uninterrupted, would have helped create an era of great social and economic progress.

Kennedy's critics, and more and more have appeared, in recent years, see things differently. His administration, they argue, was long on inspirational rhetoric and woefully short on performance. They see his errors in foreign policy not merely as owing to inexperience, but as characteristic flaws. A number have suggested that those periodic crises which occurred throughout his administration were as much due to his inept handling of foreign affairs as to external circumstances. As to Vietnam, they point out that Kennedy had in the past tended to float with the current, and that he was as sensitive to the criticism which would have followed a "defeat" as was Lyndon Johnson. There is little evidence in his political career, they claimed, to indicate that he would have handled things very much differently. Regarding domestic affairs, they have pointed out that few Presidents have been more successful than they were during their first years in office. And by promising so much but delivering so little, Kennedy made it certain that segments of the population would grow progressively more frustrated.

The Kennedy "style," which his admirers deem admirable, seems to his detractors as little more than a series of calculated poses. The cool wit, the rocking chair, the touch football games, those endless pictures of Jackie and the kids, appear as parts of a public relations package. In reality, they argue, Kennedy was far more effective in getting elected than at governing, far more adept at reading a speech than at operating the complex machinery of the Federal Government.

How will historians evaluate Kennedy after a sufficient number of years have dulled partisan feelings? One can only speculate. When he entered the office Kennedy shared that vision of the world role of the United States which developed after World War II. Stated simply, it was that this nation, as the most powerful of the "free world" states, had to serve as the world's policeman against the encroachments of expansive communism. Indeed, as indicated in his inaugural speech, Kennedy seemed to welcome this burden with his proclamation that the American people would "bear any burden, pay any price . . ." in carrying out this duty. By the time of his death Kennedy had modified this view considerably. He had come to believe that some sort of working relationship with the Soviet Union had to be reached, for the threat of nuclear holocaust outweighed all other considerations. And perhaps, one can not be sure, his more modest view of America's role in the world would have permitted him to devote more of his attention to the fissures which had developed within the American society.

A final point should be made. Some politicians get elected by playing upon a society's fears and prejudices, others by appealing to its strengths and hopes. Kennedy called upon the best the United States had to offer. As a former aid put it, with pardonable exaggeration:

> People will remember not only what he did but what he stood for—and this, too, may help the historians assess his Presidency. He stood for excellence in an era of indifference—for hope in an era of doubt—for placing public service ahead of private interests—for reconciliation between East and West, black and white, labor and management. He had confidence in man and gave men confidence in the future.

The bullet that killed Kennedy killed a great many other things as well.

"Remember the Ladies"

by Joan Kennedy Taylor

In 1776, when Abigail Adams admonished her husband John to remember the rights of women in a new American government, such rights were almost non-existent; English common law treated women little better than property. Taking their inspiration from the abolitionist movement against slavery, women campaigned long and hard for the franchise, which they finally achieved in 1920. Since then, an acrimonious debate over an Equal Rights Amendment to the U.S. Constitution has divided even the women's movement itself. In the following article, Joan Kennedy Taylor traces the long, tortuous, and still-unfinished "one step forward, two steps back" struggle for women's equality in America. Taylor is a writer, editor, and author of *Reclaiming the Mainstream: Individualist Feminism Rediscovered* (1992).

In March of 1776, when sentiment in the colonies was strong for independence, Abigail Adams wrote to her husband, John Adams, asking him to use his influence in any new government to change the legal status of married women. "In the new codes of laws which I suppose it will be necessary for you to make," she wrote, "I desire you to remember the ladies, and be more generous to them than your ancestors. Do not put such unlimited power in the hands of husbands. Remember, all men would be tyrants if they could." Today, 200 years after the drafting of the Constitution, the legal rights of women are still ambiguous.

When Abigail Adams wrote, women's legal status was governed by British common law, which treated them as children. Politically, they had no rights at all. Economically, many occupations were forbidden to them. Their main occupation was marriage, but under common law, as the legal authority William Blackstone put it, "the husband and wife are one person in law; that is, the very being or legal existence of the woman is suspended during the marriage."

A married woman had no right to buy, sell, or manage property. She could not legally own property that she inherited or that had been hers before marriage. She did not even have the right to keep any wages she earned; they belonged to her husband. She could not sign contracts, sue or be sued, or testify in court. She had no right to her children in case of legal separation or divorce, and divorce was almost impossible for her to obtain. She was legally obliged to obey her husband, who could keep her prisoner or physically punish her, although not with excessive force.

The founding of the United States did not dismantle women's common-law status. That would take a long, painful effort that has not yet been completed—some states still restrict married women's freedom to manage property, change their residence, and start businesses. Women didn't even organize to protest their status until 1848, when a Declaration of Rights and Sentiments was read aloud by Elizabeth Cady Stanton at a Woman's Rights Convention at Seneca Falls, New York.

The declaration used the format and language of the Declaration of Independence to declare it a self-evident truth that all men and women are created equal. "The history of mankind," it asserted, "is a history of repeated injuries and usurpations on the part of man toward woman, having in direct object the establishment of an absolute tyranny over her. To prove this, let facts be submitted to a candid world."

The audience was heavily composed of abolitionists, for it was in the antislavery movement that women discovered that one political right was open to them—the First Amendment right "to petition the Government for a redress of grievances." Yet they were criticized, not just for holding unpopular opinions but for being unwomanly in trying to promote *any* opinions, and many women abolitionists became aware for the first time of their subservient position. They, and the male abolitionists who worked with them, began to think and talk of women's rights as well as Negro rights.

The Seneca Falls Convention itself was organized by two women, Lucretia Mott and Elizabeth Cady Stanton, who had met at a London antislavery convention eight years before. There, they had found that they were not only forbidden to speak but were required to observe the proceedings from behind a curtain.

At Seneca Falls, Stanton also called for women's "inalienable right to the elective franchise," a demand that seemed so excessive, even to the others who had helped her draft the declaration, that only the black abolitionist Frederick Douglass would take the floor to support it. Within two years, however, women were to take the idea of suffrage so seriously that they were initiating campaigns for it in eight states, as well as continuing to agitate with increasing effect for property rights and marriage reform. But with the outbreak of the Civil War, women postponed such work to assist the war effort.

After Lincoln's Emancipation Proclamation, women collected almost 400,000 signatures petitioning for an amendment to abolish slavery. Once that had been accomplished with the passage and ratification of the 13th Amendment in 1865, the Anti-Slavery Society began agitating for suffrage, and a 14th Amendment was proposed and introduced in Congress. Its original purpose was to give the vote to slaves and to take it away from southerners who had fought against the Union, but for the first time in the history of the Constitution, it was proposed that the word *male* be used to characterize voters.

Abolitionist feminists were alarmed. Many abolitionists who had championed women's right to vote in the abstract were unwilling to make it a concrete political issue. Wendell Phillips, president of the Anti-Slavery Society, refused to support votes for women, arguing that "this hour belongs to the Negro." Senator Charles Sumner, a former advocate of women's rights, called the women's campaign "most inopportune." Such sentiments prevailed. Women were unsuccessful in gaining the right to vote through either the 14th or 15th amendments.

But had the 14th Amendment *inadvertently* given women the right to vote? "All persons born or naturalized in the United States," declared the amendment, "are citizens of the United States and of the State wherein they reside. No State shall make or enforce any law which shall abridge the privileges or immunities of citizens." In 1871, two members of the House Judiciary Committee signed a minority report holding that, under the amendment, women had the right to vote. The next year, Susan B. Anthony led 16 women to vote the straight Republican ticket.

On registration day, Anthony read both the 14th Amendment and the state election law to the election inspectors, pointing out that neither one prohibited women from voting. The women were allowed to register, and on election day, to vote. Although Anthony was arrested, tried, and convicted, she did not pay her fine and was never jailed for her defiance, which made it impossible for her to bring the case to the Supreme Court.

Women's only recourse was to get voters to amend the Constitution. This they succeeded in doing in 1920, after 50 years and what Carrie Chapman Catt, president of the National Woman Suffrage Association at the time, summarized as "56 campaigns of referenda to male voters; 480 campaigns to get legislatures to submit suffrage amendments to voters; 277 campaigns to get state party conventions to include woman's suffrage planks; 30 campaigns to get presidential party conventions to adopt woman's suffrage planks; and 19 campaigns with 19 successive Congresses."

While women were campaigning for the vote, another issue had crept up on them: protective labor legislation. Progressive legislators had enacted a whole network of laws singling out women—laws that women were divided about.

A prime example was protective legislation to limit hours and working conditions. Such laws had been held to be a violation of men's right to contract, but in 1908, in the case of *Muller v. Oregon,* the Supreme Court decided that an Oregon law limiting the working hours of *women* was constitutional.

The case was the first in which sociological data persuaded the justices to modify legal principle. The brief that was filed cited reports by state commissions to prove that women are just what the common law assumed they are—frail, and in need of special protection. The rights of men—in this case, to liberty of contract—need not be available to working women, as they had traditionally not been available to married women.

Woman has always been dependent on man, said the decision, and this is natural. "Though limitations upon personal and contractual rights may be removed by legislation, there is that in her disposition and habits of life which will operate against a full assertion of those rights. . . . Differentiated by these matters from the other sex, she is properly put in a class by herself, and legislation designed for her protection may be sustained, even when like legislation is not necessary for men, and could not be sustained."

The issue divides the women's movement to this day. An organization called the National Woman's Party, founded in 1913 to work for suffrage, became convinced that the view of women exhibited in the *Muller* decision was a threat to the idea of equal rights they had been working for. So in 1921, the party reorganized to work for the removal of all legal distinctions based on sex. At first they undertook a state-by-state campaign but soon decided to lobby instead for constitutional reform—an equal rights amendment. The amendment was introduced in Congress in 1923, and with two exceptions, substantially the same wording was submitted every year thereafter until 1972, when the ERA was finally passed by Congress and sent to the states for ratification.

From the beginning, the main opposition to the ERA was from supporters of the trade union movement. Clearly, protective labor legislation, whatever else it did, served to curb women's competition for jobs. In 1950 and 1953, the ERA was amended with a rider, urged by Eleanor Roosevelt, that would have left protective legislation intact by providing that the amendment "shall not be construed to impair any rights, benefits, or exemptions now or hereafter conferred by law upon persons of the female sex."

But it was precisely the singling out of women that the National Woman's Party opposed. So although the amended ERA twice passed the Senate, the party helped to defeat it in the House.

When Congress held hearings on the equal rights amendment in 1970 and 1971, six of the eight statements against it were submitted by organized labor, including one from the AFL-CIO. One legal expert suggested a rider to keep protective legislation intact.

During the years in which the ERA was being unsuccessfully proposed, attempts were made—also unsuccessfully—to strike down various discriminatory laws for violating the equal-protection clause of the 14th Amendment. The rationale was well expressed by scholar Bernard Schwartz, in an observation included in the record of the 1970 House hearings on the amendment by ERA for Senator Sam Ervin: "The case law has consistently ruled that, even though women are 'persons' within the scope of the equal-protection clause, the protection which that provision affords them must be interpreted in the light of the disabilities imposed upon women at common law. Thus, as recently as 1966, a state court ruled that, until the common-law disqualification of sex is removed, women are not eligible to serve on juries—and that regardless of the equal-protection clause."

In 1971, the Supreme Court finally held that a specific classification based on sex was not "reasonable." In the years since, the Court has considered a number of challenges to statutes that differentiate on the basis of sex. "While the Court has several times struck down such statutes," comments one legal source, "those occasions have been proportionately far fewer than in suits challenging classifications based on race."

Although the Court can reverse a previous ruling, and has done so, it does not do so with abandon and generally tries to support such reversals by appealing to the "plain language" of the Constitution or to the intent of those who framed the section being interpreted. Intent is discovered by examining the debates that took place at the time the wording was adopted—the legislative history. And the legislative history of the 14th Amendment explicitly did not include women, so it would require an extremely "creative" decision to hold that the amendment applies to women.

Thus, the stage is set for the sad tale of the Equal Rights Amendment. Its legislative history seemed clear at the time it passed Congress. Both its supporters and its opponents agreed that it would apply only to the actions of governments; that it would *not* address private discrimination, which could only be reached by legislation that invoked Congress's power to regulate commerce; and that it would invalidate protective labor legislation that makes women less competitive in the marketplace.

In the congressional hearings, no one, not even Sam Ervin, who voiced many of the qualms that the conservative campaign against the ERA in the '70s was to pick up, thought that the amendment would expand the power of government. It would invalidate laws, not create them. In fact, Ervin feared the ERA would bring "legal chaos" because it would "merely abolish all laws making any distinction between men and women. It would not bring into existence any new laws giving us a discrimination-free society."

And feminists agreed. "ERA will not prevent discriminations by persons or by private industry," wrote Ann Scott in the pages of the popular feminist magazine *Ms.* "It will not, directly at least, change social relations. What it will do, over the long run and on a most basic level, is to prevent the government from determining the rights of women and men on the basis of sex. And that's a hell of a lot."

Then came the conservative campaign against the amendment. Not only would the ERA change social relations by driving women out of the home and into the work force and by legalizing homosexual marriage, but it was also alleged to be "a big power grab by the Federal Government." The amendment "will eliminate all-girls' and all-boys' schools and colleges," said conservative literature. It "may compel states to set up taxpayer-financed child-care centers for all children" and "may give the Federal Government the power to force the admission of women to seminaries equally with men, and possibly force the churches to ordain women."

In response to these attacks, feminists gradually expanded their accounts of what the ERA might do. They didn't exactly *say* that the amendment would be applied to make people economically equal, but they started wearing buttons, calling attention to the statistic that women earned 59 cents to a man's dollar (a misleading figure—see Jennifer Roback's "The 59-Cent Fallacy," REASON, Sept. 1984).

The ERA was supported by a broad coalition that now included many of the union forces that still wanted to expand social legislation. They thought that they could have it all—that women could be legally equal and legally different and special, all at the same time. After all, those who made blacks their constituency had pulled off that trick by changing the interpretation of the Civil Rights Act to mean present-day affirmative action with its goals and benign quotas.

So feminists started agreeing with the conservatives that the new amendment would have broad effects. Where the conservatives called it a federal power grab, Eleanor Smeal, president of the National Organization for Women (NOW), called it "a Constitutional prohibition against sex discrimination." In a letter to supporters, she said, "Unless we fight harder and in a more organized fashion than we ever have before, women will continue to be doomed to a second rate economic status of lower pay, unequal credit and inadequate job security. After all, that's what the ERA fight is *really* all about—making the lot of women really equal to the lot of men, especially when it comes to money. That's the critical litmus test of equality."

The amendment had five years to achieve ratification, and it failed to do so. The deadline was extended until 1982, and it failed again, this time permanently. Prospects for passage of a new ERA are unlikely.

The ERA was a remnant of the classical liberalism of the early abolitionist feminists, who sought equal responsibility and laws that had neither special privileges nor special restrictions for women. It could have been used as a vehicle to enunciate that philosophy to a wide audience today, but it was not. Instead, its supporters, who began by describing it correctly, came to agree with their opponents that it would engender sweeping changes in private action. And that agreement would become a self-fulfilling prophecy should the ERA pass Congress again in the near future; it has created a climate of opinion that would provide a different and malignant legislative history, one that could make all the worst nightmares of federal power grabs come true.

So the ERA is dead, but *Muller* v. *Oregon,* the cornerstone of protective legislation, has never been overruled. And the status of women is basically what state legislatures (and majority opinion) say it is. While the ERA was wending its way through the state legislatures, it became fashionable to grant women equal treatment; several states passed state equal-rights amendments to their constitutions. But the trouble with not having the Constitution view women as fully equal and independent beings is that, if the fashion changes, there is nothing to stop the laws from changing back.

Indeed, a number of feminists are now campaigning for a new kind of protective legislation, this time aimed at helping women in the workplace with laws that mandate maternity leave and provide child-care assistance. Such legislation is a pendulum that can swing either way. In *Women and Work in America,* Robert Smuts says, "The most obvious effect of the depression of the 1930s was to throw many women out of work and intensify the feeling that working women took jobs away from male breadwinners. Many state and local governments revived old bans on the employment of married women in teaching and other public jobs, and several state legislatures considered bills to prohibit the employment of wives in public industry." It could happen again.

Vietam: The War That Won't Go Away

by George Herring

Few events have had a greater impact on American foreign policy and domestic life than the Vietnam War. In this wide-ranging interview, George Herring, Professor of History at the University of Kentucky, examines the rationale for American involvement in the war, its effects on American soldiers and their families, the growing public frustration when victory seemed so elusive, and the devastating impact of the war on domestic programs and problems. Herring also assesses the role of the media in America's first "television war" and questions whether recent military actions in Grenada, Panama, and the Persian Gulf have really cured the United States of the "Vietnam syndrome," a reluctance to commit to military intervention abroad. He warns that "wars that last longer and have negative results may have a great deal more long-term impact than a shorter war that does not have much cost attached to it." Finally, Herring cautiously draws some lessons from the Vietnam War that Americans need to apply in the future. George Herring is the author of *Aid to Russia, 1941–1946* (1973) and *America's Longest War: The United States and Vietnam, 1950–1975* (1979).

Interview with George Herring

Q. Please explain how American involvement in Vietnam grew naturally out of the post World War II policy of containment of communism.

A. The containment policy I think is the key to understanding when and how we got involved in Vietnam. Before 1941, our interest in that area of the world had been very slight, but once we were committed after 1947 to a policy of global containment [of communism], then Vietnam suddenly becomes very important to us because the insurgency against the French at that time is led by people who happened to be communist and this gives a revolution in a remote part of the world a connection with communism and is the explanation really why a whole series of commitments were made between 1950 and 1965 that eventually led to a full-scale war.

195

Q. Did the Bay of Pigs fiasco and the failure to keep communism out of Cuba encourage President Kennedy to think he had to hang tough in Vietnam? What effects did the Cuban missile crisis have on refocusing the United States to engage in limited wars as opposed to superpower confrontation?

A. There are a number of important linkages, I think, between Cuba and Vietnam in the Kennedy years in particular. Kennedy's embarrassment at the Bay of Pigs in the spring of 1961 along with other events—the agreement to neutralize Laos, the building of the Berlin wall, a rather devastating encounter with Khrushchev at Vienna in June—all of these things lead Kennedy to feel by the later part of 1961 that he is not being as firm with communism as he'd said during the election campaign that he would [be]. So when a crisis develops in Vietnam in the fall of 1961, I think there's a feeling that we must take a strong stand. So there is a linkage with Cuba. The fact that the United States had stood down the Soviet Union rather skillfully during the Cuban missile crisis gave the policy makers of the Kennedy administration—people who were later advising Lyndon Johnson—a sense of confidence that if they'd face down the Soviet Union, surely they could manage a crisis with a country much smaller, that being Vietnam. And so, I think there's a certain element of confidence in their skills of crisis management that encouraged them to escalate the war in Vietnam with the hope that they can succeed there.

Q. What were the other rationales beyond containment for pursuing the Vietnam war? Specifically, why did we aid the French in Vietnam? We didn't support Ho Chi Minh. Was it our usual policy to support colonialism in the sense of aiding the French? Was that something out of the ordinary or in keeping with our tradition?

A. Our support for France in the period immediately after World War II in Vietnam was a very complex problem for policymakers at the time. They did not feel good about supporting colonialism. We were the first anti-colonial nation in a sense. We have a long tradition of anti-colonialism, and they were embarrassed by supporting French colonialism and felt awkward about it. On the other hand, because France was so important to the United States and Europe in the early days of the containment policy, policymakers felt that if they did not support France in Indo-China, France could not support the United States in Europe, and at least until 1950 Europe was considered a great deal more important than Indo-China. The other thing was that Ho Chi Minh, of course, was an avowed communist and this made support for France somewhat easier to justify and rationalize. In other parts of the world, in Indonesia for example, where the nationalists were non-communists, [where] in fact, [they] even suppressed a communist rebellion, the United States leaned toward the nationalists rather than the Dutch. But in the case [of Vietnam], where the nationalist movement is communist and where we're committed to containing communism, I think it's much easier to accept something that we don't like, that being supporting colonialism.

[The July 1954 Geneva Conference provided for elections two years later to unify all of Vietnam under one government.]

Q. Why did the United States support South Vietnam's decision not to participate in the 1956 elections in Vietnam? Was this hypocritical not to support elections? Was it typical of the U.S. when potential communists were involved? And what were the consequences of that decision?

A. The issue of elections in Vietnam in 1956 is another example, I think, where the United States found itself in a position of going against principles that it had stood for throughout much of its history. In this particular case, the feeling was that if elections were held at that point in time, then very likely Ho Chi Minh, who had been the leader of the nationalist movement in Vietnam, would have won. Eisenhower himself at one point said that Ho Chi Minh might get as much as 80% of the vote in a national election. The rationalization that was given was that any election held in Vietnam could not be a genuinely free election because the communists would have [manipulated] that election at least in the northern part of Vietnam. But quite clearly, the basic reason was a fear that Ho and the north would have won.

Q. Do you see that as a key turning point in terms of consequences?

A. I think that the failure to hold elections in 1956 is very definitely a turning point. This eliminated probably the last chance to resolve the Vietnam situation without military conflict. And of course, once the elections are not held, within a very short time the insurgency begins in the south, certainly it's begun by 1957, and within a short time after that, the north has committed itself squarely to supporting the insurgency in the south and you're on the verge [of] what becomes called the second Indo-China war.

Q. Why did the U.S. involvement in Vietnam escalate with Kennedy first, and then especially after that between the years 1964–68? What factors shaped public perceptions of the war during those years?

A. The war in Vietnam escalates of course dramatically between 1961 and 1965. I think the reason very simply is that the perception in Washington [is] that South Vietnam is crumbling [in the] face of the insurgency and later the outside pressure from North Vietnam, and that if something isn't done South Vietnam will be lost. It will fall to communism. This in the eyes of U.S. policymakers would have serious international consequences and it might have serious domestic political consequences in the United States. So as each step fails to bring results then the tendency is to go to the next step, until ultimately you have 500,000 U.S. troops in Vietnam by 1967–68.

Q. Was the public perception during those years that we would win the war?

A. I think the public perception when the major commitment is made in July 1965, is generally cautious optimism. I think we go into the war with the feeling that we are the United States, we're in a very small country in a remote part of the world, but surely we have the power and the capacity to succeed in what we are trying to do out there at a cost that will be acceptable. This confidence or optimism begins to weaken rather dramatically in the spring/summer of 1967 and then quite sharply after Tet in 1968. And I think it's the growing feeling in the United States that we can't achieve what we've set out to do at a cost that seems to us acceptable that's the basis eventually for the significant public opposition or disillusionment with the war.

Q. How did the Tet offensive, although not a military disaster for the United States, begin to turn American public opinion against the war?

A. The Tet offensive in early 1968 is generally recognized as one of the most significant turning points of the Vietnam war. I think it's particularly important in terms of American attitudes. In the latter part of 1967, to counter what it perceived as growing public skepticism, the Johnson administration had launched a systematic, far ranging campaign to try to convince the American people that the United Stats was in fact winning the war. This had worked and public support began to rise in December 1967, and then came Tet, literally like a bolt out of the blue in early 1968. And what it seemed to be saying was that no, we're not winning, if in the face of all we have done, the North Vietnamese and Vietcong can still mount an offensive of the scope where they hit literally every city and town in South Vietnam. Where they strike right into the very heart of American power in Saigon, even getting inside the U.S. embassy compound. I think this has a devastating effect. And it persuades Americans that, if in fact we are going to win this war, it's going to last a great deal longer and cost a great deal more than what we had anticipated. And I think people began to wonder whether it's worth what by this time it seems it will cost.

Q. How and why did the war divide American families? What was the generational conflict spawned by the war?

A. The war is of course one of the most divisive events in recent American history. I think many scholars feel that it is as divisive as anything going back to the American Civil War about a hundred years earlier. Probably the reason it is divisive is that the threat to American interests or to American security is not readily apparent. It's a war that's far from home, in a seemingly insignificant part of the world. There had been no Pearl Harbor, nothing to dramatize the threat to the United States. It's a war fought for an abstract principle, containment, and it isn't always easy to convince people that this is essential. It also takes place at a time when Americans are questioning everything—the civil rights revolution, the rebellion of American youth. Nothing is sacred anymore by this time and so Vietnam is just one issue in a whole range of issues that Americans are divided about at a time when nothing is sure anymore, when everything is up to be questioned.

Q. How did the war affect the soldiers who served in Vietnam?

A. Vietnam is a very difficult war for American G.I.s to fight for a lot of different reasons, and I would add that the longer the war goes on, the more difficult it becomes to fight. In the first years, 1965 and '66, certainly America sent fine troops there, they fought very well, [and] were generally successful in the engagements they were in. The problem was that this didn't seem to produce larger results. What are we fighting for? It was not a war where you advanced from one spot to the next and took territory, it was a peoples' war. Americans found it very difficult to understand the Vietnamese. They did not find the South Vietnamese terribly friendly. In many cases South Vietnamese seemed hostile to them. They had a difficult time telling friend from enemy. Who's on our side, who isn't on our side? Among the Vietnamese it was not always easy to tell. And of course the really devastating period in terms of the morale of the G.I.s is after Tet when it's very apparent that what we're doing there is conducting a holding operation. And then when President Nixon begins troop withdrawals, it's obvious that there's going to be no effort to win this war. Americans are still out there dying in significant numbers, just so that we can escape with some degree of face. And I think the period of '68 and '70 is the period when you really have the most severe drug problems, the most severe racial problems, the most severe morale problems, fragging, the actual killing of officers, all because there seems to be no purpose anymore.

Q. How did the cost of the war affect domestic policy and programs?

A. Vietnam has many costs and many consequences and clearly one is in terms of domestic programs. It was Johnson's hope when he committed the United States to war in July 1965, that he could have both guns and butter. That's to say he could fight a war successfully and maintain the domestic society programs, which were his true love, his real commitment. But the longer the war drags on the more money it absorbs, the more divisive it becomes at home, the more the Great Society programs are its victims, in a very real sense. And so ultimately, Johnson has to abandon programs, or funds for programs are reduced. The attention of the nation turns to the war, something very much he had hoped to avoid but something which clearly has happened by 1967.

Q. Why did President Johnson pursue the war so long even after it appeared that a clear cut victory wasn't possible? Was Nixon's policy much different than Johnson's? What alternatives did Nixon have?

A. One of the most difficult questions to answer in terms of the Johnson administration, is why Lyndon Johnson persisted in the war after it was becoming increasingly clear that the policies weren't working. Why didn't he change policies at least? It's not an easy question to answer. Johnson was a stubborn man. He was a man who I think was very much committed to success, who could not tolerate the thought of failure. For those reasons he was very reluctant to back off of something he was so deeply committed to. The other thing, and getting at a much simpler level, is that nobody could show him a way out. Nobody could chart a path for him that would get the United States out of Vietnam without costs that he thought were intolerable in terms of prestige. President Nixon's decisions are very intriguing in 1969. If ever there might have been a chance to liquidate a lost venture, Nixon had not been connected with this before. He could have come in and said that the Democrats really made a mess of things and I'm going to try to liquidate this, as in fact Eisenhower had done in Korea. I think the delusive thing with Nixon is that he somehow thought he could pull off what Johnson had not been able to pull off, because maybe he was cleverer than Johnson, or maybe he was prepared to use means that Johnson had not used, namely, trying to get out of Vietnam through opening up contacts with the Soviet Union that might lead to peace in Vietnam. Also, I think he thought he could get out of Vietnam successfully, that is to say, maintaining an independent noncommunist Vietnam and getting the United States out, too. Eisenhower had gotten out of Korea by threatening to use nuclear weapons, and thus intimidating the North [Koreans] into accepting the American position. It could not work of course [in Vietnam] and Nixon paid a huge price to get the United States out four years later.

Q. What were the effects of the war protest movement on President Nixon and on the public support for the war? Also, could you comment on the impact of the media in shaping the public perception of the war?

A. The issue of the role of the media in Vietnam is still I think one of the most controversial and hotly debated issues deriving from that war. There is a perception that the reporting of the war by the media, particularly by television, had a major impact in turning [the] American public against the war. I don't really buy that. Careful studies of media coverage suggest first that at least up until 1967 media coverage of the war was generally positive or at least neutral. More often than not it reflected the position of the government. Media coverage does not become critical until '67 and particularly after Tet in '68 by which time public opinion had already started to shift. So I would argue in terms of the media that the media reflects as much as influences public attitudes toward Vietnam. The anti-war movement, in terms of its impact on [the] public and leaders, there again, there's a lot of mythology that we are still living with. It is not at all clear to me as many argue that the anti-war movement turned the American public against the war. One could even argue the reverse, I think, up to 1968. Polls show very clearly that the solid majority of Americans are very much opposed to the anti-war movement, don't approve of what it stands for, don't approve of its methods and one could even argue in a perverse sort of way that the anti-war movement up to a point may increase support for the war. What the anti-war movement does is to continually raise questions. To question the authority of government, to raise questions about a war that by 1967 and '68 Americans for other reasons are raising questions about themselves. And so, this plus creating division in the country, both leaders and the public get very weary of the division. And so it's in this indirect way, I believe, that the anti-war movement had its greatest impact, not in the more direct way of changing the minds of leaders or turning the public against the war. There is [a] very clear linkage between Nixon's demise in Watergate and Vietnam. It is Nixon's efforts to contain domestic protest to the war that lead him eventually to take extreme measures, the plumbers group [the nickname for a secret group of White House operatives under Nixon whose mission was to plug embarrassing "leaks" about the Vietnam war], all those things that eventually get him in trouble and are exposed in the Watergate revelation.

Q. How did the outcome of the Vietnam war affect American willingness to get involved in subsequent or future armed conflicts abroad? Did the relatively easy operations in Grenada, Panama, and the Persian gulf overcome the Vietnam syndrome, and would you explain that term.

A. There is no doubt that Vietnam had a tremendous impact on American attitudes toward foreign policy and intervention in particular. The outcome of the war, the embarrassment of it, the frustration of it, the cost of it, with no apparent gains, all of these contribute to what is often called the Vietnam syndrome, which is a reluctance in the aftermath of Vietnam to take on commitments that resemble Vietnam, which is to say interventions and interactions in the third world. I think quite clearly, you see [this] in Central America in the 1980's, where without memories of Vietnam, the United States might possibly have intervened more directly than it did in El Salvador, or possibly in Nicaragua. In the aftermath of the Persian Gulf war of 1991, President Bush commented that we've kicked the Vietnam syndrome once and for all. I am not at all sure that this has been the case or that this will be the case. Certainly the Persian Gulf war restored a certain confidence in the American military and a confidence in America's ability to control events internationally. But this war did not last very long. I think that wars that last longer and have negative results may have a great deal more long-term impact than a shorter war that does not have much cost attached to it. So, I would say we'll have to really wait and see to determine whether the demise of the Vietnam syndrome has been exaggerated or not.

Q. With the hindsight of some time now since the Vietnam war ended, what are the lessons of Vietnam for the American people? What are the domestic prerequisites for pursuing a successful war? What did the war teach us about the limits of American responsibilities and power in the world?

A. I think we have to be very careful about drawing precise lessons from any historical event and applying them to another contemporary situation. The first thing we have to keep in mind is that each situation is unique. It has its unique circumstances, its unique historical context. And if you extract [rigid] specific lessons from one event and apply them to another, you are as likely to mislead yourself as you are to find guidance. So, I'm in general skeptical of those lessons. I do think Vietnam indicates if nothing else that there are certain events in this world which are beyond our control. It suggests also that any foreign policy or intervention in particular must be solidly grounded in domestic support, if it can be carried out over a long period of time. I think it suggests in a broad way that you had best know the situation you are intervening in well before you [do] intervene. You also need to know your enemy, I think that's very crucial. We underestimated the North Vietnamese and the National Liberation Front [South Vietnamese opposed to the American-backed government there] and I think we should know who we are getting involved with, and who we are fighting.

Q. Would you elaborate on the financial effects of the war? Is there a direct link between some of the economic problems experienced in the 1970s, maybe even later, and the way Vietnam was financed or not financed?

A. Vietnam is one of a whole series of things that happened in the 60s that helped to bring on the economic crises of the 70s that persist on into the 80s. Usually the key thing that is cited here is Johnson's refusal to raise taxes in 1965 to pay for the war. His effort to have both guns and butter is one of the factors that is very, very important in fueling the inflationary pressures that get very much out of control in the 1970s. So yes, there is no doubt that it has important economic consequences.

I Am Not a Crook! Corruption in Presidential Politics

by Kenneth G. Alfers

President Richard Nixon's assertion in 1973 that he was "not a crook" was an astounding political statement. The very fact that he thought he needed to say it indicated the depth of suspicion regarding the conduct of Nixon and his staff. Beyond that, it is unlikely that the majority of Americans were about to believe such a statement. The unfolding Nixon scandals were causing increasing disillusionment with politics and were reconfirming widely held suspicions about politicians.

To this day, Nixon's defenders say that even if he did engage in wrongdoing, he was no worse than any other president—that is, "they all do it, don't they?" In fact, the historical evidence shows that the Nixon administration surpassed all others in the pervasiveness of its corruption. As the late Leon Jaworski, special prosecutor in the Watergate scandal, has said, there was no doubt that the former president was personally involved in many of the misdeeds of his administration.

It is true that two other administrations were noted for their corruption—those of U.S. Grant and Warren Harding. The following essay compares those scandalous administrations with that of Nixon. An epilogue has been added to the original essay, which was first published in 1980, in order to provide some perspective on the scandals which occurred during the administration of President Ronald Reagan. Ideally, a "fuller understanding of past corruption can lessen the chance that it will be allowed to reach such proportions in the future." We may have to pay the price of vigilance, but we cannot afford corruption in presidential politics.

One of the most severe tests the U.S. political system can experience is the removal of the President for reasons of corruption. What makes political corruption so abhorrent is the fact that politicians are supposed to be representative of a particular district, state, or the nation as a whole. Unfortunately, the crooked politician may be more representative than it is sometimes realized. In "non-political" affairs there is often pressure to get ahead by any means necessary. Therefore, it might follow naturally that some politicians, who on the whole are usually little better or little worse than the rest of society, engage in illegal conduct. Even though they may be given the authority to act in the public interest, some of them may not rise above the drive for selfish, personal gain.

When political corruption reaches all the way to the President of the United States, the whole country justifiably takes an interest. The President is the one politician on whom all the voters can decide, and, therefore, all citizens feel that they have a stake in how the President conducts himself. As Head of State, the President does represent the United States at national and international functions. Thus, if a President engages in, or allows his administration to engage in, corrupt activities, the nation feels a sense of betrayal.

Three times within the last century the American presidency and, therefore, the American people, have been shaken by the exposure of widespread political corruption in the executive branch. First during the era of Reconstruction after the Civil War, later in the aftermath of the first World War, and more recently as the country emerged from the Vietnam War, the American people have had their faith in their national leaders severely tested. The nation weathered each storm without collapsing, but the damage has been great nevertheless. As historian Jarol B. Manheim has said, the nation emerged

> with its confidence shaken, its trust disabused, and its cynicism predominant. Indeed, in each instance the greatest cost of scandal has been, not the dollars lost through corrupt practices or the disservice to the national interest resulting from improper policies, but rather the decline in political interest and . . . support among the American population. The greatest cost of political corruption, in other words, has been to the political system itself. (Jarol B. Manheim, *Deja Vu: American Political Problems in Historical Perspective*, p. 96. For an analysis of the three presidential scandals discussed in this essay, read Chapter 4 of Manheim's book.)

By taking a closer look at the scandals attached to Presidents Grant, Harding, and Nixon, we can more fully understand how corruption ruined each man's presidency. We can attempt to understand the forces which led to their betrayal of public trust. We can examine what forces, both inside and outside the political system, exposed scandals to public scrutiny and brought about rectification. Finally, perhaps a fuller understanding of past corruption can lessen the chance that it will be allowed to reach such proportions in the future.

The Grant Administration

Ulysses S. Grant is often considered one of America's worst presidents, primarily because of the widespread political corruption which existed during his presidency.

Ironically enough, the scandal most often associated with the Grant era was not of his making. However, the uncovering of the so-called Credit Mobilier Scandal took place during his tenure and, therefore, was associated in the public mind with all the other misdeeds.

The Credit Mobilier was a railroad construction company established by the directors of the Union Pacific Railroad. The Union Pacific was interested in building a transcontinental railroad, especially since 1864 when the government offered a grant of 20 million acres of land and a loan of $55 million to encourage railroad construction. In effect, when the directors of the Union Pacific created the Credit Mobilier, there existed two corporations, separate but with identical ownership. Once they had this dual mechanism in place, the fraud commenced.

The Union Pacific proceeded to award construction contracts at inflated rates to the Credit Mobilier, which, of course, was owned by the very people who were letting the contracts. For example, a man named Oakes Ames, a shovel manufacturer and holder of Credit Mobilier stock, received a contract to build 667 miles of railroad for $42,000 a mile. This included a stretch of 238 miles *that had already been built*—at a cost of $27,000 per mile! The two companies kept a fantastic system of duplicate books, and between December 1867 to December 1868 the Credit Mobilier netted an estimated $40 to $50 million and paid a dividend of 595 percent.

Since these financial shenanigans involved government funds, it behooved the swindlers to keep the government out of its affairs. They accomplished this in two ways. First, they simply bribed the government commissioners whose jobs it was to oversee the construction of the railroad. Second, they distributed Credit Mobilier stock to members of Congress. They were aided in the latter pursuit by the above-mentioned Oakes Ames, who doubled as a member of the House of Representatives and sat on the Pacific Railroad Committee in the House. Ames put the matter quite succinctly in a letter later made public. "We want more friends in this Congress. There is no difficulty in getting men to look after their own property."

The scandal finally broke in 1872 when a suit was filed against the Credit Mobilier for delivery of stock which the plaintiff claimed to have purchased. Documents in the suit were leaked to the press, and the resulting outcry led to a congressional investigation. The disclosures in the investigation tainted several members of Congress and the Vice President. Two congressmen, Oates Ames and James Brooks, who sat on the U.P. Board of Directors, were censured. Vice President Schuyler Colfax was shown to have cashed-in twenty shares of Credit Mobilier stock, and he escaped impeachment proceedings by the fact that his term had almost expired anyway. But in the end the House white-washed the whole affair when the investigative report said that dishonest practices had been committed but that no one was guilty of them. A later governmental suit aimed at recovering some of the money was thrown out when the courts ruled that the government had no claim against the Credit Mobilier, since the Union Pacific, not the government, had let contracts to that company. Not surprisingly, the directors of the Union Pacific did not seek to recover funds from the directors of the Credit Mobilier!

President Grant was clearly not involved in the Credit Mobilier Scandal, but it became associated with him in two ways. First, Grant proclaimed total and badly misplaced confidence in Vice President Colfax's innocence. Second, the exposure of the Credit Mobilier Scandal coincided with disclosures of wrong-doing *within* the executive branch.

As Jarol Manheim has stated, "the President's own judgment was more clearly at issue in the second great scandal of the era, the Gold Conspiracy." Briefly stated, this scheme involved the attempt by two crafty businessmen of questionable ethics, Jay Gould and Jim Fisk, Jr., to corner the gold market by manipulating the government's policy regarding the price of gold. Gold was used as a medium of exchange for foreign and some domestic transactions, so there was a demand for the commodity which was in relatively short supply. The government attempted to regulate the price of gold and stabilize the economy by selling off some of its gold every month. Gould and Fisk sought to stop government sales after they had bought gold at a low figure. When scarcity drove the price up, they would sell!

To accomplish their objective, Gould and Fisk worked through an elderly real estate operator named Abel Corbin, who also happened to be President Grant's brother-in-law. Corbin introduced Gould and Fisk to the President, who was impressed by wealth and those who had it. Gould convinced the President that the economy would benefit from higher gold prices, which would result from reduced government sales. Grant went along with this reasoning and ordered the Secretary of Treasury to halt government sales. Grant then went on vacation, aboard a special train provided by Gould.

The conspirators now began to buy gold furiously, and soon they held contracts on roughly twice the available supply. The price of gold rose sharply. Grant, finally realizing what was happening, ordered the Treasury to sell $4 million in gold on September 24, 1869, a day that became known as "Black Friday." The price of gold fell drastically, leaving Fisk and a number of innocent businessmen facing bankruptcy. Gould had sold out before the crash when Corbin told him of Grant's decision to order the government sale. The public saw Grant as a slow-witted associate in an obvious scheme against the public interest. Their confidence in his judgment was considerably lessened.

Grant's naivete was further illustrated by the Whiskey Ring Scandal, which involved his personal secretary, Orville E. Babcock. The Whiskey Ring consisted of a sizable group of distillers, shippers, and government inspectors who conspired to deprive the government of tax revenues on whiskey produced in several large cities. When Babcock was implicated to the tune of $25,000 cash, plus diamonds, rare liquors, and other amenities, Grant went to extreme lengths to protect him. At Babcock's request, Grant tried to get him a trial before a friendly military tribunal. Failing at that, Grant issued an order that essentially denied the use of plea bargaining and trades of immunity for those aiding the government's case against Babcock. When the trial began, Grant filed a deposition assuring the jury of Babcock's integrity. The deposition, along with apparently perjured testimony of defense witnesses, led to Babcock's acquittal. Afterward, Grant dismissed from the government those who had played a leading role in prosecuting Babcock, including Treasury Secretary Benjamin H. Bristow.

As one historian phrased it, the Grant presidency was "The Era of Good Stealings." Further examples include the Treasury Scandal of 1873, in which James Sanborn made $213,500 by collecting delinquent taxes. Grant's Secretary of War, W. W. Belknap, augmented his $8,000 annual salary by selling appointments of War Department positions, most notably those as traders on Indian posts, for as much as $20,000 apiece. Belknap resigned but was impeached by the House of Representatives anyway. He escaped conviction in the Senate only because most of those voting "not guilty" thought it improper to impeach someone who had already resigned.

Still other examples of political corruption under Grant can be cited. One instance involved presidential appointees to direct the customhouses in New York and New Orleans—the latter position being filled by one of Grant's brothers-in-law—who used their positions for personal and political gain. Another scandal involved the wife of George Williams, Grant's third Attorney General, who, apparently with her husband's advice and consent, accepted a bribe of some $30,000 to halt a suit in which her husband was involved. Grant's Secretary of Interior, Columbus Delano, resigned after being implicated in a scheme involving fraudulent land warrants for veterans. Finally, George M. Robeson, Secretary of the Navy, used his influence to help a Philadelphia grain dealer, as well as his own income.

The list of misdeeds could go on, but the point has been amply illustrated. The Grant Era was one of the most corrupt in U.S. history, although Grant himself was not dishonest. Rather, his weaknesses were in his inability to judge character and in his blind loyalty to unworthy appointees. He made possible and naively defended the indiscretions of others. That, more than anything else, earned for Grant his lowly position in American political history. Unfortunately, he would be joined by others.

The Harding Administration

It was another fifty years before political corruption permeated the executive branch as it did under Grant. That does *not* mean that political corruption did not exist. In fact, in the late nineteenth and early twentieth centuries it became almost an accepted fact that big industrialists kept politicians on retainer. John D. Rockefeller was said to have had the best state legislators and U.S. Senators that money could buy. However, the Presidents from Hayes through Wilson, although many of them were hardly more than adequate in performing their jobs, were not remembered for political corruption. It was not until Warren Gamaliel Harding became President in 1921 that the Chief Executive was again surrounded by scandal.

It was once said that Harding's only qualification for President was that he looked like one. A kind and friendly man, Harding had risen to the position of U.S. Senator prior to his presidential nomination. He had played along with the Ohio political machine, also known as the Ohio Gang, and was the available man when the Republicans sought to capitalize on the post-World War I disillusionment with Democrats. Harding, like Grant, was to be "more guilty of poor judgment and misplaced loyalties than of any personal corruption. Still, in a president of the United States such characteristics can be fatal, and in Harding's case were quite literally so." (Manheim, p. 109)

Before considering the infamous Teapot Dome Scandal, let us take note of several other examples of political corruption during Harding's presidency. One scandal involved Charles R. Forbes, who headed the Veteran's Bureau. Forbes was an amiable fellow who could play poker, the type of man that Harding liked. He proceeded to use his position for personal gain and to help his friends and relatives. He made appointments—one of the appointees was his brother-in-law—to government jobs which hardly demanded any work. In fact, one employee picked up an annual salary of $4,800 for two hours of work each *year*. Forbes also connived with private business firms to swindle the government out of money appropriated for building veterans' hospitals. Furthermore, he conspired to dispose of "surplus" hospital goods at a considerable loss to the government and considerable gain to himself. When Forbes' misdeeds were exposed, Harding, like Grant in earlier times, stuck by his appointee. Finally, Forbes resigned, and after a Senate investigation and nine-week trial, he was sentenced to two years in jail and a $10,000 fine.

Another Harding appointee, Thomas W. Miller, was caught with his hand in the till. Miller was the Alien Property Custodian, whose job it was to oversee the settlement of claims on alien property seized during World War I. In one celebrated case, Miller ended up splitting some $441,000 with another Harding crony, Jess Smith, after approving a fraudulent transfer of $7 million worth of alien property. When the case was exposed, Miller was sentenced to eighteen months in prison, Attorney General Harry Daugherty refused to testify on grounds he might incriminate himself, and Jess Smith committed suicide. Smith had apparently decided that his career of dispensing government positions, immunity from government prosecutions, and access to government files could last no longer. Daugherty's Justice Department, popularly known as the "Department of Easy Virtue," was under constant suspicion for illegal acts ranging from the illegal sale of pardons and liquor permits to the operation of an espionage network which shadowed Congressmen in search of blackmail material. Harding's successor, Calvin Coolidge, requested Daugherty's resignation, something the loyal Harding would not do. Daugherty later stood trial twice on corruption charges, but the juries failed to convict him both times.

Another cabinet member was not so fortunate. Albert Fall, Harding's Secretary of Interior, became the first cabinet member to be sentenced to jail for engaging in illegal activities while holding public office. Fall's conviction

208

resulted from his involvement in the Teapot Dome Scandal. Teapot Dome referred to a rock formation which set atop Naval Oil Reserve Number Three in Wyoming. The Teapot Dome Reserve and two others in California had been established prior to World War I as a safeguard for the preservation of oil possibly needed for military operations. When Fall took over the Interior Department he persuaded Harding to order the transfer of the oil reserves from the Navy Department to the Interior. Harding later wrote a letter to the Senate declaring that he not only approved the transfer but also all "subsequent acts" in the matter. Had he not died, such an admission may have brought about impeachment proceedings against Harding, for the "subsequent acts" of Albert Fall led to his imprisonment.

What Fall did was to lease to private oilmen E. L. Doheny and Harry Sinclair the rights to develop the naval oil reserves, with the government to receive a *portion* of the oil. He also improved his own finances in the process, receiving a $100,000 "loan" from Doheny and a payment of $68,000 from Sinclair. (Testimony on the Sinclair money received a humorous twist when Sinclair's secretary testified that he had been talking about "six or eight cows" not "sixty-eight thous." It seems that secretaries have to contrive some fabulous stories to cover misdeeds, *a la* Rosemary Woods with the Nixon tapes). When suspicions arose about the oil transfer and about Fall's new-found wealth, a congressional investigation was launched by Montana Senator Thomas J. Walsh. Similar to the Watergate Hearings fifty years later, other congressional business ground to a halt while the scandal was exposed.

The congressional hearings led to the appointment by President Coolidge of two special prosecutors and a lengthy series of trials which began in late 1926. By March, 1930, the trials were over, but the results were less than clear. The leases on the Teapot Dome and the other naval reserves were invalidated because they resulted from fraud, corruption, collusion, and conspiracy. But Fall and Doheny were acquitted on charges of conspiracy as were Fall and Sinclair in a second trial. However, Sinclair did serve brief sentences for contempt of Congress and contempt of court, and Fall was convicted of receiving a bribe from Doheny and was sentenced to a year in jail and a $100,000 fine. On the other hand, Doheny was acquitted of bribing Fall! The verdicts caused Senator George W. Norris to remark that it is "very difficult, if not impossible, to convict one hundred million dollars." Similarly, a historian has remarked that the decisions undermined faith in the courts and gave currency to the saying that "in America everyone is assumed guilty until proven rich."

Harding, who had also been the object of whispers that he maintained a mistress at the White House, was spared the full revelations of the scandals. His suspicions had been aroused, however, and he was heard to have grumbled about the disloyalty of his "god-damned friends." While returning from a speaking tour on the West Coast, he died of pneumonia and thrombosis on August 2, 1923. At the time, he was mourned sorrowfully and emotionally by a country unaware of the corruption yet to be disclosed. His reputation was subsequently tarnished, although like Grant, his personal honesty was not the issue. Rather, like his predecessor of fifty years earlier, his weakness in judgment and guidance submitted the country to its worst display of political corruption since Grant had left office.

Fortunately for the Republicans, Calvin Coolidge was President when most of the revelations about the Harding scandals became public. Coolidge had the image of a Puritan ascetic, and no one questioned his integrity. Years later, FDR was accused of abusing his powers of patronage, Truman was criticized for tolerating influence peddling, Eisenhower was said to be too protective of aide Sherman Adams, and some referred to LBJ as "Landslide" Lyndon for his suspicious victory in a 1948 Senate race. "But fifty years passed before another major scandal . . . the most centralized and most pernicious of all, shook the nation to its very foundations and forced the *de facto* impeachment of a president of the United States. That scandal was Watergate, and the president was Richard Milhous Nixon." (Manheim, p. 119)

The Nixon Administration

The name Watergate originally referred to a posh apartment and office complex in Washington, D.C., which housed the headquarters of the Democratic National Committee. On June 17, 1972, five men were arrested for breaking into those headquarters, and from that day on Watergate became the name for the most scandalous of all presidential corruptions. The burglars had in their possession cameras, electronic bugging devices, several crisp new $100 bills in sequential order, and notebooks which included the names of E. Howard Hunt and G. Gordon Liddy, the latter a counsel to the Committee to Re-elect the President (CREEP). Questions were thus raised about the connection between the Nixon White House, whose press secretary, Ron Ziegler, termed the affair "a third-rate burglary," and the burglars. By the time those questions were answered several years later, some sixty-three people were charged with crimes associated with the Nixon presidency, fifty-four of them were convicted or pleaded guilty, and the President himself resigned in disgrace.

Obviously, the break-in itself did not seem to merit such an extensive list of guilty parties. Had matters been handled openly at the time the break-in occurred, the fallout would not have been so great. However, the White House decided to cover up any connection between the President and the burglary. Elements of the cover-up included payment of "hush-money," frequent lies by the President and his spokesmen (the White House referred to these as "misstatements" or as "inoperative" remarks), misuse of the Justice Department, and manipulation of the Central Intelligence Agency.

Very few of the details of the cover-up were revealed before Richard Nixon had defeated George McGovern in the 1972 presidential election. During the summer following that election a Senate committee, chaired by Senator Sam Ervin of North Carolina, began investigating campaign practices. Television viewers took more than a casual interest as John W. Dean, former counsel to President Nixon, traced an elaborate White House plot to cover up the Watergate Affair, a cover-up that was denied by two top White House aides, H. R. Haldeman and John Ehrlichman. With Dean standing virtually alone, the committee needed corroboration. It got that and more when a White House assistant, Alexander P. Butterfield, revealed that a taping system in the President's office had probably recorded Dean's conversations, and all others, held in that office. The Senate Committee and Special Prosecutor Archibald Cox, who had been named earlier by Nixon to handle Watergate-related prosecutions, went after a whole series of relevant tapes. Nixon refused to turn them over on the grounds of executive privilege. A lengthy political and legal battle was now joined, with the first turning point occurring on Saturday, October 20, 1973, when President Nixon fired Cox and accepted the resignations of Attorney General Elliot Richardson and Deputy Attorney General William Ruckelshaus, who had both refused Nixon's order to dismiss Cox. Known as the "Saturday Night Massacre," this event caused a massive public outcry of indignation aimed at the President. It was becoming more obvious to the public that Nixon, indeed, must have something to hide. (See Manheim, pp. 121–122)

Numerous revelations throughout the Watergate investigation added to Nixon's problems. At the end of 1972 it was revealed that even though Nixon had become a millionaire while in office, he had paid less than $1,000 in income taxes in 1970 and 1971. Meanwhile, when the White House agreed to release tapes subpoenaed by the special prosecutor, it announced that two critical tapes were missing and one had an eighteen and one-half minute gap where a presidential discussion of Watergate should have been. In March, 1974, seven presidential aides and election officials were indicted for their roles in the cover-up, and seven for involvement in a break-in at the office of the psychiatrist for Daniel Ellsberg, who had been implicated in releasing sensitive Pentagon documents to the press. On April 29, 1974, Nixon went before a national television audience to announce that he was releasing more than a thousand pages of edited transcripts of presidential conversations. Contrary to his hopes, the transcripts only deepened public outcry, for they revealed the tone of the White House conversations as being "cynical, amoral, vindictive, self-serving, and conspiratorial." (Thomas A. Bailey and David M. Kennedy, *The American Pageant,* Sixth Edition, p. 914) In July the Supreme Court ordered Nixon to release the tapes themselves, and the discrepancies with the transcripts became obvious.

Finally, the House Judiciary Committee voted impeachment of the President of the United States. The Committee approved three articles of impeachment: the first charged the President with obstruction of justice; the second charged Nixon with abuse of the power of his office; the third accused him of conduct "subversive of constitutional government" by ignoring lawful subpoenas for tapes and other written documents. Most observers thought at least the first article would be approved by the full House of Representatives and, therefore, necessitate a trial in the Senate.

The House vote and the Senate trial never happened. On August 5, 1974, Nixon released three subpoenaed tapes of conversations he had with aides soon after the Watergate break-in. The "smoking gun" that skeptics had wanted had been found, for the tapes left no doubt that Nixon had been deeply involved in the cover-up all along. What congressional support he had left now collapsed, and on August 8, 1974, Nixon told a national television audience that he was resigning the following day. Had he not resigned he likely would have become the first U.S. President to have been impeached by the House and removed from office after conviction in the Senate. (Incidentally, resignation also allowed Nixon to receive his full retirement benefits.)

Nixon's closest associates, former Attorney General John Mitchell and presidential advisers H. R. Haldeman and John Ehrlichman, were convicted of Watergate-related crimes and sentenced to prison. John Dean, White House counsel and star witness in the Watergate investigation, pleaded guilty to charges of participating in the cover-up and served four months in jail. Charles Colson, a political adviser and reputed "hatchet man" in the White House, served six months in jail for obstruction of justice. Jeb Stuart Magruder, a high official on Nixon's campaign staff, was jailed for seven months for obstruction of justice. G. Gordon Liddy, who presented the burglary plans to Mitchell, spent more than four years in jail. E. Howard Hunt, who recruited the burglars, served thirty-two months.

The Watergate break-in, the cover-up, the resignation of Richard Nixon, and the imprisonment of his aides did not constitute the whole story of the Nixon scandals. Ten months before Nixon resigned, his Vice-President, Spiro Agnew, stepped down from his position. Agnew had come under investigation from a Baltimore grand jury investigating charges of kickbacks and tax fraud in Maryland. When evidence of his guilt seemed overwhelming, Agnew pleaded no contest to a charge of income tax evasion and resigned. Nixon, under terms of the Twenty-fifth Amendment, appointed Gerald R. Ford as Vice-President, who then became President following Nixon's resignation. A few weeks after Nixon's departure, Ford pardoned the former President for any misdeeds he may have committed while President.

There were other scandals in the Nixon years as well. Richard G. Kleindienst, Mitchell's successor as Attorney General, pleaded guilty to a charge of obstructing prosecution of an antitrust suit against International Telephone and Telegraph (ITT). There were a number of charges related to illegal campaign contributions, which led to guilty pleas from former Nixon attorney Herbert Kalmback and former Treasury Secretary Maurice Stans, who was director of fund-raising activities for CREEP. Still other illegalities involved the so-called "dirty tricks" of the 1972 campaign and the actions of the White House "plumbers."

The list of guilty parties in the Nixon scandals could go on, but it is clear that political corruption reached new depths under Nixon. The pervasiveness of wrongdoing outstripped even that of the Grant and Harding eras. Like his predecessors in corruption, Nixon had encouraged a political atmosphere which led to disregard of the law. Unlike his predecessors, Nixon was personally involved in direct abuse of presidential power.

There are some other interesting similarities in a retrospective glance at the three periods of corruption. Each occurred during a Republican administration. In each instance, the reflexive response of the President was to deny scandal and to cover it up and protect associates. Congressional hearings and special legal procedures outside the executive-controlled Justice Department were significant in bringing the corruption into the open. This supports the importance of the system of checks and balances within the constitutional framework. The press also played an important role in each case, most notably in the Nixon scandals. The dogged reporting of Carl Bernstein and Bob Woodward of the Washington *Post* will be long-remembered as an example of the press's role in exposing wrongdoing in public office.

Three additional considerations deserve comment. First, all three crises in the presidency followed extended periods of national turmoil and each followed costly wars. Secondly, each scandalous administration followed a period in which the powers of the presidency were expanded. The development of this "imperial presidency" contributed to Richard Nixon's view that the President of the United States was above the law. Grant and Harding were not seeking personal power, but their trusting nature allowed subordinates to take advantage of the presidency for financial gain. Nixon's offense was greater than the two earlier Presidents in this sense, for he sought to acquire and maintain illegal political power as well as financial gain. Finally, each period of corruption resulted in a breakdown of trust between the American people and their government. The losses here cannot be measured, but they are nevertheless real and extremely significant.

There is some scandal in almost every presidential administration and in almost every session of Congress, but the massive scale of corruption during the Grant, Harding, and Nixon eras reached shocking proportions. It seems that there is a regular pattern of a fifty-year interval between such extensive political abuses. Perhaps by keeping in mind the forces which brought about the scandals, by keeping a vigilant watch on the activities of political leaders, and by making sure that their own sense of proper conduct serves as a model for politicians, the American people can prevent such abuses of political power from happening again.

Epilogue: The Reagan Administration

Unfortunately, it did not take fifty years for serious and widespread scandal to mar the record of another president. Those who elected Ronald Reagan in 1980 believed that he stood for family values, religious ethics, and a strict construction of the law. By the time Reagan left the presidency in 1989, well more than 100 senior administration officials had come under investigation for improper conduct. Some resigned under fire, were dismissed, had their nominations withdrawn or rejected, pleaded guilty to crimes, and/or were convicted of serious offenses. Among the most prominent administration officials tainted by corruption were Michael Deaver, the president's aide and confidant, Attorney General Edwin Meese, and, of course, Oliver North, a former national security aide. At the end, the president himself escaped responsibility only because he seemed so "detached" and confused that it was hard to believe that he could have orchestrated much of this wrongdoing. Indeed, what had gone wrong?

Part of the explanation lies with the philosophical absolutes which Ronald Reagan and those around him brought to the presidency. At home, the government was a hindrance to unregulated pursuit of personal and/or corporate gain. Restrictions, otherwise known as laws, were often considered "technical, trivial, even avoidable." (See Mark Green and Peter H. Stone's article in *The Dallas Morning News,* July 12, 1987, p. 35A). Too many Reagan appointees could not make the transition from the private sector to the public service. The scandals emanating from the Department of Housing and Urban Development (HUD) under Reagan illustrate the point. It was here that administration officials and private developers schemed to defraud the taxpayers of hundreds of millions of dollars. Meanwhile, housing for the poor, which they were supposed to be rehabilitating, languished. Some pundit coined the term "the sleaze factor" to refer to the administration's failure "to comprehend ethics and outright scandals."

Abroad, the Soviet Union was simply "the evil empire," so anything done to stop the spread of this pernicious influence, even selling weapons to terrorists, was deemed morally permissible! While the Pentagon went on a spending spree accompanied by examples of gross excess and corruption, high-level Reagan administration officials engaged in one of the most contemptible scandals in the nation's history, the Iran-contra affair. Simply put, investigations revealed that Oliver North of the National Security Council, William Casey of the Central Intelligence Agency, and others secretly sold weapons to Iran, a nation branded as terrorist by the United States. They apparently believed that Iran could use its influence to help free hostages held at that time by terrorist groups in Lebanon. Despite President Reagan's pledge never to pay ransom for hostages, that appeared to be what was happening. Furthermore, the profits from the sales of the weapons was to be diverted, illegally, to aid the contras, the name given to those who were fighting against a left-wing government in Nicaragua.

The Iran-contra affair raised questions about constitutional rule and the competence of President Reagan. The threat to the Constitution involved more than the duplicity of selling weapons to terrorists. Oliver North and the others involved apparently believed that they had the right to circumvent congressional legislation. Furthermore, when the story of this unseemly affair began to be exposed in late 1986, the major operatives had already begun a coverup operation that proved to be similar to the Watergate affair of the Nixon era. The public's reaction to North was especially interesting, for a man who admitted to lies and illegal acts became a national hero to some. He played the media for all it was worth, and he wrapped himself in the flag. Or, as one commentator aptly put it, he tried to destroy the Constitution and hid behind the flag. What was President Reagan's role in all of this? Had he deliberately lied to the American people about an arms-for-hostages deal? Or was he totally unaware of what was going on in the White House? Either answer was appalling and alarming.

What should we have learned from the Iran-contra affair and the other scandals of the Reagan administration? First, we must demand that any president must know and be accountable for the actions of administration officials. Presidential styles may vary, but the president is responsible for faithfully executing the laws of the nation. Secondly, we must demand that the president's staff obey the law. The United States cannot tolerate non-elected officials (nor anyone else) taking the law into their own hands—this endangers the very foundation of our constitutional system of government. Thirdly, we must accept the idea that Congress has a legitimate role to play in foreign policy. It was not without thought that the framers of the Constitution gave Congress the sole power to declare war as well as the powers of appropriating funds and congressional oversight of executive operations. The system of checks and balances can help avoid excesses in foreign as well as domestic affairs. Lastly, the American people must be alert to abuses of power, for the price of liberty is still eternal vigilance.

How the Media Seduced and Captured American Politics

by Richard C. Wade

Ronald Reagan has been called a "Great Communicator" by some political analysts. The reasons behind this acclamation did not stem from the quality of the information the President dispensed. Rather, Reagan was effective in the *manner* in which he delivered his message, or at least many Americans of the television generation perceived him to be effective. Indeed, Reagan's background as a movie and TV celebrity may have been ideal for the age of the media campaign.

In the following essay, Richard C. Wade of the City University of New York traces the gradual expansion of the influence of television on American politics. Professor Wade's assessment of the effects of the media campaign are disturbing. Most troubling to him is the apparent correlation of the increased use of television campaigning with the decreasing number of voters who participate in our political system. As Wade notes, President Reagan's "landslide" in 1980 was delivered by "fewer than 20 percent of adults over eighteen years of age" in an election in which "just over half" of those registered actually voted.

Despite low voter turnout, inordinate campaign expenses, and the breakdown of traditional party functions, Dr. Wade does not despair. Instead he sees "no reason why the media revolution cannot . . . be made apt to democratic purposes." In order for that to happen, we must realize what has happened to our political system. Professor Wade has contributed to that realization with his timely observations.

Television has been accused of many things: vulgarizing tastes; trivializing public affairs; sensationalizing news; corrupting the young; pandering to profits; undermining traditional values. The indictments are no doubt too harsh, and they ignore the medium's considerable achievements over two decades. Yet even the severest critics have not noticed the way in which television first seduced and then captured the whole American political process.

The fact is that each year fewer people register to vote, and among those who do, an ever-shrinking number actually go to the polls. Since casting a free ballot constitutes the highest expression of freedom in a democracy, its declining use is a grave matter. How did we get ourselves into this perilous state?

Television's victory was not the result of a carefully planned and calculated assault on our political procedures; less still was it the conspiracy of a greedy and power-hungry industry. Rather it was a process in which each year witnessed a modest expansion of the electronic influence on American politics. A look at the presidential election of 1948, the first in the age of television, suggests both the magnitude and swiftness of the change. President Harry Truman ran a shoestring campaign sustained largely by his incumbency and the overconfidence of his opponent. Together the two candidates spent only about $15 million—the cost of a gubernatorial contest in New York three decades later. Both presidential candidates leaned heavily on their state and local parties for crowds and election-day support. Truman's whistle-stop tour of the country harked back to a century-old technique. Television covered the conventions but intruded no further. Radio handled the late returns, and the commentator H. V. Kaltenborn, who assumed historical patterns would hold true, waited for the rural vote to sustain his early prediction of a victory for New York governor Thomas E. Dewey.

Some of the possibilities of television emerged, however, in the next election. Sen. Robert Taft used time-honored, if somewhat questionable, tactics to line up a solid phalanx of Southern delegates at the 1952 Republican convention. Gen. Dwight Eisenhower's managers presented a more properly selected alternative set of delegates. Historically, disputes of this kind had been resolved behind closed doors and brought to the convention only for ratification. But Eisenhower strategists wanted to transform what had long been seen as a technical question into a moral one. They chose as their weapon televised committee hearings. For the first time, the public became privy to the vagaries of party rules. Viewers were let into the smoke-filled room. The result was a resounding defeat for Taft, and Eisenhower went into the convention with plenty of delegates and wearing the fresh, smiling face of reform.

A few months later Eisenhower's running mate, Richard Nixon, found himself entangled in a burgeoning scandal involving a private fund raised by large contributors to advance his political career. Though no law had been broken, the impropriety was clear, especially in a campaign based on cleaning up "the mess" in Washington. Eisenhower declared that anyone in public life should be as "clean as a hound's tooth," and many of his advisers told him to drop the young congressman.

A desperate Nixon decided to take his case directly to the public—through a half-hour paid telecast. He declared he had meant no wrongdoing, detailed the high costs facing a California congressman, noted his own modest means, and said he had always voted his own conscience on issues before the House.

Most memorable, however, was his use of his dog, Checkers, as a kind of surrogate "hound's tooth." To sophisticates it seemed like a clip out of a daytime soap opera, but the public found it plausible enough. More important, it satisfied Dwight Eisenhower.

These two episodes revealed the ambiguity of the new medium. Until 1952, conventions had been closed party affairs run by the national committees. In fact, that is still their only legal function. But television put the voters on the convention floor. Both parties had to dispense with a lot of the traditional hoopla—endless floor demonstrations, marathon seconding speeches, visibly indulgent behavior by delegates—and keynote speakers had to project telegenic appeal as well as party service. To be sure, television introduced its own brand of hoopla. Cameras zoomed in on outrageous costumes, floormen interviewed colorful if not always important figures, and networks did the counting of the delegates before the issues or nominations actually got to the decisive stage.

The Nixon heritage was less complicated. The "Checkers" speech became shorthand for slick, calculated manipulation if not deception. Critics argued it demonstrated that a shrewd master of the medium could sell anything—not only commercial products but political candidates as well.

The presidential election of 1956 was essentially a rerun of the previous one, yet one episode demonstrated the increasing influence of television. With Stevenson's renomination by the Democrats a certainty, the networks faced a four-day yawn from their viewers. Salvation suddenly appeared in a contest over the Vice-Presidency. With no obvious choice and with Stevenson himself undecided, three senators moved into contention: Estes Kefauver of Tennessee, Hubert Humphrey of Minnesota, and John F. Kennedy of Massachusetts.

Chicago was awash with whispers of deals being concocted in smoke-filled rooms to designate a running mate, and to sustain his reform image, Stevenson threw open the choice to the convention. Suddenly there was theater. Kefauver had a second chance; Humphrey got his first; and Kennedy seemed to have no chance at all. A big scoreboard behind the podium recorded the voting from the floor. The Kentucky Derby never generated more excitement. As state by state announced the results, the lead fluctuated. At the last moment Humphrey released his delegates to the Tennessean who had contested Stevenson in a dozen primaries. Afterward only historians would remember that Kefauver had won, but Kennedy's performance gave the public its first impression of a man who would dominate his party—and the media—for almost a decade.

Four years later another national election provided television with one of its greatest moments: the Nixon-Kennedy debates. It was a strange event, and it is hard to say who won. A reading of the transcripts today reveals no surprises. Each candidate expressed views already known; each circled and jabbed; but there were no knockdowns. Yet millions saw the relative newcomer under the most favorable of circumstances, and even though the contrast was sharper visually than intellectually, there was a vague general feeling that JFK had got the better of it.

In all, the new medium lived up both to its responsibilities and its possibilities. For the first time, it had brought two presidential candidates to the same podium. The proceedings were overly elaborate, but the handling of the event was scrupulously fair and nonpartisan. And afterward it would become increasingly hard for candidates, even incumbents to avoid legitimate challenges on television.

The turbulence of the sixties can only be understood in the context of television's ubiquity. It brought its first war, Vietnam, into the living room from ten thousand miles away; it showed us racial explosions across urban America; it covered the campus meetings that revealed the widest generation gap in American history; and it captured, in endless replays, the assassination of three of the country's most popular political leaders. And viewers were also voters. The decade of turbulence scrambled old allegiances and rendered old labels meaningless.

The year 1968 was a tide without a turning. Nixon's election ushered in a new era dominated by the paid commercial and an overall media strategy. Already what the press would call "image makers" or "media mavens" were on their way to becoming at least as important as campaign managers. Charles Guggenheim's twenty-five-minute TV film "A Man From New York," broadcast in the 1964 senatorial contest, purported to show that Robert Kennedy was not really from Massachusetts; four years later Guggenheim portrayed George McGovern as a bombardier in World War II to dispel the notion that he was a craven pacifist. More daringly, political manager David Garth ran John Lindsay for reelection in New York City with commercials in which the mayor admitted to endless small mistakes in office, the better to magnify presumed larger accomplishments.

Guggenheim and Garth were pioneers: the full media impact lay in the seventies, when it replaced more conventional activities. Its muscle was most obvious in determining the schedule of the candidate. Traditionally, managers had tried to get their stalwart in front of as many groups as possible. A heavy speaking schedule gave the candidate a chance to make his views known to disparate electorate, and if the newspapers covered the meetings, so much the better.

Now, every effort focused on television. Instead of sessions with political groups, the object was a contrived "event." The candidate showed up at a senior citizens' center and delivered a brief statement drawn from some position paper. Television news deadlines determined the timing; the campaign coverage of the previous week determined the issue. As election day approached, two or three of what Daniel Boorstin has called "pseudo events" highlighted the day's schedule. Nothing important was said, but the ninety-second exposure brought the candidate to the voter without the intercession of a party or political organization and showed him concerned about something that pollsters had discovered was on the public mind.

This direct appeal made parties increasingly superfluous. To be sure, they still had the critical line on the ballot; they still had enough registered members to make an endorsement worthwhile. But they were no longer the candidates' principal sponsor. Indeed, they could seldom guarantee a crowd. When that was needed, a few media celebrities could draw a larger audience than a politician's speech.

The parties also lost their traditional recruiting function. Formerly, the ambitious sought political office after a period of party service, often at lowly stations. Now the young headed directly toward electoral office with party registration their only evidence of loyalty. In fact, many considered a close affiliation with day-to-day party affairs to be the mark of a hack; a fresh, nonpartisan face appealed more to the electorate than a veteran party standard-bearer. The spread of primaries at the expense of conventions opened the way to further end runs around the organization. In addition, state after state adopted laws designed to loosen the monopoly of parties over the nominating process, thus magnifying the importance of independents. In some states, for example, an eligible voter need only appear at the polls and declare himself at that moment either a Democrat or a Republican to be entitled to cast a ballot in a party primary.

Initially, reformers rejoiced at these trends, and the regular parties seemed to be the first casualties. But media politics knew no factional boundaries. Just as surely as it undermined traditional party practices, it also withered the voluntary base of reform politics. The parties depended on patronage, reformers on participation. What regulars would do as part of the job, independents would do from commitment. Yet a media campaign did not leave much for volunteers to do.

The new media managers cared little for traditional canvassing where party workers or volunteers went door to door to discover preferences, deliver literature, and argue the candidate's case. The foot soldiers were untrained in modern interviewing techniques; they worked at odd hours; they often returned with useless material; and even good campaigns could not provide full voter coverage. Large banks of telephones were more reliable. Paid operators called scientifically selected numbers; the message was uniform; computers swallowed the responses and spit out the printouts. Ironically, phone banks had originally been a volunteer activity. Supporters took home lists and made personal calls; but better management dictated closer control. The new system is expensive, and there is no way of knowing if phone canvassing, even confined to "prime" lists, is effective; but every campaign for high office finds it necessary.

Polling, too, is an indispensable part of the media campaign. This is not new, but its intensity is. "The calls go out every night randomly, 150 or more," wrote B. Brummond Ayres, Jr., in The New York Times in 1981, of the Reagan Presidency, "to homes across the country." The interviews last a half hour; they ask every kind of question bordering on the voter's interest and public matters. Then the computers whiz and calculators click; "earlier interviews are thrown into the mix" and "in a matter of hours President Reagan and the officials of the Republican National Committee have in hand the latest intelligence needed to tailor a speech, a program or a policy." Richard Werthlin's Washington firm is paid $900,000 a year for this "tracking" of the popular mood.

Previous Presidents relied on a handful of trusted advisers and erratic, and usually unsolicited, reports of party leaders and friends from across the country. But now all campaigns use polls. Indeed, despite their frequent and sometimes flagrant errors, the press and the media treat their results as news stories; columnists scatter ratings throughout their interpretations; analysts worry that their wide use has become a surrogate election, even affecting the actual outcome. Polls are, however, so much a part of the candidates' strategy that some state legislatures have moved against the release of selected parts and require the publication of the full survey. And one poll alone won't do. Anxious managers and candidates can hardly get enough of them, especially in the climactic weeks of the campaign. What is also important is that the survey is bought and requires no use of volunteers.

The media campaign is all business. There is none of the congenial chaos that characterized traditional politics. At headquarters a few people mill about numberless machines. Everything is computerized. Paid employees run the terminals; paid telephoners call numbers from purchased printouts; rented machines slap labels on direct-mail envelopes. Mercenaries grind out "position papers," and press releases are quickly dispatched to a computerized "key" list of newspapers, radio, television stations, columnists, and commentators. "What they have created," wrote the *New York Times* reporter Steven V. Roberts, "is an electronic party."

At the center of the effort is the purchasing of paid television commercials. They are the modern substitute for conventional campaigning. The candidate is not seen live; the message, in fact, is often delivered by a professional voice. The purpose is to project a candidate who is like the viewer, but better: one who arouses but does not agitate; one who elevates but does not disturb; one who exudes morality but not righteousness; one who conveys strength but not arrogance; one who is experienced but not cynical; one who has convictions but avoids controversy. Since such people are in as short supply in private life as in public affairs, a good deal of contrivance is demanded, and the commercial permits it.

The commercial does not seek truth but plausibility. It confines itself to a handful of "issues" that are the candidate's long suit and that are reiterated until the viewer is convinced that these are of paramount interest to other voters even if they are not so to him. The idea is to define the argument on the candidate's own terms. All this is done in the context of constant polling, telephone feedback, and it must be added, old-fashioned political instinct. As the campaign continues, one spot will be dropped, others altered, and still others emphasized.

The central fact about commercials is their cost. For maximum advantage they are artfully spliced into programs with large voting audiences. Since most advertisers head for the same viewers, the price is very high. In 1980 thirty seconds in the prime-time New York market cost $5,000; ninety seconds cost $15,000. Even in South Dakota these figures ran as high as $250 and $500.

The financial risks attendant on a media campaign are borne solely by the candidate, not by the media managers. Bookings for commercial spots have to be made far in advance and the money paid on the barrelhead. In the past, suppliers of campaign materials—printers, hotels, and airlines—were more tolerant. Some creditors had to wait years for their money and then settled on a percentage, often small, of the original bill.

But now media consultants get their money on schedule. The most common plea at a fund raiser as election day approaches is, "If we don't have the money by tomorrow noon, the candidate is off the air." This is shorthand for saying, "Unless you cough up, the election is over."

The media people have so convinced the public and political donors that the commercial is the campaign that only the penurious or uncommitted will resist. And the media's demand is insatiable. If the consultant's polls show the candidate is behind, then a large buy is crucial; if ahead, then the turnout is critical. In either case, the cameras roll and the candidate pays.

Worse still, the media's demand hits the candidate when he is most vulnerable. A whole career seems to ride on the outcome. Hence, the resources of the family are called in, friends enlisted, business and professional associates tapped. For a while this feeds the tube. But except for the personally very wealthy, the cupboard is soon bare. The only recourse is to go to "political givers," old and new. They have the capacity to underwrite the big loans to cover the up-front money. Yet their liability is very small. (State and federal laws restrict total spending and the amount of individual contributions; everything above those limits must be repaid.)

For the donors it is a cheap ante: they are ultimately repaid by the finance committee. After the election a few galas retire the victors' debt. For the losers, debt is a persistent nightmare.

Many people can afford political giving, but few do it. The result is a hectic and not always elevating courtship of a handful of wealthy people by the candidate and his finance committee. Some potential donors have only a dilettante's interest in politics, but most have interests that are more than marginally related to government. They expect what the trade euphemistically calls "access" to the winner.

The influence of money in American politics is, of course, not new. But the media has introduced a level of spending never known before. In the 1960 presidential campaigns about 10 percent of the budget went to television; by 1980 it had reached 80 percent. David Garth, the most successful practitioner of the new politics, succinctly summed up the present reality when he asserted that political effort outside commercials "is a waste of time and money." The result is that the inordinate power of money in American politics is larger now than it was a generation ago.

Nothing, perhaps, better illustrates today's sharp cleavage with past electioneering than Rep. Millicent Fenwick's 1982 campaign for the United States Senate seat from New Jersey. Now in her seventies, Fenwick grew up with the old politics. "I have a total amateur approach," she told *The New York Times*, reflecting her traditional reliance on volunteer activity. But she reluctantly admitted to hiring a television consultant, studying polls, and submitting to the new fund-raising imperative. "I have never used a television person before, and all this professionalism is not happy-making, being packaged by professionals as though you were some new kind of invention like the splash-free valve on a faucet." Yet soon Fenwick commercials began the "thematic" bombardment, polls suggested tactics, and fund raisers started scrambling. Ironically, she was defeated by a wealthy newcomer who had no reservations about television.

Perhaps an even more telling gauge of the transformation of the political process was Theodore White's bewilderment in covering the presidential election of 1980. Since 1960 he had been the country's premier chronicler of the summit contests. Now, baffled by the new system, and nearly certain it signaled democracy's decline, he left the campaign trail and went home to watch it all on television. Always the quintessential insider, he now felt himself irrelevant bric-a-brac from the age of Dwight Eisenhower. He decided, "I could sit at home and learn as much or more about the frame of the campaign as I could on the road." But in fact, Teddy White, without knowing it, was still at the center of things: all the strategy, all the organization, converged on the screen in front of him, coaxing the voters' acquiscence.

And the voters, more and more, choose to stay away. Ronald Reagan's 1980 presidential victory has been called the most decisive since Franklin Roosevelt's in 1932. Yet it drew the smallest voter turnout in modern history. Just over half the registered voters exercised their franchise that year, and fewer than 20 percent of adults over eighteen years of age gave the new President a "landslide." This decline in registration and voting and the ascendance of the media is no temporal coincidence. Increasingly politics has become a spectator sport, with the public watching without participating. The candidate moves in front of the voters on film, while the continued publication of polls keeps him abreast of the latest standings. Election day thus becomes a time for ratification rather than decision. Today many just don't bother. Worst of all, there are no signs that this trend will not continue. What if, someday, we give an election and no one comes?

The media, of course, is not wholly responsible for this imperilment. The public's disillusionment with politics and politicians is another cause, and it has happened before. The very size of the country and the aftereffects of the sixties' turbulence among the young create an air of alienation, discouragement, and irrelevance. But the media revolution is truly that, and in some form it is here to stay. Yet it is not immune to change. The convention system replaced caucuses a century and a half ago; primaries replaced conventions in most states in this century; and amendments, court decisions, and congressional legislation have immensely widened voter eligibility. The process has adjusted to changing technology in printing and to the democratization of the telephone and radio. There is no reason why the media revolution can not also be made apt to democratic purposes. But that is the task of the generation that is growing up in it, not those who suffered the shock of its introduction and present triumph.

Can We Still Afford to Be a Nation of Immigrants?

by David Kennedy

David Kennedy is Professor of History at Stanford University and author of *Birth Control in America: The Career of Margaret Sanger* (1970), *Over Here: The First World War and American Society* (1980) and other works. He delivered this address at Mountain View College in Dallas, Texas, in April 1990. In it he noted that from 1820 to 1920 the United States absorbed, relatively peacefully, about 35 million Europeans into its population. According to Kennedy, three factors worked to make this process as successful as it was. First, in spite of the huge number of immigrants, the highest concentration of foreign-born persons ever living in the United States occurred around 1910, and they constituted only about 15% of the total population. Second, the immigrants represented amazingly diverse geographical, cultural and linguistic backgrounds—from Scandinavian Lutherans to Greek Orthodox to Russian Jews to Irish Catholics—and no one group was large enough to threaten the predominant cultural or political standards of American society. And last, the vigorous economic growth of the American economy in the century after 1820 offered newcomers their "piece of the pie" without taking anything away from those already here. Kennedy then focused on present and future immigration trends.

Now, let me turn to the present moment and ask what light if any, this little historical rehearsal can shed on the present situation. The biggest apparent novelty—apparent, I want to stress—about present day immigration is its source. Present day immigrants do not come from the old mother continent of Europe, but from what we broadly call the third world or less developed countries. Nine countries today account for about 60% of immigration to the United States. If we listed in rank order all the countries that contribute immigrants to the United States today, by the time we got to country number nine, we would have accounted for well over half of all immigration. I will read you that list of nine countries in rank order starting from the one that contributes the most migrants to the ninth. They are Mexico, China, Hong Kong, Taiwan, the Philippines, Vietnam, Korea, India, and Laos. I haven't named a European country yet. Those nine non-European countries contribute the great majority of migrants to this country today, both legal and illegal. Now, those nine countries, none of them European, constitute a new, novel source of immigration only if we define them culturally or geographically. If in fact, we ask ourselves, what made migration happen in the nineteenth century, we find that this is not a very new set of sources of immigration at all because all the countries I've named are undergoing historical transformations that are virtually identical with what was going on in nineteenth century Europe. They're experiencing very rapid population growth and they are experiencing their own relatively early phases of industrial revolution. The so-called newly-industrializing countries like Korea and Taiwan you'll notice are prominent on this list.

Now, let us take Mexico as the case in point. Recognizing [that] other countries contribute to this immigrant stream as well, let me just emphasize Mexico as the most conspicuous example. Mexico has tripled its population since 1950. It's passing through a period of amazingly large population growth. In the year 1950, Mexico, Central America, South America, all of Latin America and the United States had approximately the same population—about 150 million people in the United States, about 150 million people in all of Latin America. It will take, we estimate, to the year 2020 for the United States population to double from its 1950 base. So, we think we'll have about 300 million people in this country 30 years from now, the year 2020. In 2020 it is estimated that in Latin America there will be nearly one billion people, [more than] three times the population in this country, whereas in 1950 we started out at about the same numerical base. So, Latin America's population is growing at a factor of about six times over this seventy year period, 1950 to 2020, while the population of the United States is doubling. I mention that simply by way of making a point that this pressure for immigration on the United States from Latin America is not going to go away in all of our lifetimes.

As in nineteenth century Europe, this population explosion in Latin America and in Mexico has had its primary impact not on the United States, but in the cities of Mexico itself, to the extent that Mexico City is now the world's largest city with something in the neighborhood of 20 million people. It's estimated that about 100 persons per day are migrating into Mexico City from the Mexican countryside. So, what we see coming across the border into the United States as a vast stream of some legal and some illegal Mexican immigrants is in fact a kind of spillover effect from the urbanization and industrialization of Mexico. So we're seeing here something that is virtually identical with what was going on in nineteenth century Europe: enormous population expansion and reconcentration of population from countryside to city, with some incidental spillover into international migration, in this case, into the United States.

Now what if we turn to this side of the border and ask ourselves about our capacity in the present day to absorb immigrants? This is where the question that I started with, "Can we still afford to be a nation of immigrants?" begins to come into sharper focus. Now, you will remember that I offered to you three kinds of structural explanations why I think we succeeded in accommodating those 35 million Europeans a century ago. I mentioned their relatively small numbers in the American population, the variety of the immigrant stream that they composed, and economic growth. Now, what if we tried to apply those considerations to the present day and ask ourselves, do we still have the capacity to absorb newcomers at the rate at which our forebears at the early part of this century did? Well, if we look at the relative numbers of immigrants in the United States today, here I think there is grounds for considerable confidence that as a society, we still have a lot of absorptive capacity, because even if you make a fairly generous estimate of how many illegal immigrants are in the country, an estimate in the eight to ten million range, we still come up with a percentage of foreign born persons of about seven or eight percent. That's about half the proportion of foreign born persons in the census of 1910 which was, in round numbers, about fifteen percent. So here, it seems to me, there are grounds for considerable confidence that we still have a lot of absorptive capacity left as a society, since the relative number of foreign born persons in American society today is about half what it was 70, 80 years ago.

Now, if we take the second of those factors that I mentioned in historical context, the variety and pluralism of the immigrant stream a century ago, here I think we enter into a new zone altogether. Here is where, potentially at least, we are in the presence of something for which we as a country have very little historical precedent. I'm referring here primarily to Hispanic migration and even more particularly to Mexican immigration to the United States. Unlike that nineteenth century stream of European immigrants, the present day stream of immigrants to the United States is very heavily composed of immigration from a single, culturally unified, linguistically homogeneous source, which is Mexico. And what's more, that immigrant stream from Mexico is concentrated in a relatively closely defined geographical region which essentially stretches from Texas to California. The population of New Mexico, according to the inter-census population report estimates of 1988, is almost 40% Hispanic, Texas is a little better than 25%, Arizona about 20%, Colorado 12%, California 24%. More than half of all Hispanics in the United States live in California and Texas. We estimate that by the year 2000, there will be no cultural majority in California. Its population will be about 40% Hispanic, 40% what we very elastically call "Anglo," roughly 10% black, 10% Asian. Now, this concentration of a large immigrant group, Hispanic immigrants in this case, Mexican immigrants to be more particular, this critical mass concentrated in a given region is something for which we have very little historical precedent as a society, and I offer it to you as a possibility, not a prediction, but a possibility, that we could see evolve in the southwest corner of North America, something that would in the long run resemble what exists in the northeastern corner of this continent in the province of Quebec. That is, a large linguistically and culturally different group that would have available to it the real possibility of preserving its cultural heritage over a much longer period of time than any other comparable immigrant group in American history. And it would have a great degree of economic viability as well as cultural viability, and you might eventually see the demand arise for a kind of autonomous or semiautonomous Hispanic state somewhere in the American southwest. I think that is a distinct possibility in this country over the next century or so, and some of you no doubt have heard the term applied to this of the "reconquista." This is the repossession by Mexican culture of territories that were, after all, wrested from Mexico by force of arms 150 years ago.

Now, finally, let me touch on the economic factor. This is a subject of some complexity. You'll hear the argument made that one of the things that underwrote the relative tranquility of immigration in the last century was economic growth. It allowed this society to avoid questions of redistribution. Recently a lot of economic historians and economists have been turning that question around and instead of asking to what extent did economic growth make immigration possible, they've asked to what extent did immigration fuel economic growth? And in fact at the time when the last piece of immigration legislation, the so-called Simpson-Mazzoli-Rodino bill, was making its way through Congress (also known as the Immigration Reform and Control Act of 1986), there were a number of studies of this sort made, trying to determine what is the relationship between economic health and immigration. Many of those studies focused on southern California for the reason that that is the region that has absorbed more immigrants in the last twenty years than any other comparable region. All of these studies have come up with the same conclusion. One was done by the Council of Economic Advisors, one by the Rand Corporation, and one by the Urban Institute. They all came up with the same conclusion and that was that immigration measurably added to the economic vitality of southern California. So, far from constituting a net drain or depressant on the region's economic vitality, it actually contributed to it. The Urban Institute study concluded as follows, "Large scale [immigration] did not depress and probably increased per capita income in the region." Now that is a very telling finding because it really tells us that there is a great economic benefit to immigration, that often goes overlooked in many discussions of the cultural implications of immigration.

Now I'll end by summarizing for you the findings of a Stanford economist, Clark Reynolds, who is the head of a project at Stanford University called the United States/Mexico project. It's an ongoing research enterprise that brings together Mexican and United States scholars to study questions of mutual interest to the two countries. Reynolds did a study in which he projected Mexican and U.S. population growth down to the year 2000, and then did some projections of Mexican and U.S. economic growth down to the year 2000. He concluded that for Mexico to absorb its population increase into its own labor markets, to find jobs for its rapidly expanding population, the Mexican economy would need to grow over the next decade at a compound annual rate of better than seven percent, nearly eight percent in fact. And he concluded that that was a very unrealistic number. It was really unrealistic for us to expect that the Mexican economy could sustain a seven-plus percent annual compound rate of growth, which would be necessary to absorb its new workers into the work force. Then he turned to the U.S. side and he said that for the United States to grow its economy at a compound annual rate of three percent between now and the year 2000, a healthy but hardly robust rate of economic growth, a rate lower than this country experienced in the 1960s, for example, and fifties, we would need to find about 15 million more workers than we could find out of domestic sources, unless we wanted to resort to some ancient industrial practices like child labor. We've transferred in this country all the labor out of agriculture that we can; less than two percent of the American work force is now in agriculture. We have, in a way of speaking, invaded the family and drawn women into the work force to about the maximum extent that we can. So he concluded that we can't find any more workers out of domestic supply. We have a very low birth rate. We need about fifteen million more than we can get. Where are we going to get them? Mexico is the obvious place. So, he concluded that Mexico and the United States needed each other to achieve their respective goals of full employment for their citizens and economic growth rates that would be desirable. So I'll just end by saying that the proper question for this lecture is not, "Can we still afford to be a nation of immigrants?" but "Can we afford not to be?" Thank you.

Recent American Foreign Policy in Perspective

by Joseph S. Nye, Jr.

Joseph S. Nye, Jr., is Director of the Harvard University Center for International Affairs. In this provocative interview, he assesses the strengths and weaknesses of the Carter and Reagan administrations' foreign policies and the similarities and differences between them, as well as President Bush's handling of the 1991 Persian Gulf War. The breakup of the Soviet Union and its withdrawal from Eastern Europe have radically altered power equations in international relations, and the old cold war, bipolar, us-versus-them mentality no longer applies. While acknowledging the myriad domestic problems that the American people must address, Nye is optimistic that the United States can still play a leading role in world affairs—but it will no longer be based on sheer military power as much as in the past. Whether we *will* lead or not "will depend on the type of domestic leadership we have." Nye is author of *Bound to Lead: The Changing Nature of American Power* (1990) and co-author of *Canada and the United States* (1974).

Interview with Joseph S. Nye, Jr.

Q. Professor Nye, how does one explain President Carter's emphasis on human rights in foreign policy? Did it make a difference or have an effect overseas?

A. President Carter had a personal commitment, but I think even more to the point, there had been a lot of criticism by the Democrats against the lack of morality in [Secretary of State] Henry Kissinger's foreign policy. So, part of the campaign of 1976 involved criticism of Kissinger for emphasizing just balance of power and not enough emphasis on human rights. I think it did have an effect overseas. You can find some cases, Latin America particularly, where the people in power today were helped in terms of their personal lives by Carter's efforts. I've talked to some Argentines, for example, after the dictatorship gave way, who felt that Carter had made a major difference in their lives.

Q. Why were some nations criticized for violations, such as the Soviet Union, and others not?

A. One of the problems in foreign policy is that you have to think about the balance of power at the same time you think about moral issues, and if it were just a human rights policy, you wouldn't have a foreign policy at all. You'd just have a human rights policy. For example, Carter needed Iran to preserve stability in the Persian Gulf and therefore, he was softer on the Shah's human rights violations than he was on Argentina's human rights violations. So, the balance of power made a difference in terms of who got criticized.

Q. In retrospect, could Carter have handled the Iranian hostage issue and the Soviet invasion of Afghanistan much differently than he did?

A. I think Carter's handling of the hostages issue in Iran was a mistake from his point of view. He became too personally involved and the net effect was that not only did it wind up hurting him when he didn't get the hostages released, it also increased the value of the hostages as a bargaining card in the hands of the Iranian militants. With hindsight, stepping back from the issue, saying that these are American employees, they will be compensated when they are eventually released, but we're not letting hostages determine our foreign policy, might have been a better way to do it. On the Soviet invasion of Afghanistan, it seems to me that Carter acted properly. You have to respond quite firmly to as clear an aggression as the Soviet invasion of Afghanistan.

Q. Just how much influence over events abroad do American presidents exercise?

A. American presidents' influence over events abroad varies. In some areas, for example, small countries, we often have a good deal of influence. In other areas, for example, getting China to changes its policies, it's like moving an elephant, it's not so easy. So, the influence that American presidents can have varies a great deal by the issue, by the size of the country, by the particular time.

Q. What were the short- and long-term effects of Carter's policies? Did we learn any lessons from the experiences of his administration?

A. I think President Carter was successful in a number of areas. For example, if he had not succeeded in solving the Panama Canal issue, the problems in Central America would have been a lot worse. I think he was also quite successful in getting more attention to slowing the spread of nuclear weapons and nuclear proliferation. I think his human rights policy also set a standard which, even though we weren't able to meet it in every case, at least meant that the United States stood for something. So I think those policies actually were quite successful. He was a little less successful in integrating his policies, having them all fit together, figuring out how to deal with the Soviet Union, with the Chinese, and with these global issues simultaneously.

Q. Why did Reagan take such a hard line against the Soviet Union upon entering office?

A. President Reagan came into office in 1981 with the view that the Soviets were on the ascendancy, and it was widely believed at that time that the Soviets were getting close to passing us. Ironically, by the end of the 1970s, a number of Soviet analysts, realized that they had already begun to decline, but at the time in 1980 right after the invasion of Afghanistan, it looked like the Soviets were still an outwardly expansionist type of state.

Q. Reagan [not only] continued but intensified the increase in military spending. What were the economic costs and benefits of [this] in the early 1980s?

A. One of the problems with the American increase in military spending in the early 1980s is that we didn't pay for it. We didn't raise our taxes to pay for it. So, what we wound up doing was borrowing money from overseas to pay for what we were spending. The long run consequence was that we were eating up our savings and incurring debt to foreigners and that has come back to haunt us with the problem of the government budget deficit and the trade deficit of the 1990s.

Q. What were the motives of Reagan and his advisors in the Iran-Contra affair?

A. President Reagan, by his own testimony, was very concerned personally about the hostages. In that sense, he made something of the same mistake that President Carter made. President Bush was much better at stepping back from the hostages. President Reagan wanted to free the hostages. But there was another dimension to it which I think Reagan contributed to, but which some of the members of his staff, such as Oliver North, took even more seriously. They wanted to get money to support the Contras in Nicaragua when the Congress refused to appropriate the money. They used it as an end run around the Congress to carry out their own foreign policy outside the Constitution.

Q. Do you think Reagan and his advisors were trying to reestablish in the Iran-Contra situation or in general a stronger presidency in foreign policy in light of some of the frustrations that came out of the Carter years?

A. It was a view that was widely shared among members of the Reagan administration that the president should have more leeway to do what he wanted and there was a desire to have a stronger presidency, but, it's worth remembering that the Constitution deliberately divides power between the Congress and the president. If you do an end run around the Congress, you're essentially violating the Constitution.

Q. You do think then that there was a constitutional crisis in the Iran-Contra situation?

A. I think that Iran-Contra was a major constitutional problem. The idea that you can go around the right of the Congress to appropriate funds to carry out foreign policy and have the president run his own foreign policy without any congressional appropriations is outside of the constitutional mandate.

Q. Backing up just a second, when Congress cut off funds for the Nicaraguan Contras, were they expressing fear of another Vietnam situation?

A. There was a great deal of fear of another Vietnam, of Americans getting too deeply involved and the feeling was that if one thing led to another, and you wound up with American troops in Nicaragua, there'd be high levels of casualties, great turmoil at home, the public would be enormously divided about whether this was a legitimate or illegitimate thing to do. So I think Congress was quite worried that we would stick our foot in the swamp again.

Q. Please discuss Reagan's changed attitudes toward the Soviet Union after the coming of Gorbachev. Did our military buildup have an effect on that? Did he want to be remembered as a peace president? What explains this apparent shift in Reagan's last couple of years in our relationship with the Soviet Union?

A. President Reagan's change in the second half of his administration reflected the changes that Gorbachev made in Soviet policy. Gorbachev came into a Soviet situation where the economy was beginning to deteriorate. The Soviets weren't able to cope with the third industrial revolution, the information-based economy. They were going to need access to western technology and western markets, and Gorbachev realized that he was going to have to have better relations with the West. I think in that sense he began his new thinking in foreign policy quite soon after he came into office. I think President Reagan saw this as responsiveness to the kinds of things that he had been saying, and I think the net effect was a gradual coming together of the two positions through the later 1980s.

Q. Were the Soviets perceived in the late 1980's by the United States as less of a threat, and is this an accurate perception?

A. The Soviets did become less of a threat in the late 1980s. Now, this became absolutely clear after Gorbachev's statement to the United Nations in December of 1988 in which he offered to withdraw a large portion of Soviet troops [from Eastern Europe], and it became even more clear in 1989 and '90 as the Soviet empire in Eastern Europe collapsed and the troops began to be withdrawn. Without Soviet troops forward based in Eastern Europe, NATO and the West Europeans would have ample warning times to reinforce against any possible Soviet attack. So the Soviet threat in the most concrete sense greatly diminished in the late 1980s.

Q. Did the United States play any significant part in the recent 1989–1990 changes in Eastern Europe? Why did those changes occur when they did? And were Soviet economic problems a key ingredient in loosening the ties in Eastern Europe?

A. I think the problems of the Soviet economy were the central cause of the changes in Eastern Europe in 1989 and 1990. Basically, the Soviets realized that it was too costly to maintain their position in Eastern Europe and that [this] was also shutting them off from western capital, technology, and markets. So, I think Gorbachev and [Eduard] Shevardnadze, his foreign minister, made a decision that it was better to see the situation as a liability than as an asset, and in that sense, I think that while the United States contributed to it, most of the causation really came from the Soviet side.

Q. Is containment still a vital part of U.S. foreign policy? Is our policy becoming a new game with new rules?

A. Well, containment was a sensible strategy when the world was bipolar, when there were two great powers, the Soviet Union and the United States, but with the decline of the Soviet Union, containment is really no longer an adequate way to describe our foreign policy. What we're faced with now is a multiple set of problems, some of them acute, some of them less so, and we're going to have to think of a more broad based foreign policy that can't be so easily summarized by a single threat. Therefore containment is not a very good slogan for describing it.

Q. Why did we choose to fight in the Gulf? Is there a new equation or is it the same military, economic, political and ideological reasons as we've used previously in intervening in various affairs?

A There's a mixed set of motives that went into our decision to intervene in the Persian Gulf. Obviously, oil had something to do with it. As the joke goes, if Kuwait exported broccoli, we wouldn't have intervened. But, I think it was much more than that, because after all, Britain didn't import any oil and yet they were very strongly for intervention. The other point was the U.N. system of collective security. If in the first crisis of the post-cold war world, where a state crosses its neighbor's border in a clear cut case of aggression, if there hadn't been a punitive action to try to roll it back, then the whole concept of U.N. collective security would have been a dead letter as a principle of order in the post-cold war world. So, I think the issue of what kind of order there would be in a post-cold war was just as important, maybe even more important than the oil question.

Q. Why did the U.S. public respond so passionately to the Persian Gulf war?

A. The U.S. public responded to the war in part because of the reaction to the Vietnam syndrome of the past. The Americans had been defeated in Vietnam. It had been enormously divisive. It had called into question the values and capabilities of the American military, and here is a case where you had a clear cut villain who had crossed a border illegally and where there was a large public consensus behind the U.S. acting not alone, but in a broad coalition within the United Nations. I think the combination of those things produced our strong response in the case of Iraq against Kuwait.

Q. You mentioned a clear cut villain. Do we need those sorts of bad guys in the world to create public support for such an effort?

A. One of the problems in a democracy is to explain things in clear cut terms without exaggeration. But very often exaggeration is necessary. I think it was Dean Acheson, [the] former Secretary of State, who said, "When you're trying to turn an unruly team of horses, you have to tug extra hard at the reins." Similarly, in a democracy where you have many people with many different views, there's a temptation for political leaders to exaggerate their rhetoric to get the public as a whole to turn in a particular direction.

Q. What do you think President Bush means by the term a "new world order?" Is there such a thing?

A. Well, a new world order is somewhat vague as a concept. It could refer to the new distribution of power. The world's no longer bipolar. It could also refer to just world order, which isn't the same thing. Sometimes, we fail to distinguish those. For example, the cold war had a bipolar order, but it wasn't particularly just. A new world order will not be bipolar, it will be more of a diffusion of power among many actors. We don't yet know whether we can set up institutions and agreements that will get it broadly accepted as just.

Q. What new problems are likely to be generated in this situation?

A. In the post-cold war world, there won't be one single over-arching threat. The Soviet Union won't be the clear enemy. And in that kind of a world, it may be that economic friction between the United States and its allies in Europe and Japan will be more difficult to resolve than in the past. In addition, some of the problems related to self-determination when countries like Yugoslavia or even the Soviet Union itself begin to split apart will cause difficulties. Should we intervene? Who should we support? The central government? The separate governments that are trying to become free? If you support one sub-unit, what about minorities within that group? I think these are the kinds of problems that we're going to see more of in a post-cold war world.

Q. Professor Nye, are we over the so-called Vietnam syndrome?

A. The Vietnam syndrome referred to a lesson that the United States learned from its defeat in Vietnam, not to intervene again. Mark Twain said that a cat that sits on a hot stove learns not to sit on a hot stove again, but not to sit on a cold stove, either. And the United States after the Vietnam

War was not going to sit on any kinds of stoves. What the Iraq-Kuwait situation showed was that we learned to make distinctions. We [marshalled] multi-lateral support in the United Nations against a clear-cut case of aggression. So, in that sense, we have overcome the Vietnam syndrome if we think of the Mark Twain analogy.

Q. In the post-cold war world, will the United States be using that same basic framework in judging our role in the world?

A. In the post-cold war world, American citizens are going to have to be aware that you can't simplify everything down to one ever-arching threat. There won't be just a set of guys with black hats versus white hats. Many of the problems that we'll be facing will be more complicated, for example, the spread of nuclear weapons, the drug trade, the spread of diseases like AIDS; many of these go deeply into the roots of different societies and across national borders, and you can't blame it on the Russians or on this or that villain. So, in our public debates about foreign policy, we're going to have to become more careful about how we frame issues and explain them. It won't be as easy as it was during the cold war period.

Q. Has the U.S. overextended its commitments, perhaps, as Paul Kennedy [author of *The Rise and Fall of the Great Powers,* 1987] has argued, or are we still bound to lead in the world, to use one of your terms?

A. Well, the United States obviously played a major role during the cold war, but we're not overstretched. Things are becoming somewhat easier with the decline of the Soviet Union. In 1959, during the cold war, 11% of our gross national product went to the military. By 1991 about 5% of the gross national product went to the military, [and it is] projected to be about 3 ½% by 1995. So, in that sense, the idea that the United States was becoming progressively overcommitted is just the opposite of the truth. In fact, the burdens on us have become less with the ending of the cold war. So, Americans have the capacity to lead and to deal with their domestic problems at the same time, and the question is whether they'll have the will to do that.

Q. If it's not the United States, will it be anybody else that will lead the world?

A. It's hard after the cold war to see any other power that would be as broadly diversified in its capabilities as the United States. We have military power, we have economic power, we have what I call soft power, which is cultural and ideological appeal. Europe has everything except unity. The Japanese don't have the military and the soft power dimensions, so I think the Americans are going to be the country with the greatest capability. The key question is whether we want to use it or not, and there have been other times in our history when we've failed to use it. For example, in the 1920s and 1930s, we failed to stem the Great Depression, we failed to fight the rise of Fascism and that came back to haunt us in 1941 with World War II.

Q. What type of world leadership will the United States play in the rest of this century and how will that role be different from what it was during the cold war era?

A. Unlike the cold war period when we could rely upon the Soviet threat to keep our alliances together, in the post-cold war period, we're going to have to form coalitions with other countries to get them to cooperate with us. We're going to have to use international institutions, whether it be the United Nations for some of these peace-keeping operations, or whether it be economic organizations like the International Monetary Fund for some of the problems of the world financial system, and the reason is that we can't do all of this alone. You've got to get others to help. So, as the largest country, you've got to take the lead to form these coalitions to get others to cooperate. And if the largest country doesn't do its share, then essentially, the others probably won't be able to either.

Q. What threatens U.S. security in the 1990s? How serious are these threats and how will we have to deal with them?

A. The kinds of threats that we're going to face in the 1990s will be different in shape from the cold war. The spread of nuclear weapons to many countries which may be less able to control them. The spread of trans-national groups of terrorists or drug traders, or the spread of diseases like AIDS, or new types of environmental threats like global warming. All these are going to be a different shape and size of threat than we've faced in the last half century. What we've got to do is try to educate public opinion to understand what these threats are and to get others to cooperate with us in various kinds of coalitions and international institutions to try to deal with these problems, and it won't be as easy as it was when you could just point to the Russians and say it's all their fault. So a cold war foreign policy in some ways was easier than dealing with the multiplicity of the lower level threats we'll face in the future.

Q. What should our students learn from history, particularly as it relates to the United States and the world?

A. Well, the lessons of history should not be over-read. There are no perfect historical analogies. I think Mark Twain once said that history doesn't repeat itself, at best it merely rhymes. But, with that said, history does allow you to know how we've done things in the past, where we've made mistakes. Take the example of the 1920s and 1930s where we failed to play our role internationally and it came back to make our lives worse later when we got into World War II. So, in that sense I think the way to think about history is to learn some cautionary notes. How did people make mistakes in the past? How did they see things? Why did they get into things? And then to realize that the present is always different. There's no perfect trend, taking one model from the past and applying it to the present. So, understanding history for that sense of context, but knowing how to adjust it to the changes in the present, that's the key to being a well-informed citizen on foreign policy issues.

Q. Is it safe to say that the United States is in a good position in the 1990s? Are you optimistic that we will have the will to lead, to take leadership roles in the future?

A. I think the United States has a set of problems at home that have to be addressed. The question of education, of savings rates, of government deficits, of infrastructure, and so forth. We have to deal with these issues, but it's a mistake to think we have to deal with them by turning our back on the outside world. In a world of interdependence where things that happen abroad affect us at home, it's much harder to make a distinction between domestic policy and foreign policy. So, in that sense, we've got to learn how to walk and chew gum at the same time. We've got to learn how to have a serious domestic policy where we deal with some of these problems that require new investments, while at the same time maintaining our international position, because if we don't take the lead, nobody else will be able to. I think we can do it. Whether we will or not will depend on the type of domestic leadership we have.

Q. Is it really a whole new world we're entering in the 1990s?

A. I think the world in the 1990s is going to be very different. I titled my book "Bound to Lead," but the subtitle was "The Changing Nature of American Power." And unless we learn how to use our soft power, our cultural and ideological appeal, our ability to form coalitions and institutions, we're not going to be able to accomplish the things we need to get done. So, while it will be important to maintain our military strength, that won't be enough. We're going to have to learn to use the other dimensions of our power as well.

Looking Backward, Looking Forward: An Interview with Carl Degler

In this interview, Carl Degler, Margaret Byrne Professor of American History at Stanford University, responds to a series of questions about America's past and its future. He speaks on topics ranging from cultural diversity to questions of equality. Is this nation a melting pot or a salad bowl? What is equality and what is its future in America? Why does our political system seem not to function well in dealing with the problems of the modern world? How can social and political change occur in our society? Is violence a viable source of change? What is the future of the women's rights movement? These are some of the questions to which Professor Degler responds with insight and thought-provoking answers. He concludes the interview by pointing out how students should apply the lessons of history. He stresses that students should view history as continuity and realize that who you are is derived from the past.

Interview with Carl Degler

Q. On the matter of cultural diversity in this nation's history, do you adhere to the salad bowl metaphor, and please explain what that is. If not, is there a more accurate description? And more generally, how has cultural diversity affected our history, including benefits as well as conflicts and tension? How will it continue to do so in the future?

A. Cultural diversity has to be seen as one of the characteristic elements in what American society and American history are all about. It is relatively recently that we began to think about the idea of what cultural diversity consists of. At the beginning of the twentieth century, for example, the idea of the melting pot was advanced in a very popular play [Israel Zangwill's "The Melting Pot," 1908], and many historians said, this is really a characteristic of America. That is, we have great diversity of immigrants coming in, we have a lot of black people who came in as slaves, but all of these people are really coming together and creating a kind of new American society. They're all melting together in that pot. Eventually we will [arrive at a] new society, a new culture which we call American culture. Eventually all these people sort of melt together and you don't have very much diversity as time goes on.

A number of historians talked in this fashion through the 1920's and the 1930's and well into the 1950's. As they began to look seriously into the character of American society, they saw that there were Germans, and there were Italians, and there were Jews and there were blacks, and they were living together relatively peacefully. But there were also Italian restaurants, and Chinese restaurants, German newspapers and a great persistence, one might say, of this diversity which had come from Asia and Africa and Europe. Some of us began to talk about the salad bowl, not the melting pot. That American culture really was made up of a large number of groups coming from all over the world. Though they got along together and called themselves Americans, they also kept many of their cultural patterns. I think most historians now would say this country is a salad bowl rather than a melting pot. The more one looks at the American past from the standpoint of cultural diversity, one recognizes that it has had a shaping influence on American culture, for good and for bad. My favorite example of how diversity has had a shaping consequence for American society today is that in the colonial period we had such a diversity of religions, not only Catholic, Jewish and Protestant, but all kinds of Protestant religions, in an age when religion was terribly important and where all the countries in Europe took stands as to which religion was the state religion. It soon became apparent when the United States was founded in the 1780s that the way to deal with this question was not to say that we have one state religion, that we are Methodists or Episcopalians or Catholics, but that we will have a system of religious freedom in which no religion will be established, and no religious test will be needed to hold office in the United States, and that all religions will be recognized as equal and that there will be a complete separation of state and church. This came out of our diversity and it has become one of the determining elements of modern America, that we have this idea of religious freedom. We take it for granted, by and large. But all you have to do is look at countries like France or Mexico or Germany, in which religious divisions historically and in the present have been sources of difficulty and divisions. So in that sense one can see a very good example of the way in which diversity has been, I think, a plus as far as American society is concerned. It has meant that we have got a great diversity of information which I think most economic historians would say has been one of the major sources of economic growth. A great supply of workers coming in the nineteenth century and in the present time, doing jobs often that native-born Americans or earlier immigrants were not interested in doing but were necessary.

The minus side of all this, and I think it's important to recognize that diversity presents problems as well as bestows benefits, is that we've had a history of nativism, that is to say, of people who are in the country—they may or may not have been born in the country but they see themselves as established Americans—who say, well, I'm not sure that we want to treat these immigrants on the same basis, we may want to keep them out of politics or we may not want to allow them to have certain kinds of jobs and so on. In the 1850's, for example, there was a great upsurge of nativist activity seeking to limit the rights and opportunities of Germans and Irish who were coming into the country at that point in large numbers. The same thing happened in the early years of the twentieth century, during the 1920's. Legislation was passed to limit the kinds of immigrants who could come into the United States.

Q. How far have we come toward equality for minorities in American society? What do we mean by equality? Is the majority willing to grant equality in some areas rather than others? What are the prospects for the future?

A. If cultural diversity is one characteristic of American society, the one that is very closely allied to it, I think, is the idea of equality. In fact, as one talks about cultural diversity in the present, one is struck by the fact that close behind it, comes the question of how do you establish equality among all the varieties of people who have populated the United States. But before you talk about equality, one has to say, what do Americans mean by it? And here I like to distinguish at least three kinds of equality. Because what equality means to Americans shapes how they deal with particular groups or how they deal with cultural diversity in general. The most obvious meaning for equality and which is certainly one that Americans support and follow is equality before the law. We take this pretty much for granted. But we forget that there was a time in Europe in which certain people had rights that other people did not [have] before the law. The nobles, for example, were treated differently from peasants and the law was applied differently to them. And when you went to court you had to say which class you belonged to. So, in America the idea came very early in our history [that] the law treats all people equally. This of course has become one of the constitutional principles that presidents are often reminded of; that they too are under the same law as ordinary citizens.

The second principle of equality, and the one that I think is at the heart of the American idea of equality, is equality of opportunity. This I think is what Americans generally mean when they talk about equality. That is to say, that all people have an equal chance to get ahead, to realize themselves, to do what they would like to do. One of the implications of that concept is that if there is a way to get ahead, it means that the society is in some way stratified. There is some point you start at and some point you end at. You may want to go to the top of the society, you may want to go up one step, but there is an implication when we talk about equality of opportunity that you have a hierarchy, that you have a ladder, so to speak. Well, this idea can come up against another definition of equality which is that all people should be equal in what they have and where they stand. Obviously, that principle of equality is quite different to realize if your emphasis is on opportunity. Because some people are going to do better than others when they seize the opportunities that are given to them. One of the consequences of that for American society, one of the reasons why I think opportunity plays such a large role in the thinking of Americans, is the attitudes that Americans have had historically towards ideologies or principles like socialism. The United States stands out as a nation in the industrial world for having probably the least interest in socialism as a political idea. Because what socialism of course emphasizes is how all people can rise up and get a better living without reference to only equality of opportunity. There will be changes in the society in the course of which the poor will be raised and the rich may be reduced. But there will be a greater equality of result than would be the case in a society that emphasizes only equality of opportunity. There are major socialist parties in Europe or have been up until perhaps the end of the 1980's and the early nineties. There never has been a socialist party of any significance in the United States; Americans have generally opposed it. Many people say, well, you are limiting my opportunity by saying you are going to look for blacks or for women or for Mexican-Americans to fill a particular job. Why not say we'll just have competition for that particular job. And so you can get two points of view about an issue like affirmative action. And that goes back again to the principle of equality of opportunity. There's a third principle of American views of equality that I'd like to throw in here. That is, Americans also see equality meaning that all individuals in the society are intrinsically equal. If you want to put it in religious terms, we're all children of God or we're all individuals in our own intrinsic characters. It comes out most often I think in the way students deal with one another. You don't like students who put on airs. You don't like students who dress up in such a way that suggests that they are wealthy and you're poor. You don't like people who put other people down just because they are different or because they seem to have some skill or some material characteristic that you lack. So we have that definition of equality. And of course, it conflicts with and confuses equality of opportunity in America. There is a built-in conflict in American thinking about equality which comes out again and again. Do we really want equality? One person may be talking about equality of opportunity and another person about equality of worth. Others are talking about equality of results. It's important, therefore, when you ask, to what extent have we got an egalitarian society, to look at these various definitions to arrive at an answer.

Q. Why has the American political response to domestic issues seemingly taken on a cyclical pattern during the past century? How would you characterize the American political tradition?

A. Look at the nature of American reform and ask, why do we have cycles of reform? We have the progressive period in the early part of the twentieth century and another period in the 1960's and in the 1980's we moved into a period that seemed increasingly as sort of a reaction against reform. I think reforms are cyclical for reasons many historians would agree with and that is, reform requires you to change. Ignore the change, and you set up certain tension in the society. To change you have to sort of agree that the things you've been doing have been wrong and you want to do something fresh. As soon as that happens you have to start putting a lot of energy into things you didn't before. In short, I think to expect a society to be constantly reforming is contrary to human nature. That explains the rise and decline of reform and then a new cycle later on.

The American political system fits into this, too. Recently, since the second half of the twentieth century, I think our political system has run into some problems. Certainly since the 1960's we [have] found the American political system not functioning as it once did. There's Congress, which is Democratic, there's a president who is Republican. They haven't gotten along very easily throughout the 1980's. There is long standing division between the executive and the legislature. We built it into our Constitution and it worked very well in the nineteenth century. But today I question this division between executive and legislative. The European countries of course get around it and the Asian countries like Japan do, too, by having the executive as a branch of the Parliament. So that when the executive branch wants to lead it need only have a majority in the Parliament. In the United States we have one party in charge of Congress and one party in charge of the presidency. And they have to arrive at some kind of agreement to get legislation passed easily and to make reforms or to deal with problems. And I often think people ought to be thinking about [whether] we have perhaps reached the end of a serviceable division of powers, as our Constitution now specifies.

Q. How and why does political and social change occur in our society? What kinds of pressures must be brought to bear first before these changes come about? What have been the least and most effective tactics of particular groups in bringing about change in our history?

A. We have had cycles of reform and conservatism. How does reform take place, how does one get it going? As I think about the major reforms movements of the nineteenth and twentieth centuries, I would go back and try to account for their origin. De Tocqueville made the observation in the Jacksonian period that Americans are an associating people. They form organizations to achieve certain ends. And I think if one looks at the major reforms of the nineteenth and twentieth centuries, whether it's the movement for prohibition or for the ending of slavery or for the income tax or for the improvement of the labor situation, it's often groups coming together and deciding they want to have some change. But then they usually end up by moving into the political scene, forming political parties. This happened with the farmers in the 1890's forming the Populist Party, and the Democrats taking up many of the issues dealing with the Great Depression. There you got many more reforms coming out of the government itself rather than out of associations. Those have been two sources of change. Individuals forming organizations and agitating for them and getting government to respond, or the government, as in the New Deal or in the Lyndon Johnson years, proposing reforms by government itself.

Q. What are the limits of these groups? In particular, what are the limits of violent protest in America? Is that a way to bring about change? Do Americans generally resist that tactic when it comes to bringing about change?

A. The role of violence is a little hard to talk about as a source of change, though it always comes up as a question. Certainly in the days of the abolitionists there was interference with the law. To get women's suffrage there was not only picketing but there were breeches of the law. To end segregation in the United States there were many acts of violence that were carried out. By and large, however, I don't think they have been at the heart of the change. I think peaceful demonstrations have been much more effective than violence.

Q. What future directions do you see the women's rights movement taking in this country in the next ten or twenty years? What issues are still on the agenda? What tactics will they have to use? Please assess the prospects for meaningful change in these areas.

A. Probably the most recent of prominent reform efforts has been that of the women's movement. And it has been strikingly successful. Women are now in jobs that no one ever thought women should be in. We have women in the military academies. We have women officers. We probably do more in that respect, which is often thought of as the most masculine of all occupations, than any other country in the world. We certainly have proportionately more women in the armed forces than probably any country outside of Israel. So on one level there's been a great success. But I wonder whether we can continue to pursue the same approach that we have been following in the past, that is to simply open up opportunities for women by insisting that individuals have the right to enter all kinds of occupations, all kinds of positions in this society, whether it's politics or business or anything else. One of the changes that has come about in all this has been the movement of women into the work forces. And one question that I don't think has been adequately addressed by the women's movement, and whether it will be in the future it seems to me is not clear, is how do you deal with the fact that women are both bearers and rearers of the children in most cases, and yet are working? What we really need is legislation and assistance for working women who are mothers. That is to say, child care of a high quality and nationally organized, along with maternity leave with pay for a substantial number of weeks. All the countries of western Europe have maternity leave with pay. Even relatively poor countries like Italy and Spain have this benefit. American women do not. Women here are not even asking for maternity leave with pay. The women's movement ought to support it, and it would then begin to deal with the question of children, which is the other half of the women question. A great number of our children are in poverty because they are often in families which are poor, or are in single parent families headed by women. And women also usually have lower paying jobs for a variety of reasons. So there is a real need to deal with the broad group of women who don't have this benefit as mothers.

Q. How should students studying this course apply the lessons of history as Americans and in their own personal lives?

A. People always ask what are the lessons you draw from history. You have to draw lessons from history because that's the only experience we have. But there's great danger in just saying, well, let's look back in the past and see what is relevant to the problems we are confronting in the present. When you do this, you have to be very careful that the event you're looking at in the past is a true analogy with the situation in the present. My favorite example of this is how in the 1930's, after we decided that the First World War was a great disaster, we should avoid all the mistakes we had made. So what we did in the 1930's in the neutrality legislation was to say, don't let Americans travel on foreign ships. Don't lend any money to people who are likely to bring us into war because there was a possibility that war was going to break out in Europe. Make sure that you pay no money to people who have failed on their debts. In short, we were going to stay out of any involvement. And then of course what we found out is that when a new war comes along, it was a different war from the First World War. It was a war against Hitler, and the Europeans were fighting to maintain control of Europe and to keep it out of the hands of one man. So we had to repeal all that legislation, because once we thought a new war would be like the past one and it wasn't. What we should think about history is to see it as continuity. Because who you are as a country, as a person, as a member of a neighborhood, derives from what happened in the past. That's all you are. All you have to do is think about losing your mind, losing your memory, for then you don't know who you are, you have no identity. You have identity only through history. And it is the same with a nation. And what you can find out about what you should do in the case of a particular problem is, is to ask if it is consistent with what you have done in the past? Do you see a continuity between your past and what you want to do? And if there is, then you're probably following your own character. And it will be I think more likely to serve your purpose. That's why when we talk about equality of opportunity, we know this has been a characteristic of America. And when you talk about policies that fit in with that, you will likely find that many Americans will agree with you on it. So the lesson of history, it seems to me, may be that there aren't too many lessons. But, there's a lot of continuity that one ought to pay attention to in trying to know who you are, what you've done in the past, and therefore what you can do in the present.

Name Index

Subject Index